The
Courage
to Hope

The
Courage
to Hope

How I Stood Up to the Politics of Fear

SHIRLEY SHERROD

with Catherine Whitney

ATRIA BOOKS

New York London Toronto Sydney New Delhi

ATRIA BOOKS

A Division of Simon & Schuster, Inc.
1230 Avenue of the Americas
New York, NY 10020

First Atria Books hardcover edition August 2012

ATRIA BOOKS and colophon are trademarks of Simon & Schuster, Inc.

For information about special discounts for bulk purchases, please contact Simon & Schuster Special Sales at 1-866-506-1949 or business@simonandschuster.com.

The Simon & Schuster Speakers Bureau can bring authors to your live event. For more information or to book an event, contact the Simon & Schuster Speakers Bureau at 1-866-248-3049 or visit our website at www.simonspeakers.com.

Designed by Jill Putorti

Manufactured in the United States of America

10 9 8 7 6 5 4 3 2 1

Library of Congress Cataloging-in-Publication Data

Sherrod, Shirley.
The courage to hope : how I stood up to the politics of fear / Shirley Sherrod; with Catherine Whitney.—1st Atria Books hardcover ed.
    p. cm.
Includes bibliographical references.
1. Sherrod, Shirley. 2. United States. Dept. of Agriculture—Officials and employees—Biography. 3. Mass media—Objectivity—United States. 4. African American farmers—Georgia—Economic conditions. 5. Farmers—Georgia—Economic conditions. 6. Rural poor—Georgia. 7. Rural development—Georgia. 8. Georgia—Rural conditions. I. Whitney, Catherine. II. Title.
    E901.1.S54A3 2013
    975.8'043092—dc23
    [B]
                                                                    2011050718

ISBN 978-1-4516-5094-5
ISBN 978-1-4516-5102-7 (ebook)

For my parents, Hosie and Grace Miller
And, as always, for Charles

God helped me to see that it's not just about black people. It's about poor people. And I've come a long way. I knew that I couldn't live with hate, you know. As my mother has said to so many, "If we had tried to live with hate in our hearts, we'd probably be dead now." I've come to realize that we have to work together.

—SHIRLEY SHERROD, SPEECH AT NAACP, MARCH 27, 2010

Contents

The
Courage
to Hope

"The White House Wants You Out"

Interstate 75 cuts a jagged path down the center of Georgia, a busy highway where caravans of massive trucks haul their loads through the South day and night. I had driven that highway hundreds of times, traveling to Athens, where my office was, or to Atlanta. In my role as Georgia state director of rural development for the U.S. Department of Agriculture (USDA), I logged many hours of driving every week.

My practice was to spend Monday through Friday in the field and return to my home in Albany, in the southwest corner of the state, for the weekend. I usually enjoyed the ride, especially in the summer. Even when I was tired, it was my time to be alone with my thoughts, to reflect, to prepare to ease back into family life. I kept the air conditioner humming and the music on low. My phone was hooked up to a hands-free system so I could easily make or receive calls. There was always some emergency or another to address, and I liked to stay available.

But on Monday, July 19, 2010, my quiet journey was interrupted by the dark interior cloud that gripped me as I put my shaking hands to the wheel and headed for home.

Earlier that day I had been over in West Point, a tiny town on the far western edge of the state, on the Chattahoochee River, for a daylong meeting. The mood was very high-spirited among the twelve staff members who greeted me when I arrived early, ahead of the day's heat. At a time when economic good news was hard to find, the rural struggle was about to be eased substantially with the opening of a Kia plant. The textile mills that had supported this part of Georgia for most of the century had long since been shuttered and moved to Mexico and overseas, and Kia was throwing a lifeline to a dying community. When the company announced it was opening a plant in West Point, it was as miraculous as the resurrection itself. There would be ten thousand jobs from the plant and suppliers, with an estimated ten thousand more from supporting businesses. Our agency had helped the city prepare for the opening, and the city manager was going to take us over there for a tour after lunch as a way of saying thanks. We were feeling quite celebratory that day.

However, just as we were about to leave for the plant, my secretary notified me that Cheryl Cook, my boss in Washington, would be calling me and I should stand by. I told the others to go on without me and sat down to wait for Cheryl.

I had some idea of what she wanted. Behind my cheerful smile, I had been struggling with a growing personal crisis. For the last few days, my BlackBerry had been inundated with angry calls from all over the country. They were very ugly, and I was forced to listen to a steady stream of hate coming through the hands-free system as I drove.

The first sign of trouble had come the previous Thursday while I was sitting in a meeting in Atlanta. It was an e-mail on my Black-Berry that read, "You ought to be ashamed of yourself. Working for the government and refusing to help white farmers, and then bragging about it to the NAACP."

I was shocked, and I could only guess at what the person— I couldn't tell if it was a man or a woman—was talking about. A couple weeks earlier, I had given a speech to the Coffee County NAACP, but my message had not been that I wouldn't help white farmers; it had been the opposite. I had used the story of rescuing the farm of a man named Roger Spooner in 1986 as an example of how we needed to let the wounds of the past heal and reach out and help each other. I immediately texted the e-mailer back, explaining my message, and got the response "It looks like someone misrepresented your words."

That was for sure! My speech had been about healing and togetherness. I had felt so clear about the necessity of taking off our blinders and letting the light shine in, even when it was hard to face.

Sixty-three-year-old Roger Spooner was beaten down when he walked into my office at the Federation of Southern Cooperatives/ Land Assistance Fund in 1986.

Although the Federation had originally been organized to help black farmers keep their land, we regularly had white farmers approach us for various things. But that was the first time a white farmer had ever come to me for help saving his land. I offered Mr. Spooner a seat. I could see he was trying hard to maintain his pride, and I figured he must have felt uncomfortable to be talking to me about his problems. Relations between blacks and whites were still fragile in 1980s Georgia. There was a common attitude of "We'll take care of our kind, and you take care of your kind." Mr. Spooner began by speaking loudly, and at first I thought he was acting superior to me, but I later found out he was hard of hearing and he always talked like that. We stared uneasily at each other across the desk, and then, haltingly, he began to tell me his story. He and his wife, Eloise, had a family farm they were on the brink of losing. I learned that the Spooners were two weeks away from their farm being sold at the courthouse, and someone had suggested they come to see me as a last-ditch effort.

I looked at the worried man sitting across from me, and my heart just opened up wide. I had a revelation. I said, "I can help you." And I did. It took plenty of maneuvering, but my efforts succeeded, and the Spooners and I ended up being solid friends.

I told that story to the NAACP audience, describing it as an emotional breakthrough for me, because my work had always been with black farmers, but, as I told the audience, "God helped me to see that it's not just about black people—it's about poor people. And

I've come a long way. I knew that I couldn't live with hate, you know. As my mother has said so many times, 'If we had tried to live with hate in our hearts, we'd probably be dead now.'"

While I spoke, the room was hushed as the audience listened intently. It was a very powerful moment for many of us who had come through the trials of segregation and chosen not to hate. But obviously someone had decided to twist the message.

Before day's end, I had several more e-mails, and I forwarded the correspondence to Cheryl. She was a good boss, a no-nonsense veteran of rural development jobs, and I trusted her to be my advocate. I suggested that she get a copy of the tape of my entire speech, in case the department had to respond. I assumed I would get their help on this, but for the next few days the e-mails and voice mails on my BlackBerry continued, becoming increasingly virulent, and nothing was being done.

By then I knew that the instigator was a blogger named Andrew Breitbart, who had published a small selectively edited clip of my speech that Monday morning that made it look as if I was saying the exact opposite of what I said. I was being accused of reverse racism. I could not believe it. That wasn't me at all! Breitbart had also tweeted, "Will Eric Holder's DOJ hold accountable fed appointee Shirley Sherrod for admitting practicing racial discrimination?"

I expected the USDA to come to my defense and help set the record straight. But I can honestly say that the matter was not at the front of my mind that day. My plate was very full.

When my staff returned from the Kia plant, I still had not heard from Cheryl. Before they got carried away wondering what was going on, I told everyone to sit down and let me explain it, because I felt they deserved to know. "I gave a speech over in Coffee County, March 27," I said, "and someone has taken a little snippet from it and put something out there that makes me appear to be a racist. So there's some stuff going on about that." They blinked at me, not fully comprehending. "Oh, Shirley," said one of them sympathetically, "we know that's not true. How can we help?"

I was touched by their support and said so, just as my BlackBerry beeped with Cheryl's call. I stepped out of the room to talk to her.

"Hi, Cheryl," I said calmly, expecting to hear my boss outline the agency's plan for my defense.

"We're placing you on administrative leave," she said without preamble.

"Oh, my goodness." For a moment I couldn't catch my breath. It was the last thing I'd expected. I sat down in a chair and tried to steady my voice as I talked again about my message and about what Breitbart had done to the tape and how it wasn't true that I had been expressing racism. She listened without speaking, and when I was done, she said flatly, "I'm sorry."

I saw that it was hopeless. "So what do I do?" I asked. It wasn't an idle question. I was a 24/7 worker. My job was my life, and she knew it. Cheryl flippantly told me, "Go home and have a good rest."

I felt as if I'd been slapped. Was I that disposable? I pulled myself to my feet and walked slowly back to the room where my staff was waiting. "I've been placed on administrative leave," I told them, watching their faces fall. We were like family in that group, and our bond certainly transcended race. Anyone who saw our interactions would notice that.

"I'd better get on the road," I said. I had eight hours ahead of me—four hours to Athens to turn in the official car and pick up my personal car and four hours home to Albany. My staff didn't want to let me go off alone with the crisis percolating, but I said, "I can deal with it. You just continue with your meeting."

They stood around me as I put on my coat and gathered up my things, and finally one of them asked in a quiet voice if we could pray. That choked me up. I nodded, and we got into a circle, closed our eyes, and prayed to God to be with us, to be with me, in this difficult time. It may surprise some people to hear about a prayer circle in a government office, but in the small rural communities prayer was the constant glue of our lives. No matter how great the trials, prayer always helped.

I hugged each person—I was a big hugger; everybody knew that about me—and set off toward Athens. As I drove, I thought about many things. I reflected on how far I'd come from the days when

Georgia roads had been as dangerous as a war zone, and I guess they *were* a war zone during the civil rights years. I'd learned to drive at a young age, but I'd hardly ever driven alone on the back roads. When things were especially frightening, we'd traveled by caravan, even to church. There had been some safety in numbers.

There was none of that fear now, but as the hate calls continued to register on my BlackBerry, I realized that there were different ways to terrorize someone. Every once in a while, Cheryl would call, and since I was driving a government car that didn't have a hands-free phone system, I had to talk with my phone in my hand while driving, which I never liked to do. The first call came as I was leaving West Point, the second as I was driving through heavy traffic in Atlanta. In each case, Cheryl's voice was quite calm, but I could hear her underlying worry. There had to be a big problem for her to call me so many times. I wished she'd leave me alone to concentrate on my driving. I hoped my blood pressure was staying steady.

It had always been my way, when facing difficulty or confusion, to meditate on my blessings, and I distracted myself with that exercise for many miles. I was baffled and a bit demoralized, but I wasn't really worried. I figured that Cheryl and her people would sort it out. I was already planning what I'd say, how I'd be gracious and use it as a teachable moment. Lord, the teachable moments kept coming—though I didn't particularly like that expression. That was all right. I'd find a way to make it work for the good.

It was late afternoon, and I was about thirty miles from Athens, when Cheryl called a third time. This time she was extremely agitated. "Where are you? Where are you?" she shouted.

"About twenty miles out of Athens," I said.

"The White House wants you to pull over to the side of the road and submit your resignation on your BlackBerry," she said.

"Pull over? Here?" The road was busy, and the shoulder was narrow.

"Yes!" she practically shouted at me.

That's when I started getting angry. "Cheryl, I just cannot believe the administration will not support me on this. You know me, you've known me before now, and I said that was not my message.

This is wrong, and you know it!" She didn't have a response. We hung up, but she called back a few minutes later.

"The White House wants you to pull over," she repeated.

"What happened?" I felt I deserved to know.

At least she was honest with me.

She said, "Well, when Glenn Beck said you would be the topic for his show tonight, that did it."

This was about what *Glenn Beck* might say? I couldn't believe it. I kept talking to Cheryl, trying to remind her who I was and what I stood for. I was doing everything I could to avoid pulling over—first because there wasn't much room on the side of the road and I was worried about safety, but also because I couldn't fathom what the emergency could be that would make this risky maneuver necessary. I was already on administrative leave. Couldn't we discuss it when I got to the office or home? Apparently not. Cheryl was unrelenting, and at last I agreed.

"Okay, Cheryl," I said with a sigh. "I'm going to stop my car and send it in. But I want you to know you have not heard the last from me."

I pulled to the side of the road and turned off my engine. With the cars and trucks whizzing by on my left, I closed my eyes and gathered my thoughts. What should I write? What *could* I write on the tiny screen of my BlackBerry that would stand for all the years I had worked in the field?

Finally I typed, "I feel so disappointed that the Secretary and the President let a misrepresentation of my words on the part of the Tea Party be the reason to ask me to resign. Please look at the tape and see that I use the story from 1986 to show people that the issue is not about race but about those who have versus those who do not. I submit my resignation but in doing so want to put the administration on notice that I will get the whole story out." It seemed feeble and inadequate, but there it was. I bowed my head and pressed "Send." It was 6:55 PM.

Before I started up the car, I called my husband and told him what had happened.

"Charles, I've been fired. I'm on the side of the road outside Athens."

"Okay." His soft, molasses-sweet voice was immediately calming, but I still had trouble keeping my emotions together. I felt over-whelmed with the enormity of what had happened to me. "What will my babies say?" I moaned. "How can I explain to my children that I got fired by the first black president?" My head throbbed with shame.

He chuckled. "The kids will be fine," he assured me, amused that I would panic over the reactions of our adult children—who were not really babies but extremely intelligent and capable peo-ple—and our grandchildren, for whom this skirmish would hardly register. "Right now, you just concentrate on driving. Put it out of your mind, and keep your eyes on the road. Call me when you turn onto Route 300."

I put the car into drive and edged back onto the road. I stopped in Athens, parked the company vehicle, and picked up my personal car. Then I drove to my secretary's house and gave her my Black-Berry, my office keys, and my ID. I resisted her invitation to stay and have tea or coffee. I wanted to keep moving.

Just as the sun was setting, I headed south. As I drove, I started getting calls from my friends who were watching stories about me on Fox News. The word was out that the NAACP had issued a state-ment condemning me. My friends were begging me to stop and go to a hotel. They didn't want me driving alone. "No," I told them again and again, "I just want to get home."

It was nearly midnight by the time I turned onto Highway 300, the narrow road that would take me to Albany. It was dark, and the black night strained my sixty-two-year-old eyes. I peered through the pinpoints of my headlights onto the highway surface, where the deer liked to leap across without warning and the heavy summer branches fell forward at the narrow places. I had to stay alert, clear-eyed, and safe, and that's why I didn't even once consider crying during the long journey home.

CHAPTER 2

Truth to Power

I opened my eyes at 5:30 AM on Tuesday, July 20. My phone was ringing—a hate call. Someone had located my home number. The phone rang again—Tony Harris at CNN. Could I do his 11:00 show? It was starting.

When I finally got up and looked out my window, I saw a mob of media. There were satellite trucks crammed along the road bearing the logos of CNN, NBC, ABC, CBS, and Fox News. Newspaper reporters with cameras were parked on the edge of the lawn. Reporters from *The Atlanta Journal-Constitution* and the *New York Times* sat in their cars, drinking coffee, or stood in the street, waiting for me to emerge. I cringed and tried not to think of the neighbors, because before the media landed, ours had been known as the quietest block in Albany, Georgia. We hadn't lived there very long. What would our neighbors think of us now?

Before 7:00 AM the crew from CNN was knocking on my door. They set up interviews with their local affiliates and arranged for me to do a remote with CNN *American Morning* at 7:00. On *American Morning*, John Roberts took me through my speech and Breitbart's rendition of it and, perplexed, finally said, "So the question I have is, when the U.S. Department of Agriculture came to you and said you have to step down, why didn't you just say, wait a minute, you don't know the full story. Here's the full story, why should I step down?"

I sighed. He was right, but it hadn't mattered. "I did say that," I told him, "but . . . for some reason, the stuff that Fox and the Tea Party does is scaring the administration. I told them get the whole tape and look at the whole tape and look at how I tell people we have to get beyond race and start working together." I didn't know what else to say. The interview ended with a lot of answers still missing.

Charles had printed a copy of a statement made by Ben Jealous, head of the NAACP, and it was sitting on the dining room table. I picked it up with shaking hands. I'd been too tired to look at it the night before. Now I read the words with a growing sense of alarm and anger.

> Racism is about the abuse of power. Sherrod had it in her position at USDA. According to her remarks, she mistreated a white farmer in need of assistance because of his race. We are appalled by her actions, just as we are with abuses of power against farmers of color and female farmers.
>
> Her actions were shameful. While she went on to explain in the story that she ultimately realized her mistake, as well as the common predicament of working people of all races, she gave no indication she had attempted to right the wrong she had done to this man. . . .
>
> We thank those who brought this to our national office's attention, as there are hundreds of local fundraising dinners each year.
>
> Sherrod's behavior is even more intolerable in light of the US Department of Agriculture's well documented history of denying opportunities to African American, Latino, Asian American, and Native American farmers, as well as female farmers of all races. Currently, justice for many of these farmers is being held up by Congress. We would hope all who share our outrage at Sherrod's statements would join us in pushing for these cases to be remedied.

A biting feeling of betrayal clawed at my stomach. The NAACP had the full tape. It hurt me that Ben, a man I admired, had rushed to judgment without even reviewing the tape of his own event to find out the truth.

Everyone was running scared, and it sickened me. I wanted to crawl back into bed and wait out the storm, but I knew it was my duty to get the truth out. If the lies were allowed to stand, not only would they destroy me and my family, they would set a horrible precedent for reporting about racial issues.

I turned on the television and saw that every channel featured my face alongside the smug portrait of Andrew Breitbart. I was still trying to piece together exactly what had happened—how the firestorm had taken hold so quickly and ferociously. Who was this man, Andrew Breitbart? Why had my bosses and the White House so readily accepted his version, even as I was begging them to review the entire tape? Where were the responsible media that would report the truth? Why had this story gone viral so quickly? It seemed to me that there were too many people who wanted to believe the worst. They were looking for trouble, and, remarkably, they'd found it in me. It's no exaggeration to say that I was the last person on God's green earth to be at the center of public conflict.

Charles was serene as always. He reminded me, with a smile, that we had been through much worse before. I nodded silently, thinking that was probably true, but it didn't ease my heavy heart.

My mother called, crying. She wasn't the type of person to cry at the drop of a hat, but this wounded her deeply. I understood the pain of an eighty-year-old woman who had fought her entire adult life for justice and equality. No one had been happier than Mother when the Obama administration had appointed me to my position. Now she was grieving the loss of a dream that we all shared. But I told her I was all right, that this was the beginning, not the end, of the story. She reminded me to pray and told me she would pray for me. That made me feel better, because my mother's prayers were pretty powerful.

On air at 11:00, Tony Harris said, "Okay, Shirley, just a straightforward, fundamental question here. Did you discriminate against this white farmer Roger Spooner? He was facing foreclosure twenty-four years ago, and, again, this was before you were working for the United States Department of Agriculture. Did you discriminate against him?"

"No, I did not discriminate against him," I said, eager to explain the point. "And, in fact, I went all out. I had to frantically look for a lawyer at the last minute because the first lawyer he went to was not doing anything to really help him. In fact, that lawyer suggested they should just let the farm go. All of that process—that's why I tell it, because everything that happened in dealing with him—he was the first white farmer who had come to me for help. Everything that I did working with him helped me to see that it wasn't about race. It's about those who have and those who don't." I added that if I'd wanted to discriminate, I wouldn't have helped him. I hadn't been working for the government then but for a land assistance fund for black farmers.

Suddenly Harris said, "Shirley, I have someone who wants to speak to this whole controversy. Her name is Eloise Spooner. She is Roger Spooner's widow."

And then I heard the firm voice of Eloise, whom I hadn't spoken to in years, pipe up, "He's not dead. He's very much alive. He's eighty-seven and he's on his Peterbilt truck this morning."

I was stunned. Eloise explained, "Our son, he came up this morning and says, 'Mama, turn on the TV to CNN.' And he said, 'It's about your friend Shirley Sherrod.' And I said, 'What?' And we listened, and I said, 'Great days, that ain't right. They have not treated her right, because she's the one that I give credit to helping us save our farm.'"

I was touched beyond words that Eloise had called. I felt warmed by the friendship we had established so long before and well aware that the Spooners had not had to stand up for me. It brightened my day significantly.

However, in a later interview with CNN's John King, Breitbart actually questioned whether or not the Spooners who had appeared in the interview were really the Spooners! "You tell me as a reporter how CNN put on a person today who purported to be the farmer's wife?" he said. "What did you do to find out whether or not that was the actual farmer's wife?" It never ended with these people.

After my interview with Tony Harris, I stood up and looked around me. My quiet home had turned into a madhouse, with phones ringing and television cables spread everywhere. Outside, the satellite truck generators roared. "We need to get you away from here," the CNN producer said. She asked if I'd mind going up to Atlanta. They promised to link me in with other networks, because everyone wanted to talk to me. I was completely out of my league with the media. I didn't know whom to trust or what was the right thing to do, but I did know one thing: I had to get my story out. All I needed to do was tell the truth and let the nation see who I really was.

Charles and I discussed it, and finally we agreed to go. We packed a small suitcase and got ready to leave. We ducked the crowd outside and got into a car provided by CNN, and off we went toward Atlanta. Along the way, I was told that journalists had already located the full tape of my speech—at last!—and the pushback against Breitbart's version had begun.

Just as we were arriving in Atlanta, Ben Jealous called to apologize. His voice was soft and sorrowful, filled with embarrassment. "I saw the entire tape, Shirley," he said. "I can't tell you how sorry I am. I hope you'll accept my apology. I've issued an official statement. May I read it to you?" I said yes, and he did. I accepted his apology. His statement read:

> With regard to the initial media coverage of the resignation of USDA Official Shirley Sherrod, we have come to the conclusion we were snookered by Fox News and Tea Party Activist Andrew Breitbart into believing she had harmed white farmers because of racial bias.
>
> Having reviewed the full tape, spoken to Ms. Sherrod, and most importantly heard the testimony of the white farmers mentioned in this story, we now believe the organization that edited the documents did so with the intention of deceiving millions of Americans.

I would later learn that perhaps the NAACP had itself un-
wittingly triggered the incident. The previous week at its annual
convention, the NAACP had passed a resolution asking Tea Party
leaders to denounce the rampant racist behavior at some of its rallies. They were referring to things such as people carrying signs
that read, "The zoo has an African and the White House has a lyin'
African," "Obamanomics: Monkey see, monkey spend," and people
wearing buttons depicting Barack Obama as black Sambo. In one
incident, Mark Williams of the Tea Party Express penned a fictional
letter from a black person to Abraham Lincoln, reading "We Col-
oreds have taken a vote and decided that we don't cotton to that
whole emancipation thing. Freedom means having to work for real,
think for ourselves, and take consequences along with the rewards.
That is just far too much to ask of us Colored People and we demand that it stop."

Tea Party organizers were outraged by the NAACP's statement
and suggested that there was plenty of reverse racism going on—
that white folks were facing discrimination, too. Breitbart's action
was an attempt to prove just that. It was disheartening.

We checked into a hotel in Atlanta. I was naive about the media,
and when CNN explained that it would coordinate interviews with
the other networks, I agreed. I didn't know how much I needed
an independent handler. I still couldn't believe this was such a big
story.

Wednesday morning I sat in a studio at CNN and fielded interviews. At one point I viewed a briefing on the screen by White
House Press Secretary Robert Gibbs. Gibbs sparred with the press
corps for some time about whether the White House had been involved in my firing, without really acknowledging anything. The
most he would say was that I deserved an apology. He was unwilling
to speculate about whether I should be offered my job back.

Secretary of Agriculture Tom Vilsack had issued a written statement of apology on July 20, and he also held a press conference on
the twenty-first. "This is a good woman," he said. "She's been put
through hell. . . . I could have done and should have done a better
job." He spoke of offering me a different position, saying that it

would be difficult for me to return to my old duties because there would always be the perception that I could not be fair in implementing the policies of the USDA. "State rural development directors make many decisions and are often called to use their discretion," he said. "The controversy surrounding her comments would create situations where her decisions, rightly or wrongly, would be called into question, making it difficult for her to bring jobs to Georgia." That's what I call a backhanded apology. Vilsack's statement did not make me feel better; he seemed to be reinforcing the accusations against me. How is one to react when you're told that the agency made a mistake and because of their mistake people don't trust you, but nothing can be done about it? I was told that Vilsack had started crying when he'd realized he'd wronged me, but I wasn't yet convinced of his sincerity.

I didn't find out until later just how difficult Vilsack's press conference had been for him. The reporters were relentless, trying to force an explanation out of him. Apologies weren't enough. In particular, they wanted to know if the White House had pressured him to fire me. One reporter asked, "Secretary Vilsack, you say that you accept full responsibility. You clearly seem to have jumped to conclusions. . . . Why did you jump to a conclusion? Was there pressure from the White House to make a quick conclusion here?"

Vilsack said no, there had been no pressure. So, the reporter asked, had there been communication with the White House?

Vilsack didn't answer directly. "I want to make sure everyone understands," he replied a bit testily. "This was my decision, and it was a decision I regret having made in haste."

They kept pressing him, forcing him to admit that he had not seen the full tape, only a written transcript of the Breitbart segment, before he demanded my resignation.

A reporter from CNN quickly returned to the White House connection, noting that I had said that Cheryl Cook had told me the White House wanted me out. Vilsack allowed that there might have been a conversation between Cheryl and a White House liaison. He just didn't know.

The press conference went on in that vein. I wasn't the only one who was curious about how the firing had happened. There were many holes to be filled in this account. I think everyone found it hard to believe that a man of Vilsack's stature and seeming thoughtfulness had been so rash, unless there was more to the story.

On the *Today* show, Matt Lauer said he'd like me to come to New York. That was fine with me, but my CNN producer said, "Oh, that won't be necessary." I looked at her and suddenly realized that I'd been a bit too controlled by CNN. I didn't blame the network, but it didn't own me. I said I was going, and the folks there hurried to make arrangements. As we were driving to the airport, Secretary Vilsack called on my cell phone. He was obviously upset as he tried to apologize to me, saying how much he regretted the whole mess. I accepted his apology, but when he began speaking about a new position he wanted me to take, I was cool and noncommittal. He kept saying how privileged he was to have worked with me and how I was the only person who had the credentials to help the USDA fix its rocky civil rights history.

I hung up with a sigh. As much as I appreciated the secretary's apology, his kind words and praise felt hollow to me after what had occurred only two days earlier. Unless it has happened to you, it's impossible to understand how crushing it is to be falsely accused and stripped of dignity on a public stage. For me it was as if forty-five years of devotion to and hard work with the poor of Georgia and other places had been discounted as if it had never happened. Though I had experienced high levels of indignity before, growing up in segregation, I'd thought that the worst of those experiences were far behind me. I had worked hard to earn respect. Secretary Vilsack, whatever his regrets, had treated me as though I were merely a political problem, not a human being. Now he was offering me a new job, but I kept wondering why he wasn't offering me my old job back. It didn't feel right.

We flew into New York that night, and I did a live interview with Anderson Cooper outside LaGuardia Airport. Cooper had interviewed Breitbart on his show earlier, and Breitbart had claimed that when I had made the so-called racist comments to the NAACP, the audience had cheered. Cooper defended me—or, I should say, he defended the truth—saying "The fact is, there was no applause when Ms. Sherrod was talking about the white farmer. Breitbart's claim that the audience was applauding as she 'described how she maltreated the white farmer' is demonstrably false."

Cooper asked what the experience had been like for me. "It's just so unreal to me that it happened," I admitted, "because I have not lived a racist life. I've had reasons why I *could* have, but I've tried to turn what happened early on in my life into a positive. I turned it into work for people." I told him that my message was if I could move beyond race to a life of love and service, we all should be able to do that.

Thursday was another busy day, starting with George Stephanopoulos at *Good Morning America* and Meredith Vieira at the *Today* show, followed by a radio interview with Gayle King and an appearance on *The View*. Everywhere I went, the media followed. As I was leaving *The View*, the street was clogged with reporters. Someone said something about paparazzi, and I just shook my head in dismay. I watched two reporters get into a tussle and the police break them up. "I think it's time to go home," I said to Charles. I was exhausted.

At that point I was three days into a media storm that had blown apart my life and challenged my very identity and purpose. Maybe for some people the experience would have been just another episode in an ongoing political drama. But I had never sought or enjoyed the limelight. I was an unglamorous worker bee who liked to keep my head down and do my job. I was a middle-aged black woman who was normally about as uncontroversial as could be, and I didn't enjoy being the talk of the news circuit. Even as I was appearing on CNN, CBS News, *Today*, and *The View*, I longed to be back in the rural communities of Georgia, where my job was to help poor, hardworking people realize the American dream. Those folks often struggled against insurmountable odds, and sometimes they won, thanks to the efforts of our agency. It was work I knew how to do, work I loved, work I was good at. Riding in town cars and being interviewed by Anderson Cooper and Meredith Vieira were way out of my comfort zone.

As a sign of my exhaustion, I allowed myself to get into an angry argument with the black commentator Roland Martin on a CNN broadcast. Roland had criticized me harshly on air, even after the Spooners had appeared and the full story had gotten out. He said that as a government official I should have known better, and he refused to alter his opinion in light of the facts. CNN brought me on air from a remote location to have a discussion with him, and it seemed to me that Roland was intent on keeping the controversy alive. I lost my temper a bit—the first time I'd done so. "I can't listen to what he's saying because he is dead wrong," I said, overcome with frustration. "He's clearly from a very different world. He has no experience of the world I've lived in." Roland later apologized to me, but many people told me they liked the way I'd "put him in his place." I didn't feel good about it, though.

Andrew Breitbart didn't know me. Glenn Beck didn't know me. The countless people pounding away on their computer keyboards, spreading the slander across the Internet, did not know me. One of the heartening—and untold—stories of those early days was the response of the people who *did* know me. What often gets lost when there is a media firestorm is that the individual in the center of it— in this case me—is a real person, with a history and relationships. You can call names and disparage all you want, but there is a record, and I drew comfort from the fact of that. From across the nation, the people who had worked with me and had seen me tirelessly dedicate myself to creating economic opportunities for all farmers began to flood Secretary Vilsack's office and the White House with protests. At first, I'm sure they thought it was just a matter of setting the record straight and then I'd have my job back and we'd move on. But it wasn't that simple. Even after he apologized, Vilsack wasn't about to put me back in Rural Development. I knew he was embarrassed and upset, but he had created the problem, not I.

One of the first people to stand up for me was none other than Willie Nelson, my old friend from the Farm Aid effort. Few people had the public credibility Willie had among farmers. They adored him because he always came through for them. Willie wrote, "Shirley Sherrod has been a great friend to me, Farm Aid and family farmers for 25 years. She has always worked to improve economic opportunities for family farmers in the South, going back to when I first met her as the director of the Georgia Field Office for the Federation of Southern Cooperatives/Land Assistance Fund. Like Ms. Sherrod herself has said, she's always tried to help those who don't have so that they can have a little more."

There were many others. The Rural Coalition put together a compendium of support from fifty-eight rural and farming organizations. I was moved and somewhat shocked to see the outpouring, but as I remarked to my husband, "It feels kind of like a eulogy."

I had never needed my friends so much, and they came through. Their letters were not just about me personally but about learning from this experience—reminding the secretary of the USDA's troubled history. Many of them were outraged that during all the years of overt discrimination against minorities and women, not one USDA executive or administrator had ever been fired for civil rights violations—yet here I was being fired. The irony was bitter.

Rudy Arredondo, the president of the National Latino Farmers and Ranchers Trade Association, wrote, "For years, numerous administrations could find no way to even reprimand the former director of loan servicing for USDA, who had a noose in his desk and by failing to take action on civil rights complaints, allowed thousands of families to loose [sic] their land. How could the USDA allow him to quietly retire a few months back while forcing Shirley out on the basis of a 'you tube' video without apparently giving her an opportunity to come to DC and state her case?"

Ross Racine, the executive director of the Intertribal Agriculture Council, wrote, "The administration and career staff at USDA have allowed 70 years of preferential treatment of 'traditional partners' . . . Yet someone who has made a career of truly helping others has been held up as an example. This just stinks of political manipulation!"

Of course, I had the full support of my former colleagues at the Federation of Southern Cooperatives/Land Assistance Fund. The director, Ralph Paige, wrote a lengthy and scathing letter to Secretary Vilsack, defending me. He, too, pointed out, "We find it ironic that in the one hundred years of USDA's history of discrimination, not a single white person has been dismissed for discrimination, however, a Black woman who is doing her job well is falsely accused of discrimination in an altered video and you decide that she can no longer do a credible and nondiscriminatory job of dispensing USDA rural development programs and must resign."

The flood of support lifted my spirits. But I was weary of the media and wanted to get away. Finally we were in a car on our way to the airport, accompanied by the ever-present CNN reporter. My cell phone rang, and when I noticed the 404 prefix for Atlanta, I answered it. Congressman John Lewis's booming voice came over the line. "Shirley," he said, "Lillian and I have literally been in tears over this." John Lewis was a good friend. Back in the 1960s, as the head of the Student Nonviolent Coordinating Committee, John had been a courageous force in the Georgia civil rights movement. We had worked with him on many occasions, helping to register black voters and integrate public facilities. His call meant a lot to me.

By now my BlackBerry inbox was full of messages. I saw that I had a text message from the White House saying that the president was trying to get in touch with me and asking me to call a number. I did and was told that the White House wanted to set up a call with the president immediately.

"I'm on my way to the airport," I said, and they promised to patch the call through. I turned to see the CNN reporter pulling out her camcorder, and I put out my hand to stop her. "This is private," I warned. She turned it off and put it away.

We drove in circles around the airport, waiting for the call.

"You are very hard to reach," the president of the United States said to me with a chuckle. "I've been trying to get you since last night."

I was huddled in the backseat of the town car, with a cell phone pressed to my ear. In any other circumstances I would have laughed at the sheer absurdity of the icebreaker. Imagine! The president had trouble tracking *me* down! I'd also have been flattered that President Obama was talking to me at all. But I was exhausted and demoralized, and I knew I was being played. The president was on the phone with me for only one reason: to solve the Shirley Sherrod problem. So I didn't have it in me to laugh. I felt embarrassed by the whole mess, which wasn't of my making, but I also felt a strange calm, a resolve to drop the pretense.

I believed that Mr. Obama was a decent man. I had voted for him, and I could still summon up a visceral memory of the awe I'd felt when a man of color won the White House. Until a few days earlier, I had worked in his administration and been proud to serve as Georgia's first black director of rural development. The president and I had never met face-to-face, but I had seen him from afar only three weeks earlier, when Charles and I had attended a picnic on the White House lawn. We'd had a great time that day.

If I, a child of segregation, had once dreamed of standing shoulder to shoulder with our first black president, I'd never imagined I could be so deeply shamed by his administration. It was a horrible blow. I realized that what had happened to me wasn't directly Obama's doing, and I doubted he'd known anything about it until after the fact. But I did feel that he had set a tone in his administration that had allowed it to happen. There was zero tolerance for anything that would bring race to the forefront. We were supposed to be color blind, which was another way of saying that our supposedly race-transcendent president was *terrified* of race. Many black folks I knew shared that fear. It's as if we'd sneaked in the back door by electing Obama and they were afraid someone might notice and kick us out.

I wasn't buying that attitude. I was determined to hold on to my dignity, even as the president's main goal was to minimize the fallout. He confirmed that he and Vilsack had come up with a job—not my old job but a new position, deputy director of the Office of Advocacy and Outreach. I was reluctant to accept it, because I couldn't figure out what kind of job it was, and I didn't trust them. I could hear in his voice that the president was frustrated by this. "Look," he said, "I can understand what you've experienced and the issues you've been talking about in the last few days. If you read my book, you'll see that."

His tone was not apologetic, but it was conciliatory. I appreciated that. But I also felt that it was very important that I speak the truth to this man, to send him a message, not to let this conversation just be about damage control. And there was one very important truth: in life experience, the president and I were worlds apart, both geographically and generationally.

"With all due respect," I replied, "you don't understand issues the way I do. We haven't lived the same kind of life. I'm not saying you would have had to live as a black person in the rural South to understand it, I'm just saying we are coming from different places."

I couldn't help thinking that if Obama had grown up black in segregated Georgia, he would not have acted so precipitously. If he had known me and known my experience, maybe he would have said, "Wait. Let's look at this first." I was disappointed that he had caved so easily at the first hint of trouble. I was sad that he was so easily cowed by right-wing bullies. Neither the White House nor Secretary Vilsack had even bothered to check the facts before they threw me out. The mere mention of Glenn Beck and his intention to do a show about me had been enough to send them running for cover. It was so cowardly. Where was my *audacious* president?

All of those thoughts were going through my mind as Obama spoke into my ear with an attempt at camaraderie that felt very forced. He wanted me to read his book—which, by the way, I had—but his book didn't speak to my life, and it seemed irrelevant to the matter at hand.

"Have you ever been to south Georgia?" I asked, knowing he had not.

He grabbed on to the idea like a lifeline. "You know, Congressman Bishop has been telling me I need to come down," he said eagerly. He was referring to Sanford Bishop, Jr., Albany's nine-term congressional representative, a black man who himself had been raised in the segregated South.

"He's right," I said with a smile. "And when you come, be sure to bring Michelle with you."

He promised me he would, although he has yet to make the trip.

After the call, the press all wanted to know if President Obama had apologized to me. "Well, he didn't exactly say the words 'I'm sorry,' but I didn't need that," I told them. "He's the president of the United States!" Overall, I thought it was a good talk. That's what I told the media, and I meant it. It also confirmed what I already knew—that President Obama just wanted me and my embarrassing drama to go away. He hoped I'd take the new job, disappear into the bureaucracy, and never be heard from again. Believe me, I would have liked to do just that.

But it wasn't that simple. I suppose if they'd immediately offered me my old job back, I might have taken it and moved on. But they didn't, and that spoke volumes to me. Vilsack was concerned that white folks would never be able to trust me again, but I wasn't going to take that as the last word. I had spent my career earning trust across Georgia, from both blacks and whites. I refused to accept that I had lost it.

People would later ask me, "How could you be so calm?" I wasn't as calm as I looked. Still, for me the primary focus was getting the truth out. When you're coming from truth, you don't have to curse and shout and cry.

Charles had a different way of putting it. In his characteristic way, he told a reporter, "The attack on my wife has opened up an avalanche of discussion on a tabooed subject—race. It is a blessing to be an instrument of God's grace."

That was Charles, always able to find a blessing in the worst situation. He was right, though, that the conversation about race, long dormant, was opening up once again. I began to see that my story provided an opportunity that hadn't been there before. There was something about the incident that made people sit up and pay attention and then not to quite want to let go. I am in the odd position of going from a complete unknown to a person who is greeted by name—hugged or glared at—wherever I travel. I'm humble enough to realize that it's not about me so much as it is about what my name and face represent to people. I've been handed the chance to say some things that need to be said, so I will tell my story.

———— ◆ ————

CHAPTER 3

Freedom's Whisper

When I'm out speaking, I always tell my audiences to please say the Twenty-seventh Psalm all through the year. My father got us into the habit when we were kids. It just fit our circumstances somehow: "The Lord is my light and my salvation; whom shall I fear?" We were very poor, but we were never made to feel that way. My father had a farm outside Newton, Georgia, 180 miles south of Atlanta, that had been in his family since at least 1890. (They didn't include black people in the census by name before 1870, so I'm not sure when they bought the land.) He was a Hawkins—a name so revered in our area that today the land they farmed and the whole surrounding area is called Hawkins Town. They were sharecroppers whose dream was to be landowners, and they achieved that dream in the decades after the Civil War. Hawkins Town eventually reached five thousand acres.

When my paternal grandmother—a Hawkins—got married, her father gave her twenty-eight acres of land. My grandparents did well enough to acquire another five hundred acres. My father, Hosie Miller, grew up farming on the land; when his father died, he deeded land to each of his children, and my father's allotment was sixty-two and a half acres, down a long dirt road outside Newton. He grew cotton, corn, peanuts, and cucumbers and raised cows, goats, and hogs. There he brought my mother, Grace, to the farm, and they began their life together. My mother was a very young girl when she got married, and she barely knew how to boil an egg. But she was strong and intelligent, and on the farm you learn fast. Life in the Miller household was hard but happy. The entire community helped each other. People who worked for my father were like family to us, and some of them still attend our family reunions.

I was the oldest child, and I worked the fields from the time I was four years old, and so did my four sisters when they came along. I still remember being shaken out of bed, eating a simple breakfast, and walking out into the field just as the sun was coming up over the horizon, my stubby little legs powering me across the field.

We had two mules, and when we planted corn Daddy and I were a team. Daddy drove the distributor, pulled by one mule, making burrows and letting out streams of fertilizer. I followed with the planter, pulled by the second mule, dropping seeds into the furrows and covering them up. I was so tiny that all I could do was hold the planter in the row and get to the end, and then Daddy would have to come and turn the mule around.

I was proud of myself. It felt so good helping Daddy. Later we got a tractor and I learned to drive it, although I wasn't always so steady. I remember one incident, after we had been working in the field all day and we were coming home, me driving the tractor. The yard was full of kids as we approached, and I decided I was going to show off for them. I yanked the handle, and the tractor sped up and I lost control of it. I hit a tree, and the engine stalled, saving me and the kids, who were running for cover.

Daddy hurried over, his face filled with a mixture of relief and anger. He pulled me off the tractor and was about to give me a beating when my mother rushed to stop him. "Leave her alone," she said. "She's too young to be doing this, anyway." That was surely true.

We also grew cucumbers, which was a big deal because it gave us a crop that provided income in the spring. Cucumbers had to be picked every other day. So each Monday, Wednesday, and

Friday during May and June, Daddy would collect us early from school to pick.

I hated picking cucumbers. It left a green stain on your hands, which was very hard to get off. You could always tell the kids who picked cucumbers because their hands would have that ugly stain. It was embarrassing.

Cotton was picked starting in August, the hottest time of the year. Those Georgia cotton fields could be blistering. My sisters and I slung burlap bags over our shoulders and worked all day. When a bag was filled, we dumped its contents onto a burlap sheet and started over. By Labor Day we had most of it done, but sometimes we had to take off from school to do the last picking.

That was life on the farm. If you had told me when I was a child that I would devote my life to farmworkers, I would have laughed my head off. My daydreams in the field took me far, far away. But in spite of its hardships, it wasn't farm life that really got me down; it was a different kind of oppression, one of which I became increasingly aware as I grew older.

Georgia was segregated both by law and by custom. Black folks could not sit at lunch counters, use public restrooms, or drink from white water fountains. Black children could not study or play with white children. The year I was born, Herman Talmadge, a dedicated segregationist, was elected governor of Georgia. He immediately advanced his "Four Point White Supremacy Program" before the legislature, which included such remedies to integration as a poll tax to prevent blacks from becoming a large voting bloc and a qualifying test for registering to vote, which was broadly interpreted by local officials. In one case, registrants were required to count the drops in a glass of water.

We were still under the thumb of old Jim Crow laws established by the state of Georgia to keep blacks in their place. They seemed almost silly, but they were voted on with dead seriousness by the legislature. If it weren't so real, it would have been amusing to imagine our legislators burning the midnight oil, thinking up every possible scenario by which blacks and whites might mix and declaring them illegal. Among Georgia's Jim Crow laws:

- It shall be unlawful for a white person to marry anyone except a white person. Any marriage in violation of this section shall be void.
- No colored barber shall serve as a barber to white women or girls.
- All persons licensed to conduct a restaurant shall serve either white people exclusively or colored people exclusively.
- It shall be unlawful for any amateur white baseball team to play baseball on any vacant lot or baseball diamond within two blocks of a playground devoted to the Negro race.

In 1955, Governor Talmadge published a book called *You and Segregation*, in which he set forth the principles of a separatist state. He was scathing in his criticism of the fledgling NAACP, writing "If they can't swim with the White people, they don't want to swim. And they don't want White people to swim. Instead, they yell for the Supreme Court like spoiled brats." He also invoked God as being in favor of segregation, based on the fact that "nature has produced white birds, black birds, blue birds, and red birds, and they do not roost on the same limb or use the same nest." Sadly, that was not an uncommon view. The establishment church had been twisting its theology for centuries in order to support first slavery and then segregation.

When I first started school, the black children were housed in an old army barracks sent from the base in Albany. It was rickety, and during the cold weather, the icy air would pour in through the cracks. Some days we'd have to bring wood from home if we wanted heat. There was no indoor plumbing; we used an old outhouse in the yard.

When the landmark Supreme Court case *Brown v. Board of Education of Topeka* was passed, declaring it unconstitutional to have separate schools for blacks and whites, it had little immediate impact in Georgia. Mostly, it was just ignored.

The benefit to us black students, if you could call it that, was that we were moved to a new school in 1957. We were so excited about the nice buildings, the indoor toilets, and the hot lunches that we barely considered the downside—Baker County's refusal to abide by the law. In our young minds, integration was a questionable goal. Did we want to go to school with white children? The seemingly benevolent culture of separation made us suspicious of integration. We didn't think whites liked us or would treat us nicely if we were in the same classrooms. No child wants to be ostracized.

In spite of the talk about being separate but equal, there was nothing equal about our schools. The books were hand-me-downs, in terrible condition with pages torn out. The school buses were on their last legs.

Many times those buses would travel out the rural dirt roads to the plantations, dropping students off at home, and a fire would start under the hood and the students would leap out the windows and the door. The bigger kids would open the hood and throw sand under the bus to put the fire out.

Was there fear? Sometimes. In Baker County, where the last vestiges of racial brutality were on a slow collision course with history, we learned very young not to be in the wrong place at the wrong time, not to drive down Highway 91 after dark, not to look a white person in the eye, not to argue a point. Even then, our safety was never a given. Violence could rain down on us without notice and for no good reason. There was a speed trap that was set up on the highway, and no one, white or black, could ride through the county without being stopped. If you were white, you just paid on the road. If you were black, you might go to jail, and going to jail was a terrifying prospect for a black person. Anything could happen when you were in the hands of the law.

I was a good girl and a serious student, and I made sure never to get into any trouble. But by the time I reached high school, my eyes were opening. Every once in a while a black person who'd moved north would visit and tell stories about the land of equality and prosperity. I was lulled by these stories, which I now realize were vastly exaggerated. But one thing was true: racism in the North didn't have sharp teeth. I dreamed of a life of freedom. In my Georgian world, if you played by the rules and stayed deferential, you might be all right, but that wasn't always the case. Mostly, I wasn't thinking of ending racism, which seemed an irreversible reality. But I did want to escape. By the time I turned seventeen and got ready to graduate from high school, I had a secret I didn't share with anyone: I was going north. I hadn't even applied to any colleges in the South. I wanted to know what it was like to be free.

People have often asked me what it was like growing up in segregated conditions, often being treated as less than human. Was I angry and bitter? My parents did not allow such feelings to be expressed in our household, but as I reached my teens and began to wake up to my own identity and the world around me, I found myself wondering—why? I was like any other young girl, bright and full of life. Why did people look at me with disdain? Why did they not want me in their presence? Why did they cross to the other side of the street or shrink from me? What had I done to deserve their scorn? I didn't understand the constant shadow of danger that hung over my head or the necessity of staying in line just because someone who was no better than I said so. I knew about the legacy of slavery, but that seemed very long ago. This was the 1960s! No one ever explained why in my lifetime we had to settle for being less than everyone else. I know my father thought that if he just worked hard and played by the rules, eventually everything would sort itself out. He was as well respected as a black man could be in our town, and that gave him a sense that justice would prevail. He and my mother relied on faith as a salve to their difficulties. They believed that God would intervene. We were raised to have a deep faith in God, but for me that faith showed cracks, because I wondered how we could pray about being all God's children one day and be less than that the next. When would God make things right? I believed in the power of faith—I was a person of faith, as I still am today—but I also knew I had to save myself.

I was only thirteen when a gangly young "Freedom Rider" named Charles Sherrod got off a bus in nearby Albany, about twenty miles away, to begin his work desegregating southwest Georgia. I was blissfully ignorant of the serious work of the civil rights movement at that point and couldn't have dreamed of the role that man would play in my life. He had been appointed regional field secretary and director by the Student Nonviolent Coordinating Committee (SNCC, pronounced "Snick"). I'd heard a little about the Freedom Riders, the daring band that rode interstate buses and tried to integrate bus station waiting rooms and restaurants, but I'd never met any down in Baker County. We were off the bus line, out of sight and out of mind.

Charles was born in Petersburg, Virginia, in 1937, one of six children. For most of his childhood they lived with his maternal grandmother, "Big Ma," at the end of a long row of two-story houses with outdoor toilets. As a boy Charles developed a strong sense of ethics and religious conscience, working his way through college and the Union Theological Seminary in Richmond.

At the seminary, the scales were lifted from his eyes. Before then he had always been the perfect patriot. To him, the government could do no wrong. But his understanding began to grow. He started attending meetings of the Richmond Human Relations Council, a group of black and white people discussing race issues and strategies, and eventually he joined the Freedom Riders to try to desegregate the South. He quickly gained notoriety. As graduation approached, he turned down a teaching job to work in the movement full-time.

In 1960, Charles, along with three civil rights legends—Charles Jones, Diane Nash, and Ruby Doris Smith—participated in a major action in Rock Hill, South Carolina, after nine college students from Friendship Junior College were arrested for sitting down at whites-only lunch counters at F. W. Woolworth and McCrory's. As the group's leader told the media, "We don't feel that sitting next to a white person will help us digest our food any better. We just want to sit down and have a cup of coffee like other students." Charles and others led a protest sit-in against the arrests and were arrested themselves. They refused bail in the new "jail, no bail" strategy and spent thirty days behind bars.

In 1961, after hundreds of Freedom Riders were jailed in Mississippi, Charles was part of a small group of movement leaders who met with Attorney General Robert Kennedy, seeking the federal government's help. Kennedy appeared annoyed with the Freedom Riders. He challenged them to stop aggravating the already explosive situation in the South and just concentrate on voter registration drives. Charles seethed at his dismissive tone. "It is not your job, before God or under the law, to tell us how to honor our constitutional rights," he said. "It's your job to protect us when we do." Kennedy stared at him for a moment and then coolly ended the meeting. There was no doubt that he was echoing the sentiments of his brother, the president, and the entire administration.

President John F. Kennedy had been a bitter disappointment to blacks, who had voted for him in 1960 and probably sealed his narrow victory over Richard Nixon. The president had openly said that the Freedom Riders were unpatriotic "sons of bitches" who were bent on domestic disruption during a period of intense international crisis. He felt that it was best to leave it to the states to manage the process of integration. As a practical matter, that left blacks fully in the hands of the oppressors. "Outside agitators" such as Charles had no protection under the law. Charles was left to wonder, must they die before the federal government stepped in and stopped compromising with the bigots?

With the tacit support of the federal government, the southern establishment continued to paint an ominous picture of integrationists as angry radicals bent on destroying their communities—in spite of the reality, which was that they all abided by Dr. Martin Luther King, Jr.'s principles of nonviolence. To read those principles today is a startling experience, because they seem extreme in their call for passivity in the face of violence. But they also show a movement born of humility and obedience to God, dedicated to principled Christian love and patience. In the fliers he made for distribution, Charles summarized them as follows:

1. Use active non-violent resistance to evil.
2. Never seek to defeat or humiliate your opponent, but
   to win his friendship and understanding.

3. The non-violent resister seeks to defeat the forces of evil, not the persons who happen to be doing evil.
4. Avoid external physical violence, but also internal violence of spirit.
5. Accept suffering without retaliation.
6. Have confidence that the universe is on the side of justice.
7. Recognize that the center of non-violence is the love of God operating in the human heart.

The genius of King's insistence on nonviolence was the understanding that it was not the same as passivity. He believed that the radical power of peace was fiercer and more persuasive than the authority forced with a gun. Charles, a thoughtful, deeply religious young man, was a true believer in the cause of nonviolent action.

When Charles, just twenty-three years old, boarded a train in Atlanta heading south for his new position with SNCC, he was immediately faced with a decision: would he ride the "Jim Crow coach," for colored people only, or would he protest and ride in the whites-only coach? If he chose the latter, he knew he would certainly be arrested and he'd be all alone to face jail, with no support. If segregationist citizens or police killed him—and that was always a possibility—who would know? He argued with himself, and finally his higher voice won, as he saw it. How could he best achieve his goal, which was to get to Albany and help the people there? So he rode in the colored coach, silent and brooding.

Albany had once been the slave-trading center of Georgia. It was tucked down in the southwest Georgia "black belt," a beautiful area on the Flint River ringed by spectacular plantations whose elegance harkened back to an older era. The civil rights movement Charles found there might generously have been called fledgling, but it felt almost nonexistent. He and his partners, Charles Jones and Cordell Reagon, set up a small office near the all-black Albany State College, but they weren't welcomed by the black community. In fact, blacks didn't want anything to do with them. They were suspicious of the passionate outsiders, with their rhetorical swagger, who threatened the fragile peace of their repression. Sometimes Charles and the others would be walking down the street, and the kids would start shouting "Freedom Riders, Freedom Riders" and the black folks would cross to the other side of the street. They didn't even want to meet their eyes. Albany had a more moderate atmosphere than many other southern cities, such as Montgomery and Selma. Whites and blacks formed an uneasy but benign collaboration that kept segregation alive. The overriding sentiment was "Things aren't so bad. Just let it be. Change will come by and by." Even the local chapter of the NAACP was opposed to the arrival of SNCC, declaring its members Communist agitators.

Fear was the daily diet that kept the status quo alive. Everyone had heard the stories of other places where churches were bombed and homes shot at. It wasn't just fear of physical harm, though, but more pragmatically of economic disaster. Most blacks knew that to join protests could mean dismissal from their jobs. It was a spoken and unspoken understanding that the livelihoods of families were dependent on silence and cooperation.

Unable to budge the older blacks, Charles turned to the young people and began recruiting students from the college and high school. The young people were more pliable and also braver. Fear had not corroded their sense of purpose. They were searching for meaning, and they found it in civil rights action. Charles set up nine committees—typists, clubs, writing, telephone, campus, communication, Sunday school communication, Boy and Girl Scouts, and a central committee. He held workshops every night at different churches to teach their members about nonviolent protests and to inspire them with stories of the movement that was sweeping across the South.

Charles wrote an eloquent statement of purpose:

The threads of freedom form the basic pattern in man's struggle to know himself and to live in the assurance that other men will recognize this self. The ache of every man to touch his

potential is the throb that beats out the truth of the American
Declaration of Independence and the Constitution. America
was founded because men were seeking room to become.

We again are seeking that room. We want room to recognize our potential. We want to walk in the sun and through
the front door. For three hundred and fifty years, the American Negro has been sent to the back door in education, housing, employment, and the right of citizenship at the polls. We
grew weary.

The Movement is a protest and it is an affirmation. We
protest and take direct action against conditions of discrimination. We affirm equality and brotherhood of all men, the
tenets of American democracy as set forth in the Constitution, and the tradition of social justice, which permeate our
Judaic-Christian heritage. Thus, we came to Albany, the
Egypt of Southwest Georgia.

Charles set his sights on a first test—integrating the Trailways
bus station—and began enlisting students to take a stand. By law,
interstate travel had been recently integrated, but in southern communities such as Albany, the stations were still segregated. Nine volunteers agreed to go to the station, and at three in the afternoon
the neatly dressed students walked down the street headed for the
depot. People, both black and white, came out onto the street to
watch them pass. It was the first time anything like that had hap
pened in Albany.

The bus station was full of policemen with guns and billy clubs
ready. The students marched past them into the terminal. They
bought tickets to Florida and then sat down in the white waiting
room. They were asked to leave by police officers under threat of
arrest, and in silence they stood up and walked out of the terminal. That had been planned—it was like a warning shot that change
was coming. Charles filed affidavits with the Interstate Commerce
Commission, stating that the students' rights had been violated. It
was a formality. He didn't expect a response, and he didn't get one.

Like the antiwar movement of the late sixties, the Albany Movement was born through the determination and fearlessness of the young. The students were the catalysts for a reluctant adult population. They brought awareness to the black establishment that this fight was not going to go away. Finally, the NAACP and black churches decided they had little choice but to support some type of organization, and the Albany Movement was officially formed. At an evening gathering at a private home, they laid out their purpose and decided on their first action, which was an appeal to the mayor and the City Commission to end segregation. They elected Dr. William Anderson, a thirty-four-year-old osteopath, as their president. Anderson had initially been reluctant to get involved in civil rights. It had been enough of a struggle for him to establish a practice in a city where hospital privileges were regularly denied to black doctors. But his wife's brother had gone to school with Martin Luther King, and the families were very close. It was inevitable that he would be pulled into the movement. The others thought he was a good choice for president because his conservative demeanor might make him more palatable to the establishment.

At the first meeting, a formal letter was drafted to the Albany City Commission:

> We the members of the Albany Movement, with the realization that ultimately the people of Albany, Negro and white, will have to solve our difficulties; realizing full well that racial hostility can be the downfall of our city; realizing that what happens in Albany, as well as what does NOT happen in Albany, affects the whole free world, call upon you tonight to hear our position.
>
> It is our belief that discrimination based on race, color or religion is fundamentally wrong and contrary to the letter and intent of the Constitution of the United States. It is our aim in the Albany Movement to seek means of ending discriminatory practices in public facilities, both in employment and in use. Further, it is our aim to encourage private businesses to offer equal opportunity for all persons in employment and in service.

The night of the first mass meeting of the Albany Movement, which took place at Mt. Zion Baptist Church, there was a huge crowd. Charles was astonished to see people jammed together in the pews, hanging over the railings of the upstairs balcony, and sitting in the choir stands. Every available space was taken. A group of almost thirty ministers sat in a row beside the pulpit. The mood was electric as speaker after speaker challenged the community to join the sacred mission for freedom. When the congregation rose to sing "We Shall Overcome" at the end of the speeches, the rafters shook with the power and beauty of the notes. "It was as if everyone had been lifted up on high and had been granted voices to sing with the celestial chorus," Charles wrote.

But the next day it was back down to earth. As the Albany Movement leaders presented their petition to Mayor Asa Kelley and the City Commission, the SNCC continued recruiting students to shake things up. The first big incident came when five students from Albany State College again agreed to protest at the Trailways station by sitting in the whites-only waiting room. That time they didn't leave when asked. They were promptly arrested and subsequently expelled from school.

That event was the spark that finally lit Albany's fuse. At a mass meeting at Mt. Zion Baptist Church following the arrests, the atmosphere was electric. Fathers and mothers spoke for the first time, stating that they could not let their children stand alone against oppression. Charles saw an opportunity to exploit the community anger over the arrests, and he arranged for a group of Freedom Riders from Atlanta to come south. When the Freedom Riders arrived at the Trailways station, there was a crowd of four hundred people cheering them on. Charles never forgot that scene: "In the crowd were eight hundred eyes in joyous thought as they walked together from the terminal, smiling from the toes upward in dignity; four hundred minds would never forget the Sunday they met both white and Negro friends from Atlanta, Georgia, in spite of the possibility of arrests; four hundred mouths would tell the story at least four hundred times and four hundred different ways to thousands of aunts and uncles, brothers and sisters, mothers and fathers, all night they would talk and all day the next day."

The reality on the ground was less poetic. Albany Sheriff Laurie Pritchett arrested the Freedom Riders and declared that outside agitators would not be tolerated.

Following the arrests, Charles organized the first mass protest in Albany's history, with hundreds marching on city hall. More than 250 marchers, including Charles, were arrested that day.

Pritchett, not wanting to create a media spectacle of overflowing jail cells, arranged to have those arrested distributed to other facilities throughout the region. Charles and twenty-five others were sent to the jail in Dawson, which was in the notorious Terrell County—dubbed "Terrible Terrell" by blacks. Locked in a cell for two weeks, he had little to do but watch ants crawl up the walls and jump when a rat darted out of a hidden corner. He and his companions entertained themselves by holding bug races—but they also sang and talked and told jokes, in a bonding process.

Charles marveled as he sat in the cell that there he was, a highly educated man, accomplished even, yet it did not matter in that context who you were, how much education you had, or even how much money you had; if you were black, that marked you as disposable. He contemplated the indignities: if you were black in 1961 Albany, you could be smacked, beaten, arrested, or killed for no reason. On a more mundane level, the indignities mounted. You could not look a white person straight in the eye or talk to a white girl or boy your own age. You could not try on a hat in a white clothing store unless you wore a stocking cap underneath, and you could not work the cash register in any store.

Charles was a deeply religious man, and being in jail during the civil rights struggle taught him what it really meant to live in Christ. "I would learn through experience just how much fear, day by day, a man can stand," he said later. "Every day you wake, you thank the Lord because you do not know how long you have to live."

One incident was burned into his memory. The thuggish sheriff of Dawson, Z. T. Mathews, and his deputy lined the prisoners up in the hallway outside their cells. They proceeded to walk up and down the line, slapping heavy flashlights against their palms with an ominous smack, and spitting on the floor. Charles was at the end of the line, and finally Sheriff Mathews stopped in front of him. He looked him up and down and then said, "What you boys come down here for? Is you looking for trouble? Is you looking for trouble?" Charles calmly gazed back at him, preparing to answer. The sheriff and deputy moved closer, their hands resting on their gun holsters, and Charles said as loudly as he could, "No, I'm not—" Before he could finish his sentence he was hit by the deputy and knocked to the floor. Charles slowly pulled himself to his feet, wiping blood off his face, and said, "We are still human beings and children of God." Mathews was livid. "You are not coming into my county and taking it over. You are not the law. I am the damn law, and you will hear me one way or another." From the corner of his eye, Charles noticed a white man sitting in a chair to the side carving shavings from a stick. He called out, "The Flint River is mighty deep, and they're building boxes every day." The tension was thick. Then Mathews ordered the men returned to their cells.

Later, reflecting on that period, Charles mused, "People would always ask us how we could stand the cursing at us, the spitting on us, the cattle prods and pistols pointed at our heads, the bombings and beatings. The answer was faith in God and the fresh nourishment for our souls, which was our music." Music was the healing salve and the motivational driver. The songs that inspired them the most they called "freedom songs." Some they wrote on the spot, such as "Ain't scared of your jail because I want my freedom" and "Open dem cells." Others they borrowed from the slave era, changing the words slightly, so that "Go tell it on the mountain that Jesus Christ was born" became "Go tell it on the mountain to let my people go"; and "Woke up this morning with my mind stayed on Jesus" became "Woke up this morning with my mind stayed on freedom." The rich harmonies of "Swing Low, Sweet Chariot," "We Are Climbing Jacob's Ladder," and "Ain't Gonna Let Nobody Turn Me Round" wafted from the cells. "All the songs told a story or held a meaning or expressed an emotion," Charles said. "The music burned inside of us, and it was there for us when we needed it."

From one of the cells in Albany, Diane Nash, who had followed SNCC to Georgia, wrote lyrics to the tune of the Negro spiritual "Rockin' Jerusalem," directed at Sheriff Pritchett and Mayor Kelley:

> *Oh Pritchett, Oh Kelly, Oh Pritchett*
> *Open them cells*
> *Oh Pritchett, Oh Kelly, Oh Pritchett*
> *Open them cells*
> *I hear God's children*
> *Crying for mercy*
> *I hear God's children*
> *Praying in jail*
> *Freedom, freedom, freedom*

Charles used songs as nonviolent weapons, and he believed their enemies were afraid of the singing. "It scared them. They didn't even want us to *hum*. We had guns pulled on us to stop us from singing. We whipped them with our songs."

Music would continue to be integral to the movement's work. One of the most stirring voices belonged to Charles's SNCC partner Cordell Reagon. Cordell had put together a small group composed of Albany locals Bernice Johnson (who would later marry Cordell) and Rutha Mae Harris, along with a national civil rights worker, Charles Neblett. They called themselves the Freedom Singers and raised the rafters at mass meetings with "Oh, Freedom," "This Little Light of Mine," and other inspirational songs. At one point Pete Seeger visited Albany, and when he heard the Freedom Singers at a mass meeting, he suggested they go on the road to raise money for SNCC. They set off on a tour of the country, performing alongside Seeger, Bob Dylan, Joan Baez, and Peter, Paul and Mary. To this day Bernice Johnson Reagon carries on the music and the message, even singing old freedom songs at the White House. Rutha Harris still sings once a month with a new group of Freedom Singers at the Albany Civil Rights Institute. Music carried the movement into the twenty-first century. But it was a very long road, and back in 1961, it was difficult even to get started.

*   *   *

Charles found that the primary obstacle to confront was not the stupid meanness of the white authorities but the stark terror of the black citizens. They wanted to move, but were terrified of the consequences. He told them there were worse chains than jails and prisons—the system that imprisoned people's minds and robbed them of creativity. He was intent on winning the hearts and minds of the people—to move them to reject the idea of being good Negroes and instead become good men and women.

Meanwhile, the leaders of the Albany Movement were still convinced they could negotiate with the city government. Anderson petitioned Mayor Kelley to establish a biracial committee to talk over the issues. He appeared before the City Commission and was told that the petition was not worth being considered as an agenda item, since there was no common ground to be had. The day after the meeting, the segregationist newspaper *The Albany Herald* derided Anderson as a radical troublemaker and published his address and phone number in case any readers wanted to tell him how they felt.

Finally, in December 1961, Anderson reached out to his friend Martin Luther King and persuaded him to come to Albany and help inspire the citizens. King arrived with an entourage that included movement luminaries such as Reverend Ralph Abernathy, Reverend Wyatt Walker, and Reverend Andrew Young and spoke to overflow crowds at Shiloh and Mt. Zion Baptist churches. King had planned to spend a day or two to invigorate the movement, but when he spontaneously decided to march, his plans were irrevocably changed. Along with one hundred others, King was arrested on charges of parading without a permit, disturbing the peace, and obstructing the sidewalks. Using the "jail, no bail" strategy promoted by Charles, the entire band refused to pay the fines and went to jail.

In his jail diary, King wrote, "I will never forget the experience of seeing women over seventy, teenagers and middle-aged adults— some with professional degrees in medicine, law and education, some simple housekeepers and laborers—crowding the cells. The development was an indication that the Negro would not rest until all the barriers of segregation were broken down. The South had to decide whether it would comply with the law of the land or drift into chaos or social stagnation."

Sheriff Pritchett was a savvy operator who understood that having Martin Luther King imprisoned would do him more harm than good. "God knows, Reverend," he told him bluntly, "I don't want you in my jail." It was the first time King had experienced being kicked out of jail, and he was not happy about it.

The SNCC and the Albany Movement kept chipping away at the stonewalling local government, but an opportunity arose when a courageous young woman—Albany's own Rosa Parks, she would later be called—refused to give up her seat to a white man on a city bus. Eighteen-year-old Ola Mae Quarterman, a freshman at Albany State College, told the bus driver, "I paid my damn twenty cents, and I can sit where I want." When the bus driver tried to pull her out of her seat, she yelled, "Get your damn finger out of my face!" Ola Mae was arrested, and she was convicted in city court, not for refusing to move but for saying "damn"—a public obscenity. She spent sixty days in jail. Reenergized, the Albany Movement declared a bus boycott, which actually hurt the black community the most since the majority of customers were black. The movement believed that the economic pressure exerted by the boycott would lead to concessions from the City Commission, but that didn't happen, and the bus system was shut down as a result. It was a hardship for many people, but the shutting down of the bus system was hailed as a victory for the Albany Movement.

King returned for trial in February of the next year, but the judge put off his decision until the summer. Finally, in July 1962, King and Ralph Abernathy were convicted and sentenced to a fine of $178 or forty-five days in jail. They chose jail, and King issued a statement explaining the decision:

> We chose to serve our time because we feel so deeply about the plight of more than seven hundred others who have yet to be tried. The fine and appeal for this number of people would make the cost astronomical. We have experienced the racist

tactics of attempting to bankrupt the movement in the South through excessive bail and extended court fights. The time has now come when we must practice civil disobedience in a true sense or delay our freedom thrust for long years.

Pritchett, however, was determined to put an end to it as soon as possible, since King had the world media in his hands and all eyes were on Albany. He arranged for a private citizen to pay King's bail and convinced the Albany city government to offer some meager concessions if King would vacate the premises. Finally King agreed. The concessions went unmet, and it was a psychological blow to the movement.

Over the signatures of William Anderson, Slater King, and Martin Luther King, a new appeal was sent to the Albany City Commission: "We implore you to realize that our legitimate aspirations for freedom cannot be snuffed out by a series of evasions and legal maneuvers. We therefore beg of you once more, in the name of democracy, human decency and the welfare of Albany, to give us an opportunity to present our grievances to the city commission immediately." There was no response.

Unwilling to help but frustrated from afar, President Kennedy remarked, "The U.S. is sitting down at Geneva with the Soviet Union. I can't understand why the city officials in Albany cannot sit down with Negro citizens to work out racial problems there."

Pritchett's master strategy was to do an end run around the Albany Movement's protest efforts by being the soul of patience. He bragged about adopting King's nonviolent strategies to mute the impact of the demonstrations, realizing that pictures in the press of dogs and police with fire hoses attacking demonstrators would just stir up more trouble.

However, the marches showed no signs of abating, and with news of a new King protest rally scheduled, Mayor Kelley moved to halt the protests on another front, requesting a federal injunction to stop outside agitators like King and others from marching in his city. The day before the march, Federal District Judge J. Robert Elliott ruled in the city's favor and barred a list of people, including

King, Abernathy, Anderson, Sherrod, and others, from participating in the march. Kelley must have believed that the injunction would end the matter, but that night more than seven hundred citizens filled Shiloh Baptist Church. The mood was one of gloom until Reverend Samuel B. Wells took the pulpit. Waving the federal list of banned marchers at the crowd, he roared, "I see Dr. King's name, and I see Dr. Anderson's name, and I see Charles Sherrod . . . but I don't see Samuel Wells, and I don't see Mrs. Sue Samples, and I don't see Mrs. Rufus Grant. Nowhere do I see those names." He told them he planned to march the following day and urged them to join him.

One hundred and sixty people marched, and all of them were arrested. But King was already turning his attention away from Albany. He experienced a sense of discouragement during that period, fearing that he had failed the Albany Movement by taking an approach that was too broad-based. He had been unable to create the dramatic impact of his other efforts across the South. Sad but true, the nation needed a constant infusion of scenes of brutality to stir its collective conscience, and Albany had not provided that.

Many people believed that Pritchett had outsmarted the movement with his nonviolence, but Charles never bought the facade. He'd watched Pritchett supervising many acts of violence by his police force. He'd seen Reverend Wells pulled from a paddy wagon and dragged to jail by his genitals. And he'd observed the coldness in Pritchett's eyes when he'd said to him, "Sherrod, it's all about mind over matter. I don't mind, and you don't matter."

After a year of effort, Albany's black community was faltering. People were not mentally or emotionally prepared for the long battle, not willing to lose their livelihoods and security to sit in jail cells. The status quo did not feel oppressive enough to fight. Quiet repression seemed to be winning the day, and King's verdict was disappointing. Still, Charles and others working in the field understood that it was not King's movement, it was the *people's* movement, and they never gave up, always seeking a way of calling ordinary citizens to action. It was a battle they were unwilling to lose, and, indeed, they did not lose.

While the leaders of the Albany Movement continued to work

on strategies for moving the City Commission, the people themselves showed flashes of daring that had a great psychological impact. One incident would be remembered by people for decades to come. It became known as "the great Tift Park pool jump." The Tift Park pool was a public pool, but it had always been off limits to blacks, with the understanding that black bodies and white bodies could not possibly mingle. Finally, fearing that civil rights legislation might open it to blacks, the city sold it to James Gray, the publisher of *The Albany Herald*, who had stalwartly resisted integration. As a private pool, it could safely be kept open for whites only without fear of legal interference.

But some of the youths had other ideas. They wanted to swim in that pool! One day about seventy-five black youths converged on the park, but only three of them had the nerve to scale the high steel fence and go over. They leapt into the pool, and, as one person recalled it, "When they hit the water, all the whites in the pool were sprung straight into the air onto the deck." Everyone was so shocked that the three boys were able to simply walk away without being harmed or arrested. It was quite daring, and the incident might have ended differently. Instead it became a symbol of freedom that everyone relished. I imagine it heartened the weary minds of Albany's discouraged blacks, who might have wondered if change was even a possibility in their own lifetimes.

Charles would not give up on southwest Georgia. He refused to even consider the organization's efforts in Albany a failure. Instead of quitting, he expanded the mission.

———— •◆• ————

CHAPTER 4

My Father's Dream

Charles had received a taste of Terrell County during his prison stay in Dawson, and he headed back there in 1962 for a voter registration drive. Terrell was a different pot of stew from Albany, which at least maintained the pretense of civility. In "Terrible Terrell," registering blacks to vote was fraught with danger. In 1962, only seventy blacks were registered to vote in the entire county.

Charles and several other SNCC workers were given lodging at the home of Lucius and Emma Kate Holloway, who were early stalwarts of the movement. Lucius's father had been a sharecropper on the Chickasawhatchee Plantation in lower Terrell, and as a boy he had worked alongside his family members in the cotton, peanut, and corn fields. Even when he was very young, Lucius bristled at the disrespect the foreman showed his father. He couldn't wait to get away, and he joined the army after high school, serving with distinction in the Korean War. When he returned home, he joined the newly formed NAACP and traveled the county drumming up membership.

Holloway was fearless. People talked for years about the time he had voted in a whites-only section of the courthouse and lived to tell the tale. The Holloways lived in a modest house with their four children, but they were warmly welcoming of the SNCC workers. They suffered as a result. In short order, Holloway was fired from his job at the post office for working with the SNCC. He refused to beg for his job back and instead took a couple of part-time jobs. Emma Kate also went to work to help make ends meet.

The first time SNCC workers went to the courthouse to register voters, they were met out front by Sheriff Mathews and his deputy. "You boys got this mixed up with New York City," he chortled with ominous sarcasm. "You looking for something, and damn if we ain't gonna help you find it. We gonna put you so far back in jail, you won't see your shadow." He patted his holster and added, "If that ain't good enough, I got something to help you sleep and solve all your damn problems." The terrified citizens retreated.

It wasn't just the sheriff who was full of threats. Bringing scared residents to register, Charles would often be stopped at gunpoint by regular people who traveled in small mobs. One leader called out, "You nigger-loving sons of bitches, get your niggers back to the holes they crawled out of." Another yelled, "Somebody's gonna die today, goddammit!" And they'd surround them, cocking their pistols. It became a regular occurrence. If, by luck, the SNCC workers got their charges inside the courthouse, there were other barriers. Sometimes the registrar would be "out to lunch" for three days. Or he would administer tests, requiring registrants to explain obscure passages from the Constitution and read legal textbooks without faltering.

In spite of the dangers, the SNCC workers kept canvassing, traveling the back roads in old cars or on foot, often returning to the same people over and over again, trying to persuade them to register. Sometimes they would spend entire afternoons at one house, talking and creating trust. They peppered the area with fliers that read:

CITIZENS OF SOUTHWEST GEORGIA
THE CONSTITUTION OF THE UNITED STATES
SAYS:

1. Anyone born in the United States is a citizen of the country and the state where he lives.

2. All citizens of the United States have a right to vote
   that no state can deny because of race and color.

On one occasion, three workers for the SNCC were attempting to register voters when a deputy town marshal named D. E.
Short shot at them and chased them out of the county. Charles was
outraged. He appealed to the Justice Department, and it did file
charges against Short on the grounds that he had violated their civil
rights. But it was a hollow suit in a pile of hollow suits. Short was
ultimately acquitted by an all-white jury, which took a mere half
hour to deliberate.

Disheartened and outraged, Charles cabled President Kennedy,
warning that the federal government must protect voter registration workers or "our blood will be on your hands." There was no
response.

One of the courageous leaders in Terrell County was the president of the NAACP, D. U. Pullam, a short, light-skinned man of seventy, who was soft-spoken but tough as nails. He was often mistaken
for white, a fact that amused him. Once, returning home from an
NAACP meeting with Lucius Holloway, they were stopped on the
road. Holloway was driving, and Pullam was dozing in the passenger
seat. The cop asked Holloway, "Where you going?" Holloway said,
"I am going home." The cop asked, "Where you been?" Holloway
said, "I have been to the NAACP convention."

The cop got loud, and Pullam woke up and asked, "What the hell
is going on?" The cop shone his flashlight at Pullam and, seeing what
he thought was a white man, said, "Sir, I stopped this boy speeding in
your car. Tell him to slow this car down. You can go on now."

The local black families who put up the workers suffered great
harassment that added to their economic hardship. The Holloways
were no different. One day during the coldest month of the year,
their heat suddenly went off. Lucius was baffled. He'd just paid for a
full tank of gas. But when he went outside to look, he found that the
gas tank had been disconnected and stolen. They all realized that it
was retribution for letting the Freedom Riders stay there.

Sometimes there was violence. A household belonging to Carolyn Daniels, a beautiful, soft-spoken local hairdresser, was the hub of movement meetings. Carolyn was a wonderful woman who was always very brave and dedicated to the cause. But her dedication increased greatly after her beloved son Rochester was slapped in the face by Sheriff Mathews when he was helping a woman register to vote. You didn't mess with Carolyn's son! That had to be the slap heard 'round the world because it solidified her commitment. Such commitment did not come without a price, however. Mathews liked to harass Carolyn. After a mass meeting, he stopped her on the road and took her license away, and she couldn't drive for three months.

There were worse things. One night shots were fired into Carolyn's house. There were six workers there, including Charles. One worker was hit in the arm, and Charles felt the wind from a bullet going past his ear. It was a miracle that no one was killed.

The attack was reported to the Justice Department, the FBI, and the Georgia Bureau of Investigation, as always. They came out, took notes and fingerprints and collected shells and bullets, and then were never heard from again.

A few weeks later, a bomb ripped a gaping hole in Carolyn's house, throwing her out of bed and collapsing part of her roof. Her hairdresser shop was destroyed. She left the area after that.

One night, as Charles gathered nervous locals at the church for a mass meeting, sixteen white men walked in fully armed with pistols, shotguns, cattle prods, billy clubs, and high-powered rifles. They were Sheriff Mathews and four other sheriffs and deputies from neighboring counties.

Charles saw death in their eyes, and he knew he had to do something fast. So he put on his preacher's hat, reading from Romans 8:28–39, his quietly resonant voice piercing the scared silence:

> We know that all things work together for good for those who love God, who are called according to his purpose. . . . If God is for us, who is against us? He who did not withhold his own Son, but gave him up for all of us, will he not with him also give us everything else? Who will bring any charge against God's elect? It is God who justifies. . . .

No one stirred. The intruders stood in the back, their hands on their guns, as Charles led the congregation in singing "We Are Climbing Jacob's Ladder." When they were finished, Charles raised his head and looked Sheriff Mathews in the eye. "Would you like to speak?" he asked in a soft voice.

Mathews stepped forward. "Our Negroes live well enough here," he said. "They live better than they do up north—all mushed up like hogs fit to wallow in their mess. We want our Negroes to live just like they have been living for the last one hundred years, happy and peaceful. We don't need northerners confusing them about who they friends is. And I'm gonna tell you right now. We just not gonna have it."

Charles stood there wondering if this was the night he was going to die. He kept speaking to them courteously and introduced others present, including freelance writers for the *New York Times*, *The Atlanta Constitution*, and the Associated Press. The media presence probably saved them. But still, when they left the church there were a few slashed tires, sand in their gas tanks, a couple of broken windshields, and a few gunshot holes in their cars.

That incident solidified Charles's reputation as "the wild man of nonviolence."

In the summer of 1962, two black churches in Terrell County, including the one where the SNCC held its mass meetings, were burned to the ground. It was obviously arson, although the official explanation was a lightning storm. Charles refused to be intimidated. He purchased a large tent and pitched it in a field, announcing "This is where we will hold our meetings." That humble tent housed some renowned guests, among them Martin Luther King and Jackie Robinson. They sang songs of the movement, including

Satan, we gonna tear your kingdom down,
Ain't no use you hangin' round,
Might as well put your shotgun down,
Satan, we gonna tear your kingdom down.

From its safe position in the nation's capital, the Justice Department kept encouraging Charles and his people to continue registering black voters. Injunctions were issued against the resistance to registration, but for the workers on the ground in Terrell they were just pieces of paper. The local whites in government did not believe that the federal government could touch them.

Throughout Georgia, governments continued to erect road-blocks to integration. Down in Baker County we remained frozen in time, getting by the best way we could.

By 1965, my father had reached a point when he was finally achieving his goals. He had his farm and his family, and his greatest happiness was the anticipation that at last he would have a son. When my youngest sister was eight, he convinced my mother to try one more time for a boy.

I didn't realize at first that my mother was pregnant. I was a senior in high school, busy with my life, but I was concerned because my mother had been feeling sick for some time. One day my best friend at school asked, "How's your mama doing?"

I told her, "She just doesn't seem to be getting any better."

She laughed loudly. "Girl, your daddy was up at the store yesterday giving out cigars. Your mama's going to have a baby." So that's how I found out.

After five daughters, my father just knew this one was going to be a boy. He loved us girls, but we all knew and accepted how much it meant to him to have a boy to carry on his name. He'd even given us boys' nicknames—I was "Bill"—so we understood his passion about it.

Daddy's farm was doing well. He was involved in the community and a deacon at the church. He was the first black person to get a loan to build a home in Baker County, and that was quite a distinction. Of course, even in that case, as a black man he couldn't get all he asked for. He wanted to build a brick house, but the county supervisor told him he could get approved to build only a wood or block house. Only white people had brick houses. It sounds silly today, but that's the way it was then. So he picked out the smallest blocks he could, and they looked almost like bricks. The house was just about finished, complete with a baby room painted blue. I was dreaming of college. My sisters were thriving. I always remember that as the happiest time for our family. We were feeling successful.

On Sunday morning, March 14, we were on our way to church, and I was driving. Daddy was sitting next to me in the front passenger seat. A car pulled up alongside us, and we saw that it was Mr. Cal Hall, who owned the farm adjoining our property. We were on polite but chilly terms with Mr. Hall, although I later learned that we were actually related. He was my mother's uncle. Her father, Joe Nathan Hall, was the bastard child of Cal Hall's father by his Negro maid.

Daddy leaned across me to talk to him from the car. Mr. Hall said that one of his cows was on our land, and he wanted to arrange to retrieve it. This wasn't a new issue. Mr. Hall's cows had wandered into our pasture sometime earlier, and all of them had been retrieved except for one intransigent cow that was difficult to separate from our herd. Daddy said, "Come over to the pasture tomorrow morning and I'll get some help to get him back." They arranged to meet at nine o'clock, and Mr. Hall drove off. It was a completely innocent, noncombative conversation between two farmers.

The next morning we went off to school, and Daddy took a black farmhand and my mother's brother out to the pasture. When they arrived, Mr. Hall was there with a black farmhand, and he was angry. He pointed to several of Daddy's cows and claimed that they were his and that they, too, had wandered onto our land. Daddy couldn't believe it. It felt like a robbery attempt to him. But he was not one to get hot under the collar. He finally said, "I don't want to keep arguing with you. We'll go to court, and they'll settle it." He turned and began walking away, and Mr. Hall pulled up his rifle and shot him in the back.

I was in my classroom when I got a call to go to the principal's office. I was surprised by that. I wasn't the kind of girl who ever got called to the principal's office, which usually meant you were in trouble. When I arrived, everyone was standing around looking very upset. They told me Daddy had been shot. Soon my sisters also came in, and we huddled together, crying. Even now thinking about it, I experience the utter despair I felt with the revelation of Daddy's shooting. It was the worst moment of my life. A teacher offered to take us to the hospital, and we piled into a car. I tried to comfort my younger sisters, but how could I when I was so devastated myself? Daddy was our hero, our rock. And we didn't know whether he was alive or dead.

By the time we arrived at the hospital in Camilla, they had already moved our father to Phoebe Putney Memorial Hospital in Albany, which was thirty miles away. We didn't get to see him until the following day, and when we walked in he was lying completely still on a hospital bed, unconscious, with tubes going in every which way. It was a terrible sight. Mama gathered us to her, and we all prayed. She knew from her brother what had happened, but she didn't tell us the details then. And to see Daddy lying on a bed like that was unspeakably horrible.

Daddy lingered for ten days before he died, and then we were thrown into deep mourning and a sense of unbearable loss. I couldn't look at my father dead, that was the one thing I couldn't do, so I didn't go up to the casket to say good-bye. I said it in my heart.

My mother was strong throughout. I can only imagine what she must have felt—a young woman with five children and another on the way. But she never let us see a hint of panic. She was a great comfort to us, at what I now realize was enormous personal cost to her.

Cal Hall was never prosecuted. The grand jury said there wasn't enough evidence, although there had been three black witnesses. That didn't surprise us. Even if the law took him in, a white jury would have acquitted him. Everyone understood that.

After my father's death, it was hard to have faith, although we were serious church people. He had been a deacon, and my mother used to joke that every time the church doors opened, we were there. She was seven months pregnant, and the prospect of continuing the farm without my father was unthinkable. But you could hear her singing every day around the house the spiritual "The Lord Will Make a Way Somehow," and those words meant something to her.

Like a ship that's tossed and driven,
battered by an angry sea;
when the storms of life are raging,
and their fury falls on me.

I wonder what I have done,
that makes this race so hard to run;
then I say to my soul, take courage,
the Lord will make a way somehow.

But why? Why had Cal Hall shot my father? I pondered the question endlessly. The only reason I could think of was that he couldn't stand having a black man speak up to him. I tried not to feel hate, but hate seemed the only emotion available toward the man who killed my daddy. My mother cautioned against it, reminding us of our faith, but I struggled with it.

I was seventeen, and I prayed hard for guidance. I needed a new vision of what I could do. Growing up, all I had wanted was to get out of southwest Georgia and go north to escape the daily experience of segregation and fear. Could I still go? Should I stay? The night my father died, our house was full of people, and I went into a back bedroom to be alone. There was a full moon, and I stared out the window at its brightness and prayed to God for an answer. Thoughts of getting a gun and killing my father's murderer came to me, but they were fleeting. Finally I decided that I had to stay and try to make things better. I felt a great sense of peace and clarity when I resolved it. That night I made a promise to stay in the South. Escape was no longer an option.

—— • ◆ • ——

CHAPTER 5

Sheriff Gator's Law

I didn't fully appreciate until after my father's death just how strong my mother was. She took immediate action to save the farm, renting out parcels. She could not work the farm herself. Two months after Daddy died, his son, Hosea (Hosie), was born. It was a bittersweet event, because how could one hold such great joy and such great sorrow together in one heart and not have it burst? We all knew one thing, though. That innocent little baby had some mighty big shoes to fill.

My mother was not willing to let my father's murder go un-avenged. If the criminal justice system refused to act, she would try to get satisfaction in the civil court. She approached C. B. King for help. King was a legend in our area, the only black lawyer any of us had ever met. He had a powerful voice and an unrivaled command of the English language. Sometimes, when he was questioning jurors or witnesses, they'd stare at him blankly, not understanding, and then complain, "Judge, tell him to ask me something I know." C.B. loved those moments of linguistic superiority. He couldn't abide the ignorance that was the cornerstone of racism. C.B. was key to the movement in our area. So many people relied on him for help. He had also suffered and been beaten for his actions. His brother, Slater, also active in the movement, had had his share of tragedy as well. In

1961, Slater's wife, Marion, pregnant at the time, had gone with a friend to visit the friend's daughter in the Camilla jail. The girl had been arrested in a protest march. Marion had stood at the fence, trying to speak to those in the jail cell, and a sheriff had ordered her to step back. She hadn't complied quickly enough, and the sheriff and a deputy had punched her and kicked her to the ground. Her baby was born dead.

C. B. King helped my mother file a wrongful death lawsuit against Cal Hall, seeking $330,000 to recover present and future lost wages, medical expenses, and funeral costs.

The trial was held in the Newton courthouse in the heat of summer 1966. The big fans rotated in the packed courtroom, and the mood was tense and ominous, especially in the segregated Negro section, which was overflowing with people from the community who had come there to support my mother.

This case would not be decided by a jury of our peers, because the jurors were all white. It's not that blacks weren't eligible to serve; they were on the rolls just like anybody else. But the rolls listed whites first, then blacks at the end, so most jury selections were completed before any black names came up.

King spent a lot of time questioning potential jurors, waging an uphill battle to root out discriminatory impulses. He asked each man if he felt that whites were more inclined to tell the truth than blacks. Except for one person, all of the jurors said they believed whites were more truthful. King repeatedly requested that juror after juror be struck, on the ground that they had admitted bias right there in open court, but the judge denied each request.

The trial went on for several days, with Cal Hall sitting smug and self-satisfied next to his lawyer. He felt no remorse and was confident of the outcome. People told me that he still carried the shotgun he used to kill my father in the back of his truck. Not surprisingly, the jury ruled in Hall's favor.

I was sickened by the outcome of the trial. I asked my mother, "How do you bear it?" She told me her faith was getting her through, but in my eyes it was more than faith; it was a deep sense of resolve and responsibility. My father's death gave Mother her voice. Cal

Hall's unexpected legacy was to create a powerful force in the burgeoning civil rights movement and to make our humble farmhouse the center of activity there. My quiet, prayerful mother became a leader.

Years later, quite a few white people came up to her and said they didn't like what had happened but had been afraid to come forward at the time. She was very understanding and forgiving. She knew how things were. In a twisted way, black oppression was also white oppression. No one was free under that system.

Sometimes it seemed that the civil rights movement had left Baker County behind. Encased in poverty, its citizens trod wearily along pitted dirt roads in the brooding shadow of trees dripping with Spanish moss. Large plantations with fields of cotton and peanuts were tended by thousands of black sharecroppers, their annual salaries peaking at below $1,000. Segregation's tentacles were as firmly rooted as the aged cypress trees. When the civil rights movement stormed through the South in the early 1960s, no sounds of freedom drifted our way. Even if they had, the movement would have been a hard sell to the cowed black population, which earned its keep by silence and compliance. It was not unusual for me to hear the older folks clucking with disapproval at the antics of the Freedom Riders or laughing at the supreme naiveté or even insanity that would make the black rabble-rousers think they could overcome centuries of repression by getting carted off to jail. Even the federal government was aware that Baker was an outback. A report from that period read, "On the surface, Baker County appears isolated from the modern world."

In Baker County there was an excellent reason for keeping your head down if you were black. His name was L. Warren Johnson, and he was the sheriff. Everyone called him "the Gator." He'd created that nickname for himself because he liked to make the loud, rattling sound of a gator when he was trying to scare black people. He was a huge, intimidating man who inspired fear in all of us. The Gator was a testament to the fact that guns, whiskey, and hate were a deadly combination. People were sure he'd murdered at least four blacks in cold blood, and he inspired tremendous fear because he just didn't have civilized restraints.

The Gator had learned his ways at the knee of his predecessor, a brutal sheriff named Claude Screws, who had lynched a black army veteran named Bobby Hall in 1946. (Bobby was also a cousin of ours.) Hall was arrested on the charge that he had stolen a tire, although that was not true. Screws and two deputies handcuffed him and drove him to the courthouse, where they dragged him out of the car and beat him with blackjacks and fists before dumping him unconscious in the jail. He died there. Charges were filed against Screws, but they were not for murder, as one might expect, but for depriving Hall of his rights. An all-white federal jury convicted Screws and his deputies of the charge, but the conviction was overturned by the U.S. Supreme Court with the astonishing reasoning that the prosecution had not proved that they had *willfully* deprived Hall of his civil rights. The convoluted logic was that they had to prove that while they were beating Hall to death, they were *thinking* of depriving him of his civil rights. It was a shameful case. Today, when visitors come to southwest Georgia for tours of civil rights sites, I usually take them to the courthouse in Newton to show where Bobby Hall's body was displayed.

The Gator was an apt pupil of Screws. Nobody messed with the Gator. He owned a gas station in town that had a big sign outside: "We Want White People Business Only."

When the civil rights movement made its first tentative incursions into Baker County, the Gator and his allies were on hand to stop it. They would hang around the courthouse wielding ax handles to discourage blacks from registering to vote. They would set traps along Highway 91 where anything could happen. *The Atlanta Constitution* reported at one point that the Gator's take on the road was at least $150,000 a year—and that was in 1960s money. It was nothing for the Gator to burst into people's homes and harass them. Violence and fear imposed a simmering quiet on our community. The whispers of intimidation grew around the case of a man named Charlie Ware.

Charlie Ware was a small, thin man, just an ordinary husband and worker. On the evening of July 4, 1963, after attending a large picnic for blacks at a nearby plantation, the Gator and his deputy showed up at Charlie's door, handcuffed him, and dragged him away from his terrified wife. It was never entirely clear what had precipitated the arrest. Some accounts held that Charlie had flirted with a black woman at the picnic who was the mistress of the white overseer of the plantation, others that he'd cursed out a policeman while in a drunken state. Whatever the case, the Gator wasn't much interested in due process. While driving to the jail, he suddenly called out over his police radio that Ware was coming at him with a knife. The radio transmitted the sounds of three shots fired into Ware's neck. He miraculously survived, but the Gator didn't worry too much. Ware, he said, had attacked him, and the shots had been fired in self-defense. Ware was charged with felonious assault. At his showcase trial in the Newton courthouse, Ware was found guilty by an all-white jury and was sentenced to three to five years in prison.

Elizabeth Holtzman, who would go on to become a U.S. representative from New York, was a young law student who had decided to spend the summer working for C. B. King. The image of Charlie Ware's trial was burned in her memory decades later:

> The courthouse itself was right out of *To Kill a Mockingbird.* Huge fans turned slowly overhead hanging from the high ceilings. There was a tiny balcony for black observers and witnesses. White farmers in overalls peered in through the open windows, chewing on stalks of grass. And on a platform, the judge in his black robes spat into a brass spittoon.

Soon after Ware's conviction, a student group picketed a supermarket owned by Carl Smith, one of the jurors. Smith's store was located in the black section of Albany, and it had black customers. The students picketed for only an hour on a Saturday afternoon, but on Monday Smith closed the store. He claimed the picket was in retribution for his jury vote, but the students denied that, saying they were there because Smith had refused to give blacks jobs as cashiers and butchers. Their account seemed to be correct, since they had been after Smith to employ blacks for months before the Ware trial. But Smith's cry of jury tampering held sway with the Albany Bar Association, which called upon the U.S. Department of Justice and Attorney General Robert Kennedy to investigate this possible violation of the federal law against intimidating a juror. In contrast to the Department of Justice's usual lackluster response to our civil rights pleas, this time it mobilized for action. Kennedy sent a large contingent of FBI agents to investigate whether the students had picketed Smith in retaliation for his jury vote. Sixty people were subpoenaed to testify before a federal grand jury. Although the grand jury did not find evidence to indict, the incident left people discouraged for a long time. We'd been waiting for the federal government to shower us with its powerful attention, but no one had expected it to happen that way.

Ware's conviction was later overturned because of the unconstitutional exclusion of black jurors, but at the time it cemented the belief that the Gator was allowed to operate outside the law. Indeed, it is amazing to reflect that even given his history of known brutality, the sheriff's version of events was taken at face value. No one ever breathed a hint that the Gator, not Ware, should be called to account for his actions. He ruled Baker County.

For that reason, we were late coming to the idea of equality and civil rights. We watched from afar as others waged the long battle, and we stayed on the sidelines. By 1965, the year my father was killed, the civil rights movement had long ago parked itself down the road in Albany, where Martin Luther King, Jr., himself led demonstrations. But it required a special effort to take on the Gator and his cronies. And so far no one had dared to step across that bloody border.

My father's death changed everything in Baker County, and for that I imagine he would have been proud, although he was not a fighter. He was, however, a principled man and a leader, and I'm certain that if he'd lived he would have been a quiet force for change.

Now, however, the quiet had fled with the sound of a bullet piercing all our dreams. The black community was in a frenzy over Hosie Miller's murder, and by the summer of 1965 the Baker County Movement—once unthinkable—was born. Inspired by events, Charles and his SNCC workers finally made their way into "Bad Baker" County.

I wasn't there at the beginning. I'd graduated from high school in June, and my father's sister, who had a doctorate from Atlanta University and was the principal of a school in Atlanta, had arranged for me to participate in a pilot Upward Bound program. Everyone always said I was a lot like Aunt Carrie, and in some ways that was true, because she, too, had grown up on a farm but had striven for more. Many of my peers seemed resigned to a humble fate, but I had a role model in Aunt Carrie, and she showed me I could reach higher. I was happy to escape for a few weeks, and I was almost two hundred miles away when everything changed.

My brother was a newborn when the Baker County Movement launched its first protest march. The Gator was determined that it wouldn't reach the Newton courthouse. Before the marchers even got close, he sent his brother, Deputy Sheriff Ben Johnson (did I mention that all of his deputies were relatives?), to lay down the rules. The protesters were told that only seven of them could form a line to march in intervals. In other words, tiny groups on the sidewalk. Seven volunteers, including Charles, began walking, and almost immediately they were assaulted from behind by an angry white crowd. The attackers carried ax handles (provided by the local grocer), chains, baseball bats, hammers, sticks, and shovel handles.

One group surrounded Charles and began beating him with ax handles, driving him to the ground. He might have been killed if an old woman had not thrown herself on top of him and yelled, "If you want to kill him, you'll have to kill me first." Seeing her fierce determination, the men backed away.

Bloodied and broken, the protesters retreated to St. Matthew's Baptist Church, while the seriously injured were carted off to the hospital. The movement nicknamed the day "Bloody Saturday." It never made much news north of us, but Georgia state troopers were sent to offer protection for a continuing series of protests. Again, the Gator stood in the way, announcing his rules for demonstrators: they were permitted to march only behind the courthouse and away from Main Street, out of public view. That was so patently ludicrous that the marchers simply went ahead and marched in front of the courthouse. They were arrested, and the state troopers, who were supposedly there to protect the marchers and ensure their constitutional rights, helped escort them to the jail.

Filled to overflowing, the jail cells were putrid steam baths that made breathing hard. When the Newton city attorney arrived to record names, my Aunt Josie, one of the arrestees, had the idea that they should give historical names, such as Harriet Tubman. One of the young men declared that his name was Booker T. Washington, and the city attorney punched him with his fists.

That night, with the sultry July heat unrelieved, the Gator gave the order to have the jail sprayed with a mosquito-killing chemical that made everyone violently ill. Three people were so sick that they had to be taken to the hospital. The leering Ben Johnson volunteered for the task, and on the road he pulled his gun and told them that if they got killed no one would do a damn thing about it.

The protesters remained in jail, suffering through the heat and subsisting on a paltry diet of bologna, beans, and bread. On the third day Gator turned the water on full force inside the jail, and as it rose up their legs, they clung together, wondering if he was planning to drown them. They were finally allowed to go outside.

I arrived home for the July 4 weekend to learn that three of my sisters had been jailed with the marchers. There was a hearing the night I returned. Hearings were often held at night because we didn't have a full-time court and the judges were on a circuit. They got to us when they could.

At the courthouse, we found C. B. King representing the protesters. As we sat in the hot courtroom and listened, we were relieved when the judge said he was ordering the release of the minors, including my sisters. The adults would remain in jail.

The judge ended the hearing and left the courtroom. As we were preparing to leave, the Gator, who had been standing at the back, swung his booted foot against the door, slamming it hard. "Sit your goddamn asses down!" he bellowed. There were about fifteen of us, and we sank back down on the benches, afraid to say a word.

He stormed in front of us and began a tirade that seemed to last forever. He was cursing and shouting and telling us we'd better watch ourselves and threatening us with violence.

Finally spent, he barked, "Get up and get your goddamn asses out of here!" We were glad to oblige. We gathered in the parking lot, noting the inky black of the night. It was the worst possible time for us to be out on the roads. We decided to travel in a caravan, which was the safest way. About three miles out of town, the Gator's son Scroot, who was a deputy, was waiting for us on the road, swinging his big flashlight in our direction.

I was in the lead car, and Scroot swaggered up to us. "You didn't stop at the stop sign back in town," he said with a smirk. No one even considered answering that how would he know since he had been ahead of us on the road? We understood the game that was being played and kept our mouths shut. Finally he waved his flashlight in the air and told us to go on.

Afterward, the Gator sent out word that he was looking for that "nigger Sherrod," and when he found him he was going to kill him.

I was proud of my sisters because I felt they were standing up for all of us and also doing something healing for themselves. In today's world, if your father were murdered, there would be therapists lining up to help you. Then we had nothing but our grief and our powerlessness. And my sisters had struck back against the powerlessness.

The next week I went to my first mass meeting in Baker County. And I knew then that that was the way. I sat in the church with tears streaming down my face as I reconfirmed my commitment. I didn't know what I would do or how I would do it, but I was deeply inspired by the people I saw that night—people who had every reason to be afraid yet who testified and planned and talked about the fight as if it were their second nature. I couldn't wait for the Upward Bound program to end. I needed to get back home and get to work.

*   *   *

It had been more than ten years since school desegregation had become the law of the land, but Baker County schools were still segregated. So far they had managed to defy all federal efforts, and in that they had the backing of the state. Georgia had been very slow to integrate the schools and from the very start had bullishly stood against the law. For a time Georgia schoolteachers had been required to sign a pledge that they would not teach in integrated schools under penalty of losing their licenses. The edict was brutally clear, and it carried the full authority of the state:

> Be it resolved by the State Board of Education, duly assembled in the State Capitol . . . that any teacher licensed to teach in the public schools of the State of Georgia who supports, encourages, condones, or agrees to teach in a mixed grade shall have his or her license and salary automatically forfeited, and the same shall not be renewed for a period of two years from the date of forfeit.

Eventually the edict had to be rescinded on constitutional grounds, but Georgia still lagged behind, and nowhere more than in Baker County.

At last, in the summer of 1965, it was announced that around fifteen black students would be allowed to enter the white elementary and high schools. My mother registered three of my sisters.

The first day of school, she took my sisters by car and the Gator met them and told them to go back home. They returned home and called the Justice Department. On the second day, a school bus collected the black students, and it was allowed to go forward. As it approached the school, the students looked out their windows and saw angry whites, both adults and children, lining the road, shouting at them.

When the bus stopped, the male students descended first, and my sisters and the other girls watched in horror as they were set on by whites who hit and kicked them. The next day state troopers were there to escort them inside.

Those kids grew up fast. The daily indignities and threats—even by some of the teachers, who referred to them as "Nigras"—made studying difficult. Several of the students dropped out immediately and returned to the black schools. Not my sisters, though. It might not have fully been their choice to be on the front lines of integration, but my mother was firm that it was the right thing to do. It's hard to imagine parents today deliberately subjecting their children to such violence and emotional cruelty, but those parents believed in their hearts that it was the only way.

My sisters suffered in that environment. There were signs around the school referring to my father that read, "Another coon gone," and I'm sure that was heartbreaking. People did everything they could to drive them out, children mimicking the evil of adults.

My sister Sandra was up late doing homework one night about two weeks after school started when she heard cars coming down the road. That was unusual because we were far out in the country. She peeked out the window and saw a large cross burning in our front yard and a group of men standing around laughing and hollering. Sandra screamed for my mother, who was asleep. Mother was not afraid; she was furious. She grabbed a rifle and told my sister Nan, "Get on the telephone and start calling some people to come out here." We had already set up a phone tree for emergencies.

Mother and Sandra went out on the porch, and Mother shouted to the men, "I see you, and I know who you are."

Soon several friends and relatives arrived, carrying rifles. They surrounded the men in the yard, and there could have been a bloodbath—people were that angry. But they didn't fire a shot, just drove the men off our property.

At that point, the Gator and Ben Johnson appeared out of the night, as if they'd been there all along. We were pretty sure they had been involved. No one ever found the perpetrators, but the community men stood guard over our house for several weeks.

School segregation was not achieved overnight. It was a long, slow, and usually painful process, school by school. Many years after the first black children walked into white classrooms, there were deliberate efforts to halt the entire process. For example, in 1969 the intimidation was ongoing, as reflected in the story of one young girl.

Dorothy Young was fourteen years old when she got into an argument with a white boy her age on a school bus. She apparently called him a "bastard" and other profanities after he threw a spitball at her. The superintendant sent Dorothy and all her siblings to the youth detention center and didn't even bother to inform their mother. She didn't know what had happened until the bus failed to stop at their home that afternoon. Dorothy's siblings were released, but she was sent to the Regional Youth Development Center, a reform school in Sandersville. Her mother was frantic, but even with C. B. King's efforts and intense lobbying by national figures, the judge would not budge. At Dorothy's hearing in juvenile court, Judge Bowie Gray stated that there was no other way but the reformatory to deal with a girl who would utter profanities. He said, "Dorothy Billie Young is in a state of delinquency in that said juvenile did use vile, obscene and profane language to one Will Aultman, another juvenile about fourteen years of age, and in the presence of numerous other juvenile children, knowingly, willfully and without just cause."

It took the movement an entire year to secure Dorothy's release, and everyone regarded her jailing as a form of intimidation toward black families who would put their children on buses with whites. Anything could happen!

One of the saddest aspects of the attempt at school desegregation was that the blacks shunned the students who participated, so they lived in a friendless no-man's-land between two communities that reviled them. Their old friends treated them with suspicion and thought they were betraying them. The high schoolers were barred from attending the prom at either their new white school or their old black school. The black kids who integrated the schools were deeply hurt by the treatment they received from other blacks. It was bad enough to deal with the pain of being attacked every day. It was shattering to have no comfort zone among their people. The experience left deep scars that are apparent to this day. Some of the area's leading citizens still shy away from public gatherings, their bruised psyches forever afflicted with the pain of being outcast from their own community.

—— • ◆ • ——

CHAPTER 6

Love in a Land of Hate

I was miles away in Atlanta the first time Charles Sherrod came knocking on our door. He'd arrived in Baker County with the movement, and every day he drove or walked along the back roads talking to folks about registering to vote. He stopped by our farm to speak with our mother. She wasn't home. My sisters were there, though, and they were happy to sit on the porch with the charming young man, who complimented them on their beauty and intelligence.

"Well, we have a sister even more beautiful," one of my sisters said coyly, "but she's up in Atlanta studying."

Charles asked, "You got a picture of this girl?"

They said yes and invited him in. My graduation picture was sitting on the piano, and they showed it to him. As Charles has always recounted it, "I knew right away I was going to marry that girl." It's a typical romantic exaggeration coming from my husband. True or not, Charles could certainly have had his pick of girls. He was a legend by that time.

When I came home, my sisters told me, giggling, about the man who had come to our door, and I didn't think anything of it. I'd never heard of Charles Sherrod, and the first time he returned and walked up on our porch, I wasn't too impressed. He was all glasses and very skinny. I glanced at my sisters, hovering nearby. *This* was supposed to be my heartthrob? I was pretty cool to him, but he didn't seem to notice. He was almost cheerful in the face of rejection, as if he knew I'd come around.

The following evening, I attended a mass meeting, and suddenly I saw Charles for who he really was. I was spellbound. The church was packed with people, many of them workers on the big plantations who I knew were jeopardizing their homes and livelihoods to be there. I was moved by their lack of fear of either the Gator or their bosses. They were standing tall, singing and talking and full of newfound self-esteem. And Charles, leading the meeting, was transformed before my eyes from a quiet, skinny man with glasses into a powerful preacher. I saw the way everyone respected him and looked up to him, and I probably started to fall in love with him a little at that meeting.

I began to spend more time with Charles, working on the voter registration drive. It was slow going. Often the Gator would meet us on the steps of the courthouse and block our way. He was an immovable force. Finally we decided to go to Washington, D.C., and try to get an injunction against him. We held meetings and raised enough money for five carloads of people, and we set out in a caravan on a Sunday night. It was our intention to talk to as many politicians in Washington as we could. We had high hopes.

The obvious route would have been up Highway 91, but we knew the Gator would be out there waiting. So we drove east into the next county and then went north from there. In Washington we spoke to a panel of U.S. senators and to people from the Justice Department, and we eventually got our injunction, and things became a little better but not much. Everyone realized that as long as the Gator was the law in Baker, progress would be slow and agonizing.

I had never known anyone like Charles. He was a complex man with deep reserves of religious conviction. But he was also sweet and joyful. When I considered what he'd been through those past years, I was amazed that he never showed the slightest hint of bitterness. I was young to the movement, and I tried to put myself into his shoes and found it hard. My parents had often counseled love and forgiveness, and in Charles I saw the personification of that spirit. I wanted to be part of that, to walk that path and learn to be half as good as he was. Recalling my previous intention of running off to the North and my belief that I would never find the right kind of man to marry in southwest Georgia, I marveled that Charles had walked up to my door and knocked on it.

I would probably have become involved in the movement even without Charles. But he was a great teacher and inspiration who continually stoked the furnace of others' commitment. He eased all my doubts with his moral clarity and resolve. I knew that if I was going to be with Charles, I had to accept that the movement was his life and it would be my life as well. "I'm nothin but a soldier," Charles told me, singing a verse from a song he'd written:

Told Judge Jim Crow slowly, I may not be brave,
You can jail my body, but I'll never be your slave

Nothin but a soldier, nothing but a soldier . . .

Within months of our meeting, Charles and I were talking about getting married. I have to say that there was some disappointment in my family about my plans to join the movement and stay in the area. I had always been the person people expected to go away and do great things. Everyone loved Charles, but they would say to me, "Are you sure that you want to marry a Freedom Rider, Shirley?" They didn't consider the fact that he was so well educated and brave and had come in and helped change our lives for the better. They only worried that he would lead me into a dangerous, not very prosperous life. But by then I was determined to live the way Charles and I had planned.

We didn't get married right away, though. At the urging of my uncle, who was a vocational education teacher in the next county, I applied to Fort Valley State College, a historically black college in Peach County, about eighty miles away. Charles also left for a year to finish his master's degree at Union Theological Seminary in New York. We communicated by letters and saw each other at Christmas, eager for the time when we'd be together full-time.

Charles was an assiduous letter writer, and I began to learn more about his family in Virginia and his upbringing. He had been raised mostly by his grandmother. She and many of his other relatives were light-skinned and could pass for white. He'd never known his grandfather, who had been run out of town for openly objecting to the lynching of a black man.

Charles had been a hardworking boy, and he'd had an after-school job at fifteen working in a five-and-dime for the princely sum of $15 a week. What had happened there had given him his first experience of fear. One day the manager had sent him down to the stockroom to collect some inventory. When he'd started down the stairs, he'd encountered a beautiful blond girl with a devilish grin on her face. She'd stood in his way, so he would have had to squeeze against her to get by, and then she'd reached out a hand and touched him intimately. All he could see was the rope around his neck. He'd left the store at a run and never returned.

Charles had a supple mind, and throughout his school years he was able to figure out that the world needed to change. He had enormous faith in God, not the passive faith of his ancestors but a sense of responsibility to act.

While Charles was at Union Theological Seminary, he kept a hand in the SNCC work in southwest Georgia. In the spring of 1966, he began recruiting white divinity students to come down for the summer and help with the voter registration and other projects. He ended up with twenty-five volunteers, and he was enthusiastic about how much they could accomplish. But Charles hadn't reckoned on the conflict those white volunteers would create.

For years Charles had been accustomed to viewing the major roadblock as the resistance of the white establishment. Now he faced an upheaval within his own organization. The direction of the movement was changing, and he didn't like the change one bit.

That spring, a new chairman had been chosen to head SNCC, replacing Charles's old colleague John Lewis. His name was Stokely Carmichael. Stokely was a hard-liner who had coined the term "Black Power." He resented whites, even those who were helping us. He wanted to abolish all white workers from SNCC because he felt the black struggle must be waged and won by blacks and that whites needed to work in their own communities. Charles vehemently disagreed. He was still committed to a nonviolent effort, with blacks and whites working together. But the tide was turning.

The incident that radicalized many blacks and put them into line behind Stokely and other Black Power proponents was James Meredith's March Against Fear in June 1966. Meredith, who was well known for his dramatic and successful effort to break segregation at the University of Mississippi, had devised the march as a solitary trek of 220 miles from Memphis, Tennessee, to Jackson, Mississippi. But he hadn't walked very far when a sniper shot him with bird shot and he was hospitalized. Others in the movement, including Martin Luther King and Stokely Carmichael, continued the march, and it became a much bigger event than it would have been had Meredith gone it alone.

When the group reached Greenwood, Mississippi, near the end of the walk, they planned to camp on the grounds of the Stone Street Negro Elementary School. The police forbade it, and Stokely had words with them, which led to his arrest. Fearing an outbreak of violence, the police changed their minds, and the campsite was opened. A mass meeting was arranged for the following evening, and the main speaker was Stokely, who had been released on bail. A crowd of more than six hundred listened to Stokely's electrifying speech, not knowing it would set a new course for the movement.

"This is the twenty-seventh time I have been arrested," he said, "and I ain't goin' to jail no more." The crowd roared as he went on, "We want black power. That's right. That's what we want. Black power. We don't have to be ashamed of it. We have stayed here. We have begged the president. We've begged the federal government—that's all we've been doing, begging and begging. It's time we stand up and take over. Every courthouse in Mississippi ought to be burned down tomorrow to get rid of the dirt and the mess. From now on, when they ask you what you want, you know what to tell 'em. What do you want?"

The crowd thundered, "Black power!"

It was in the aftermath of that incident that Charles brought his twenty-five white divinity students to southwest Georgia. Stokely was enraged, and many other SNCC workers, who had adopted the Black Power attitudes, felt the same way. When the whites walked in for their orientation, one of the blacks commented loudly, "God-damn, it looks like the roosters outnumber the Panthers. Panthers are hungry. Panthers *eat* roosters."

One of the members of the group was a serious young man named Joseph Howell, who arrived with his new wife, Embry. The Howells were there to help run a Head Start program, for which SNCC had arranged funding. From the very first, Joe recalled, there was a great deal of tension between the two camps, and they were often cautioned to stay far away from the Black Power workers. In his book *Civil Rights Journey*, published in 2011, Joe wrote about some of the tense meetings, in particular one showdown between "Sherrod's volunteers" and the rest of the SNCC workers:

> The first issue was over Baker County and how Sherrod had broken his truce by letting us go into the county the previ-ous evening when we attended a mass meeting. SNCC did not want white people "messing around" in Baker County. The cli-max came when [one person] got up and shouted that he didn't want whites at all in the movement. . . . The Baker County issue was finally resolved by the fact that white people were needed to get fifty thousand dollars from the federal government on the Head Start program. So we must go, but we were to work *only* on Head Start. . . . By one o'clock in the morning every-body had gotten a chance to say what was on their mind, and all of a sudden things seemed OK. It was the strangest thing. Everything had been said. The hostility was out in the open. Communication was reestablished. We all stood up and sang some songs. Sherrod began a spiritual, and everyone joined in. Then came "Oh, Freedom." It felt great to be alive.

Such was the mixed emotional tangle that was faced throughout that summer: one minute hostile, the next minute holding hands. But the undercurrent of Black Power was growing, in spite of Charles's efforts to keep whites in the movement. Charles was always dedicated to unity, and he lifted his voice in a particularly strong and stirring baritone when he sang the words of "We Shall Overcome":

Black and white together.
Black and white together,
Black and white together someday,
Oh, deep in my heart, I do believe,
That we shall overcome some day.

Throughout the summer, Charles tried to do SNCC work while leading the divinity students and keeping them out of the way of Stokely's people. It was uncomfortable for everyone, and by the end of the summer Charles was frustrated and worried, but I wouldn't permit him to get too down about it, because at the beginning of September we were getting married, and that would be a happy time. I knew that whatever difficulties lay ahead, we would face them together and that would make everything possible.

Our wedding took place on a warm September day, in the last sun of the summer. A large crowd of family and friends gathered at my mother's house, where tables in the yard were loaded with food. We were honored to have that brave, wonderful man Reverend Samuel Wells officiate, and his face, which was capable of breaking into such fiery passion, showed simple calm delight as we said our vows.

Later, we sat out under the stars at the end of a perfect day. Charles and I held hands and felt blissfully content in the knowledge that we were embarking on a great adventure.

After our wedding, we moved into a house on Holloway Avenue in Albany, which we shared with other movement folks. We always had a houseful of people, but we didn't mind. That was the way our lives were going to be for some time. Besides, I had another year at Fort Valley State College before I transferred to Albany State College, so we were due for more separation.

A month after we were married, Charles was arrested for having four hundred-dollar bills in his possession. It was typical of the petty harassment that went on then. I had received a student loan from a bank in Calhoun County. There hadn't been time for me to go to the bank with Charles to open an account because I had to go up to school and register for classes. So I'd given Charles the money to open an account in both of our names at the First State Bank in Albany.

A few days after arriving at school, I received a call from a detective with the Albany Police department. He wanted to know if I had given my husband any money. I said yes, I had given him twenty-, fifty-, and one-hundred-dollar bills. He was satisfied, and hung up. I was concerned that something was going on, and I called the house we were staying in with other movement folks. I learned that Charles had gone to the junkyard to buy a part for one of the old cars we used, and he'd tried to pay with a hundred-dollar bill. The junkyard dealer had called the police, and they'd taken him to jail. He was released after they talked to me, but the indignity burned me. Charles, as always, shrugged it off. He'd long before learned that if you were going to let every slight get you down, you'd be buried in your own bitterness.

In 1967, Stokely announced that all whites would be expelled from the SNCC, saying "Before a group can enter the open society, it must first close ranks." Charles grieved over the decision. He thought it was plain wrong—that the struggle wasn't for a different kind of segregation, it was for integration. Charles believed that using white workers side by side with blacks was a strong demonstration that they were equals and whites were not superior. But by then the Black Power movement had gained tremendous momentum in cities and towns across the country, led by young men who liked the idea that they could inspire fear instead of feel it. Older movement leaders, such as Martin Luther King, Ralph Abernathy, and Andrew Young, were concerned about the new direction, but even King didn't speak out too harshly against it.

As an aside, let me say that one of the great ironies of the accusation that I practiced reverse racism was that my husband and I were so staunchly opposed to the Black Power movement and the separatist ideology. All we ever wanted was for all people to work together and prosper together.

Charles and I had long conversations about what we would do once whites were ejected from the organization, and Charles felt he had no choice but to step down. He resigned from the SNCC, stating "I didn't leave the SNCC, the SNCC left me."

Stokely was soon replaced at the SNCC by a firebrand named H. Rap Brown, who increasingly collaborated with the Black Panthers. Later he would change the name of the organization, replacing "nonviolent" with "national." By then, the SNCC we knew was dead.

We always believed that the movement was inside us, buried so deep in our marrow that it could not be eradicated. Leaving SNCC was merely a transition, not an end. We considered what we would do next and felt that educational and economic empowerment were the next steps in the black journey. I returned to Albany to finish my studies, and with only a few nickels to rub together, we started a new nonprofit organization called the Southwest Georgia Project for Community Education. Our mission was to promote social justice through economic and educational opportunity.

Along with a group of like-minded colleagues from SNCC, including the white students who had been working with us, we decided to incorporate the Southwest Georgia Project. We agreed that we would pool our resources to keep the organization going. We put all the money we made into the common treasury to help pay rent and other expenses, and each member received a small stipend. We continued the practice for many years. Until about 1979, my paycheck went into the account, and our rent and utilities were paid. Charles and I received a stipend of $65 a week for food and other personal necessities. From time to time a grant would be received for different parts of the work or the family of one of the white students would send money to help with purchases of equipment or transportation.

Our main goal was to help people. There was always a job to do, and increasingly that job was focused on practical solutions. We were still registering people to vote and trying to get black people elected, but we saw that the real key to the future was financial stability and economic clout.

After the civil rights struggle of the early and mid-sixties, we faced a tough economic reality. Although progress had been made in areas such as integrating facilities and black voter registration, blacks still had little in the way of good jobs and property ownership. We had almost no influence in the political or civic processes and no organization beyond the protest movement. It was time to take a hard look at what our needs were and how we could ensure the stability and prosperity of our community. Our focus was on real, long-lasting opportunities.

The Southwest Georgia Project served people in thirteen counties. We taught old people how to read, trained people for jobs, and opened day care centers for working mothers. We operated a professional printing shop that provided apprenticeships to young people. And we lobbied for jobs in the local businesses.

Charles would say, "Where we do business, let there be black hands ringing the cash register." He thought nothing of walking into a store and telling the manager, "If we are doing business here, then we should also benefit from some of your business. Have some of our people work here. We're not asking for all of our people to work here, we're asking for some to work here." He went to every business in southwest Georgia.

For a while times were really hard. We barely had enough money to feed everyone. One day a farmer from Lee County told the men in our group that if they would come out to help catch wild hogs on his place, he'd share the meat with them. That seemed like a good deal, so the men left the house very early on Saturday morning while it was still dark. They were gone all day long. We women were at home that day, anticipating being able to prepare a large meal that would include at least half but maybe a whole hog, since the farmer had said there were several hogs. When the men arrived home that night, they didn't look too happy. Although they had caught several hogs and even helped the farmer clean them, he had given them very little meat. The pieces they'd brought home were not the most desirable pieces, and they definitely were not enough to feed the whole group living in the house. I never forgot that, because our hunger had given us high expectations and they were dashed.

In a sense, our mission, the quest for economic equality, was more threatening to the establishment than marches and demonstrations. Economic power was the truest and most significant form of equality, and there were plenty of people who couldn't stand the thought. By then we'd grown used to some degree of harassment, but our enemies were invigorated by our new emphasis.

By this time, Albany had reached an uneasy compact with integration. Schools and public buildings were open, and many of the obstacles to voter registration were removed. But things were far from settled. We still received threats. No one enjoyed answering the phone, because chances were they'd be subjected to a barrage of profanities and threats. When I learned I was pregnant, Charles and I were overjoyed, but my mother was worried. "Shirley, you've got to stop," she said. "You have a baby to think of." I hugged her and said that she shouldn't worry. I didn't remind her that she had fought segregation with a baby in her arms.

The dangers were real, though. One day I stayed home to rest while the others went out to distribute our newsletter. A group of white men came to the house early in the day, looking for Charles. I was in the bedroom, and I heard them talking to Grady, a young child who came around our house every day. He'd stayed with me when the others went out. Grady stuttered, and the men had trouble understanding him, so they asked if he'd take them to find Charles. They left, and I didn't think anything unusual was happening because people were always looking to talk to my husband. They were gone for about forty-five minutes. When they returned, they went to the back of the house and then burst into my room. I began screaming at them. One of them continued to approach me but stopped. They went out of the room and left the house.

Grady walked outside with them, and when he came back into the house, he went to the back and then came running to my room to say the house was on fire. The men had set a fire in the office. God was with me that day to protect me, but as I watched our home burning, I wondered if the harassment would ever end. I knew God would forgive me if I occasionally fantasized about a simpler, quieter, safer life. But those thoughts were short-lived. I believed with all my heart that we had to be about providing a better future for the child growing inside me and for all the other children. If I were going to bring children into the world, I had to commit to doing better by them.

Our greatest disappointment during those years was the way the Black Power movement continued to dominate the civil rights conversation. Anger was a palpable presence, splashed across television screens. The cauldron was being stirred, not just in the South but across the nation. Martin Luther King struggled with the goals and strategies of Black Power, and he gamely tried to redefine the notion to mean economic power, but there was no way to halt the unstoppable momentum of a movement that signified violence and separatism. Contemplating the new reality, he wrote:

> I guess I should not have been surprised. I should have known that in an atmosphere where false promises are daily realities, where deferred dreams are nightly facts, where acts of unpunished violence toward Negroes are a way of life, nonviolence would eventually be seriously questioned. I should have been reminded that disappointment produces despair and despair produces bitterness, and that the one certain thing about bitterness is its blindness. Bitterness has not the capacity to make the distinction between some and *all*. When some members of the dominant group, particularly those in power, are racist in attitude and practice, bitterness accuses the whole group.

For us, Black Power was a step backward in our efforts to achieve economic and educational equity and prosperity within our community. Some people viewed us with new suspicion, wondering if we were some of those crazy radicals. But the heat was spreading, and all it needed was an accelerant to turn it into an explosion. That occurred on April 4, 1968, with the assassination of Martin Luther King.

Many black leaders urged people to respond nonviolently, but

Stokely Carmichael led a different charge, gathering a large crowd in Washington, D.C., that went on a rampage breaking store windows.

"White America killed Dr. King last night," he said, fanning the fury of the people gathered. "She made it a whole lot easier for a whole lot of black people today. There no longer needs to be intellectual discussions, black people know that they have to get guns."

The angry crowd took over the nation's capital for four days, fighting back against the National Guard and the military. At one point marines set up machine-gun posts on the steps of the Capitol. In the end, Washington neighborhoods were smoldering and rubble-strewn. To this day many people believe that the riots of that week sparked an unprecedented period of white flight and sealed D.C.'s fate as a city dominated by the black poor.

The nation's capital wasn't the only city to see an explosion. By some accounts there were riots in 125 cities after King's assassination, including Chicago, where an entire black neighborhood was burned to the ground.

We watched the news reports with alarm and found it hard to contain our despair. We could not understand why black people were burning their own communities, driving their own mothers and brothers and sisters out of their homes, destroying businesses that blacks had worked so hard to build. Wasn't it clear that blacks would pay the greatest price for their actions?

On April 9, King's funeral service was held at Ebenezer Baptist Church in his hometown of Atlanta. More than three hundred thousand people showed up to pay homage in a quiet, nonviolent way. Inside the church, the eulogy was delivered by King himself, through a tape of his last sermon.

But the prevailing message to the nation was not King's nonviolent ministry but the ruins of the cities. It was a presidential election year, and the unease caused by the riots, along with continued resistance to black equality, formed the centerpiece of the Republican election campaign, in what was called the Southern Strategy. Richard Nixon ran on a platform of states' rights and law and order, a thinly veiled appeal to the traditionally Democratic southern states. He was tangentially aided in getting the message out by the third-party candidacy of former Alabama governor George Wallace, who was not shy about putting his cards on the table, stating "I draw the line in the dust and toss the gauntlet before the feet of tyranny, and I say segregation now, segregation tomorrow, segregation forever." Nixon was able to appear more moderate than Wallace, and that added to his appeal to those who viewed themselves as reasonably opposed to the new era.

By contrast, Vice President Hubert Humphrey, the Democratic candidate, was intimately connected with the civil rights achievements of the 1960s. He was also burdened by the Vietnam War and the uprisings among the young. Although he lost to Nixon by a narrow margin, he didn't carry a single southern state with the exception of Texas. The Southern Strategy had worked. Indeed, it is practiced to this day. In 1981, Ronald Reagan's campaign strategist, Lee Atwater, laid it out to a political scientist, Professor Alexander P. Lamis, for his book *The Two-Party South:* "You start out in 1954 by saying, 'Nigger, nigger, nigger.' By 1968 you can't say 'nigger'— that hurts you. Backfires. So you say stuff like forced busing, states' rights and all that stuff. You're getting so abstract now [that] you're talking about cutting taxes, and all these things you're talking about are totally economic things and a by-product of them is blacks get hurt worse than whites."

After the 1968 election, some Democrats charged that the voices of radical youths more than racism had lost the election for them. It was probably a combination of both, but Charles and I found it hard to relate to either camp, even though we were young, too: I was only twenty, and Charles was thirty-one. But we refused to join what we thought of as the path to destruction that the Black Power advocates were walking. We believed in black empowerment. We agreed that black was beautiful. But the form of activism we chose was one of community, not division. We set our minds to the task of building bridges and opportunities and dreamed of the time when we would all stand as brothers and sisters in our own eyes.

CHAPTER 7

At Work in the Fields

Our daughter, Russia, was newly born when Charles came to me with an announcement. "I'm going to Israel next month," he said.

"Israel?" I thought he was joking.

He told me that the Norman Foundation had funded the trip for Charles and six others to study the kibbutz system. It would be the first step in the fulfillment of a long-held dream. We'd been talking for some time about ways we could empower black families, and we had been working toward that end. But one vision compelled us and stunned us with its audacity and possibility: a farming collective that struggling black farmers could join to pool their efforts for the common good.

Charles and Slater King had been discussing the idea seriously. Slater, whose thriving real estate agency continued to be a force for economic opportunity for blacks in the area, was deeply committed to issues of financial solvency and housing for poor blacks. He introduced us to a remarkable man named Robert Swann, who was a pioneer of the collective farming movement. Swann was enthusiastic about our idea. They then talked to people from the Jewish National Fund, which had helped develop the land trust (kibbutz) movement in Israel. And now they'd been invited to Israel to see for themselves how a kibbutz worked.

With our infant in my arms, I smiled and told Charles that of course they should go to Israel—although it seemed a very, very long way away. In my mind there was a beautiful synchrony to the Jews in Israel and the black farmers in the United States drinking from the same cup to ensure their futures. It was natural to feel a kinship with those who had defied oppression by creating an independent land of their own. Self-sufficiency had been a path out of the darkness for the Jews. We hoped it could be that way for us, too.

On the ground in Israel, Charles, Slater, and their group visited several kibbutzim, and they were impressed by the structure and dedication of the farmers. The land-lease covenants, held without rancor or dispute, were a perfect application of democratic principles. However, our men were less impressed by the family arrangements, which seemed foreign and unacceptable to them. In the kibbutzim at that time, family identity was absorbed by the community, with children living in separate houses from their parents and raised by community minders while their mothers worked. Charles and Slater balked at the rigidity of the system, and they knew it would never work for the black community in Georgia, where family autonomy was so prized. The legacy of slavery was still on our minds, that time when children had regularly been ripped from their families and sold to others far away. We tended to hold our children close. What we were seeking was something less communal and more collective—a land trust operation that would boost economic sustainability while also helping individual families maintain their own residences.

Our people left Israel having learned much and made friends but more determined than ever to craft a unique arrangement, borrowing pieces but not the whole of the kibbutz system. We ultimately settled on an organizational plan that involved individual homestead leases and cooperative farming leases. We decided to call it New Communities, as a symbol of a brighter future.

Through his real estate office Slater became aware of a property of almost six thousand acres in Lee County, just outside Albany, owned by two brothers. Lee County was a very insular place, closed in on itself and resistant to change and outsiders. During the height of the civil rights movement in the early 1960s, in spite of its majority black population, it was solely ruled by the Forresters, a family that controlled everything, including the sheriff's office. When the SNCC had first gone there in 1962, the word went out: "Anybody keeping a Freedom Rider or associating with a Freedom Rider had just as well dig his grave and stand by it."

However, Charles had fond memories of his time in Lee County, thanks to their local sponsor, an eighty-year-old woman named Mama Dolly Raines who lived in a backwoods corner down a long, dark road. She possessed an iron faith, a strong constitution, and a sweet disposition. Charles and others, black and white, stayed with her and coordinated their work out of her house in the company of a flock of geese, turkeys, brood sows, pigs, a milk cow, and a twelve-gauge shotgun. Every day the phone would ring repeatedly with vile death threats. Mama Dolly was not intimidated. Recalling her younger days as a midwife, she remarked that she'd brought many white children in Lee County into the world. And she added with a smile, "I may have to take some of them back out of this world." That was Mama Dolly.

Still, recollecting that period, Charles realized that only six years had passed and they could not expect the area to magically set out the welcome mat for a community of black farmers. He knew there would be battles ahead.

New Communities was incorporated, and we immediately began attracting black farmers. They were excited by the opportunity and the realization that we could do so much more collectively than they could do individually. We would have buying clout to purchase supplies such as fertilizer—one hundred thousand tons being a much more attractive order than one hundred tons. We'd have greater opportunities to sell our crops. We were out to promote trade from the rural areas to the urban areas, and we planned to introduce organic crops, which was a new idea at the time. Buyers in the cities would see that they'd be getting high-quality goods at a reasonable price.

But before we could do anything, we had to purchase the land, which was no easy matter, because people in Lee County didn't want a large black farming operation out in the open for all to see. Slater helped us get an option on the property, and we prepared an application for funding from the federal Office of Equal Opportunity.

We received a planning grant from the OEO. The Washington, D.C., firm of McClaury and Associates assisted us with studies and collaborative design sessions, called "charrettes." While the charrettes and studies were being done, people were also registering to move onto the property when the plans were complete. The sites for three villages were selected, along with the types of houses to be built. We also identified the site for industry, which would be on Highway 19, since there was a spur onto the property from the railroad that passed through. We planned the farming and health and education systems. At the end of the year, all of the plans were completed for the funds we had been assured of getting from OEO.

However, as word of our intentions got out, we began to experience opposition. Sometimes people would drive by the property and vandalize it. Then the rumor spread that we were Communists, and, of course, that was an inflammatory word that really riled folks up. The local congressional representative even filed a motion in Congress declaring us a Communist organization. White people from the local and state offices let it be known that they were determined to block the OEO funds that had been promised. The local government denied our application without explanation, and the matter went to the governor's office. With a single stroke of his pen he had the power to accept or reject the local verdict. And the governor at that time was a famous segregationist named Lester Maddox.

Before his rise to political influence, Maddox had owned a restaurant in Atlanta called Pickrick. After the Civil Rights Act was passed in 1964, he refused to let blacks into his restaurant, and he often said publicly that he'd close down before he did. He kept pickax handles—dubbed "Pickrick drumsticks"—hanging on the wall, and he sold them for $2 apiece. When a group of blacks tried to enter the restaurant, customers and employees grabbed the pick handles and drove them away. Eventually, true to his promise, Maddox did sell the restaurant, and he walked away without ever having served a black person.

Maddox ran for governor on a platform of states' rights and segregation. He was sworn into office in 1967. As most of the country was making slow steps toward integration, Maddox was defiant. He believed in the cause of segregation. He once stated, inexplicably, that discrimination was part of America's greatness. "Yes, sir," he said. "Inequality, I think, breeds freedom and gives a man opportunity." One can't imagine what he was talking about. It was nonsense. But enough people believed him to elect him.

Now he was holding our fate in his hands. There was no suspense about it. Maddox accepted the local recommendation, as we expected him to. In the process he managed to get in a dig, calling New Communities "Sharecropper City."

Once the governor wielded the ax, there was a great sense of discouragement among the farmers. We had counted on the OEO grant. How could we begin farming without money? It just wasn't possible. But Charles was typically undeterred. He lectured us, "We can't give up. We'll just have to find funding elsewhere."

With a hope and a prayer and what was left of the original OEO money, we started farming, but we faced foreclosure since the initial grant had been for just one year until the major grant was set up. Finally, without any government funding, we were able to raise private money and also secure long-term financing with Prudential, but that process was full of drama. Even with private funding and the Prudential loan we were still $50,000 short of the purchase price, and the deadline was looming. In his memoir, *Peace, Civil Rights and the Search for Community*, Robert Swann recalled the heart-stopping race to get the final money before the option closed. The day before the deadline, a black church group in South Carolina announced that it would donate the $50,000 and have the check delivered to C. B. King's Albany office in time for the noon closing:

The next morning we arrived early at C. B. King's office. Everyone assembled had an interest in the project, including, of course, the two brothers who owned the property. They were nervous and clearly hoped the sale would not go through because apparently they had been threatened by some of their neighbors. As the hands of the clock moved to twelve noon and past, the two brothers jumped up and gleefully shook hands, saying "too bad." C. B. King, however, called their lawyer aside, and after a brief consultation with the two brothers their lawyer announced that his clients would extend the time for another twenty minutes. At that very moment a messenger arrived with the $50,000 check. Now it was time for our group to cheer. Everyone, of course, wanted to know what C. B. King had said to their lawyer, but he said only that he had certain information that their lawyer would not want reported.

We were off and running, and our future looked bright. We planted crops that other farmers were not planting at that time, such as muscadine grapes. We built a farmer's market right on Highway 19, and in addition to eight acres of grapes located behind the market for pick-your-own, we built a greenhouse and a sugarcane mill for making syrup. We put up an old-fashioned smokehouse. Instead of taking the hogs to market, we would have them slaughtered, and we'd carve up ham and bacon. We also made sausage. We sold the fresh cuts in ten-pound boxes. We proudly erected a sign on the highway: "Welcome to New Communities, the Land of Pick Your Own."

It was wonderful. We had 2,200 acres under cultivation, growing soybeans, peanuts, corn, grapes, watermelon, and various vegetables. We had a beef herd of 250 and several hundred hogs. With two and a half miles of highway frontage, our market got plenty of traffic.

We also started implementing various programs, such as bingo games, to raise money and bring folks together. We kept the day care center running. We planned ahead to a time when we could expand and create more jobs for blacks. We envisioned putting up more than a hundred housing units and building a recreational park, a nature trail, and a retreat center. We had long-range plans and ambitious ideas.

It was a very special operation, and it held deep personal meaning for me. I often thought how proud Daddy would have been to see our thriving collective. Sometimes, as I worked in the market, with Russia and her little brother, Ken, running around outside, I reflected that I had come full circle. I had been born on a farm, and here I was again, this time at a much higher level. We had the potential not just to save ourselves but to save our communities.

In addition to Russia and Ken, we had a group of about thirty children we were working with all the time. Some of the children lived in Albany, some on the farm. Children wanted to be part of the group because of all the activities.

Every Sunday morning, we would get a vanload of them and go to either the Kinchafoonee Creek or the day care center we operated on the farm to have Sunday school and Bible study. The children fished and played. They also learned to pick and shell peas and how to grow food to eat. During the summer, they picked vegetables on the farm, and we paid them when they worked. They saved some of their money for trips and activities, including a visit to Disney World in Orlando, Florida. Once Eastern Airlines offered the opportunity to fly for $15. The children worked hard to pool their earnings to spend a weekend in Atlanta that included a flight from Atlanta to Birmingham and a trip to Six Flags. I cannot forget the reaction of the children when the airplane lifted off the ground at the Atlanta airport. There was a loud chorus of "Oooooooooh!" That flight was probably the only one that some of them ever experienced.

Our children were thriving, although there were times when I trembled for them. Intermittent violence plagued us. Our son still talks about the bullet hole in the wall over his bed, from an incident that scared me to death but was mostly a source of curiosity for Ken. Sometimes Charles and I would sit up at night after the children were asleep and wonder if we would be able to protect them. We were always open with the children about our work and its dangers. They grew up *knowing* they were in the movement. We refused to shield them from the truth, but we did our best to protect them from danger. As a parent, you can always fret and second-guess your decisions, but seeing the remarkable, caring, engaged adults Russia and Ken became, we are confident of the choices we made.

Sadly, Slater, who had been such a supportive, wonderful part of our beginnings, did not live past our early days. He was killed in a car accident in Dawson in 1969, and we mourned him deeply and missed his friendship and wise counsel. But the collective was growing, and those were mostly happy years, full of new plans for the future.

Twenty miles to the south, Baker County was showing incremental signs of change in 1976. There were two significant events: one, the Gator announced his retirement; and two, my mother, Grace Miller, announced her candidacy for the school board. The Gator's retirement wasn't all good because he was fronting his son, Scroot, who was a chip off the old block. It was a strange election. We were canvassing for my mother, and we'd run into the people canvassing for Scroot. At our meetings, Charles would tell people, "Don't put another Johnson in office." I'm sure word got back to the Gator that his old nemesis, Charles Sherrod, was campaigning against his son.

On election night, we all gathered in the lobby of the Newton courthouse to watch the ballots being counted. I was surprised by the number of white people who came up to us and said they'd voted for my mother. They said it in a quiet, almost shamefaced way that made me realize they were people who had been on our side all along but had never had a chance to show it before.

As we were standing with our children, watching the votes being counted, suddenly the Gator strode out of a back room. I hadn't seen him for some years, and he was definitely older but still big and bad-looking. He walked right past us without looking in our direction, greeting us out of the side of his mouth as he went by. Then he stopped and swung around and saw who we were, and marched straight back. Glaring at Charles, he said, "I take that back. I didn't know it was you."

Charles and the Gator stood there eyeballing each other with mutual disdain. The air felt smoky with the tension. I was nervous. The sheriff had a gun in his holster, and he was just mean enough to pull it out and shoot Charles right there. Luckily, someone ran outside and got Scroot, and he came in and grabbed the Gator by the arm and said, as if speaking to a child, "C'mon, Daddy, just leave 'em alone." He pulled the Gator out the door, and he was gone. I never saw him again.

Scroot won the election, and that was a big disappointment. But his victory was dwarfed by the tremendous joy we felt when my mother also won. We were delirious with happiness. She was the first black ever elected in Baker County, and we savored that moment. It was hard to get your head around how far we'd come since that awful day eleven years earlier when my father had died. Before our eyes, Grace Miller had grown into a woman of great substance and ability, lit from within with an inner strength and faith that allowed her to do anything she set out to do.

My mother still recalls her first board meeting. She'd been hearing a lot of enthusiasm for her election from blacks and whites alike, but she understood that the reality was going to require patience and an open mind—two qualities she had in abundance. At the time the superintendent of schools was a Hall, as was my mother. (You'll recall that the black and white Halls were related.)

Before the meeting, Hall walked up to my mother and started asking her about family members he had not seen in several years, and she queried him about people on the white side of the family. When they took their seats, Hall rose and said he wanted to introduce them to the newest board member. "This is Grace Miller, Joe Hall's daughter," he said.

An elderly man in the audience spoke up. "Was that the nigger Joe Hall?" he asked loudly.

Before my mother could respond, he added, "That was an honest man. I dropped my wallet one time and Joe Hall found it and brought it back to me. All the money was there."

My mother smiled and remarked, "I realize he is old and probably doesn't understand what he's saying, but I want everyone else to understand that I don't expect that from you."

Another young white man mentioned that he'd heard about some of the things that had happened to our family, such as my father's murder and the cross burning. He said, "You seem like such a nice and positive person. How do you deal with it?"

My mother appreciated having the opportunity to talk about not letting hate run you. It was a big theme of her life, which she passed on to her children. To this day, my mother, now eighty, serves on the Baker County board of education, and she is quite popular. Several streets have been named after her. I keep telling her that maybe it's time for her to step down, and she always looks at me as if I'm crazy.

Scroot Johnson didn't have such a blemish-free tenure. In 1982, federal authorities charged him with embezzlement and tax evasion. He spent a few months in jail. The Johnson regime officially ended that year when his brother, Herbert, was defeated in the election. In 1996, Isaac Anderson became the first black sheriff of Baker County. Surely the Gator was turning in his grave.

We were politically active on another front during that period, seeking representation for black farmers. The Agricultural Stabilization and Conservation Service (ASCS) was the USDA agency that made all the decisions about which farmers would get loans, subsidies, and other aid. It operated through local committees, which were elected by farmers and farmworkers. For many years, going back to SNCC, we had tried to get blacks onto that committee, but it had been an uphill battle. Election tampering was common, farmer education was almost nonexistent, and intimidation was high. In the 1960s, SNCC contested elections in numerous counties throughout the South and began working with black farmers to prepare them for the election. They faced the same violent backlash they had with voter registration. The USDA eventually ordered that ASCS elections be conducted by mail to avoid voter intimidation. The problem was that mailed-in ballots were more likely to be "lost" or messed with.

In Baker County one year, SNCC sponsored a write-in campaign for three black candidates. The ASCS leaders confused the issue by placing several other black names on the ballot (which they were allowed to do without the agreement of the individuals), creating confusion and diluting the vote. That was a common tactic.

At New Communities, we worked with all the black farmers in the area, educating them about the process and convincing people to put their names on the ballot. We had rare victories but also plenty of disappointments. In one case our candidate actually won the election, but his opponent, a white woman, appealed, and a new election was ordered. Her supporters, knowing how many votes our side had cast, made sure that there were enough new votes to put her over the top. It was an ongoing struggle, completely ignored in the press, but essential to the livelihoods of farmers.

In the late seventies and early eighties, our region experienced a series of terrible droughts. Like all farmers in the affected areas we applied for an emergency loan from the Farmers Home Administration (FmHA), the arm of the USDA that administered grants and loans, so we could install an irrigation system and save our crops. Such emergency loans are the lifeblood of farmers when nature turns against the land. It took nearly three years to finally get the first emergency loan. The FmHA knew we would be severely hurt by its stalling. Three years without the necessary financing was too long for an operation our size, especially since the droughts continued.

When Charles first walked into the local FmHA office to apply for the loan, the supervisor looked him up and down in an unpleasant way and said, "You'll get a loan over my dead body."

Charles stared back at him with disbelief. Who was this backward character? New Communities had been in operation for twelve years at that point, and he thought we'd conquered the worst opposition and had become accepted, however reluctantly. He hadn't expected to be slapped in the face in a manner reminiscent of the early sixties.

We complained to Washington, and eventually three people from the national office, the district director from Albany, and the lone black person who worked in the state office in Athens went with us to the local office. We got the application that day, but we still had to work with the local representatives to submit the application and then suffered lengthy delays. We learned years later that plantations owned by wealthy landowners had received financing for irrigation at the same time as we were denied financing.

By way of background, the plight of black farmers had grown

increasingly dire during the last sixty years. In 1920, there had been 925,000 black farmers. In 1981, there were fewer than 25,000. There were several reasons for the decline, but the primary one was their lack of access to the funding sources upon which all farmers rely. Although the FmHA was a federally funded organization, the decisions about grants and loans were made on the local level, usually by a committee of white farmers and ranchers. There was hardly any black representation on those committees. Black farmers thus found the deck stacked against them.

Black farmers across the country had complained to the USDA about discrimination by the local committees, which regularly denied or delayed applications, or approved them for meager amounts that didn't even begin to meet their needs. The only avenue open to a farmer who believed his application was denied on the basis of race was to file a complaint with the USDA's Office of Civil Rights Enforcement and Adjudication. But in 1983, the Reagan administration dismantled OCREA, the complaint files languished in storage cabinets, and new complaints were often sent directly to the trash. Civil rights violations did not end with the closing of OCREA—just the means of adjudicating them. Most farmers had no idea that their claims were being filed in the garbage bins.

The drought conditions continued, and at one point we were forced to cut trees and sell lumber for $50,000. Money was extremely tight. Sometimes I'd sit up alone late into the night, crying over bills and not knowing how we'd make it. We were still trying to get a loan from the USDA, which told us that as a condition of a loan we had to give it our $50,000 in lumber proceeds. That was tough, but we had no choice, so we turned it over. Still nothing happened. Meanwhile, the agency made us jump through all kinds of hoops. At one point we were informed that we might not meet the definition of a farm because we weren't a "family" farm; we were something different. The representative came out, looked around at the fields, and asked, "Where are your children?" Now, our children were young then, and they weren't going to be working in the fields during schooldays, as my sisters and I had. Even so, we had to explain over and over again the difference between a family farm and a collective farming operation. It took us three years to get approved for our "emergency" loan, but by then it was too late. The USDA wasn't allowed to foreclose on farms then, but we also had a loan from Prudential. We had to find $100,000 a year to pay it. With the USDA demanding all of our receipts with the false promise of a loan in the offing, we didn't have the money to pay Prudential. It was a real catch-22.

Prudential foreclosed on the property in 1985. It was worth $5 million, and for want of $100,000 we lost our land. The land was quickly sold to a white businessman from Atlanta for $1 million, and Prudential turned around three weeks later and gave him a loan for $950,000. The new owner dug holes and pushed all of our buildings into them. That was adding insult to injury. I remember feeling that he wanted every trace of our existence buried.

We were heartbroken. We had poured our blood, sweat, and tears into New Communities, and it was impossible to believe that it had died just like that. Charles was so devastated that he wouldn't even talk about it for years, and he was the one we always relied on for hope. It was small comfort that New Communities would become the catalyst and a model for the community land trust movement in the United States, which produced hundreds of similar operations.

During the period when we were losing our land, I became a part of the Rural Development Leadership Network and was able to start working on a master's degree through an RDLN link with Antioch University. I was scheduled to spend a month in California studying at UC Davis, and when it became clear that our land would be sold on the courthouse steps, I was eager to go. I didn't want to be there to see it happen. It turned out that the sale was delayed, though, so I had to see it.

I was in RDLN's first class, and it was a new experience for me to get to know Hispanics, Asians, and Native Americans. We found common ground in our rural efforts. Shortly after my graduation, I was asked to serve on the board, and I continued to work with the organization over the years.

We had to feed our family, so I took a job with the Federation of

Southern Cooperatives/Land Assistance Fund, an organization dedicated to helping farmers keep their land. Because of our experience,
I was burning with commitment to make farming work for others.

The Federation of Southern Cooperatives/Land Assistance
Fund was established in 1967 to provide education, training, and
assistance to farmers. It was the only organization that had as its
central purpose the retention of black-owned land. An important
part of my job was to help farmers navigate the difficult loan process. I'd had a lot of experience with that, and it was becoming an
urgent matter. The U.S. Commission on Civil Rights was beginning
to sound the alarm, saying that unless something was done to help
them, within fifteen years there would be no black farmers left.

At the end of the Civil War there had been a short-lived policy
to give freed black men "forty acres and a mule" so they could make
their livelihoods from the land. We'd come a long way since then,
but discriminatory policies were setting back the dreams of black
farmers across the nation. My job was to stem the tide of foreclosures. Plainly put, I was out to help farmers figure out how to make
more money from what they were growing.

When I started working out of a tiny office in Albany, the Federation didn't have much of a presence in our area. I was mostly a
one-woman show. At first I relied on VISTA volunteers. Eventually
the USDA enabled us to hire staff. I loved the work. The demise of
New Communities had been such a terrible blow, and now I found
the small blossoming of hope that would allow me to carry on.

CHAPTER 8

Saving Farmers

A funny thing happened as my work with the Federation gained notoriety across southwest Georgia: I started getting appeals from white farmers. Although the Federation had originally been organized to help blacks, it had quickly grown to encompass a mission of outreach for all rural farmers.

You already know about the Spooners, the couple from Iron City, Georgia, who came to me for help. Roger Spooner says when he was sent to me he had no idea that I was black until he walked into my office, and he didn't care. A proud World War II veteran who fought in the Battle of Midway, Roger had watched two of his brothers lose their farms, and he was getting ready to lose his, too.

I've always been glad I was there in that office when Roger needed me, because he was in even worse straits than he recognized at the time. At that point, he was faced with foreclosure; only a temporary injunction against the USDA preventing foreclosures was holding it off. He knew that as soon as the injunction was lifted he could receive a foreclosure notice. That injunction gave us time to work on his case.

During his first visit with me, Roger talked nervously about his service to his country. I didn't perceive it as nervous talk because I didn't know him at the time. I perceived it as a white man showing that he was asking me for help but at the same time showing me he was superior. He talked about having been on a submarine and his service to his country. Referring to the foreclosure, he said, "I don't believe my country will do this to me."

I looked him straight in the eyes and responded, "If you sit back and do nothing, you will see what your country will do."

I told him I didn't think he would qualify for Chapter 12 bankruptcy because he did not meet all of the criteria. For him to qualify, at least 50 percent of his gross income had to come from farming in the year preceding the filing. Normally, that wouldn't have been an issue. But Roger hadn't farmed the previous year because while he was struggling, the county supervisor had rented his farm to another farmer even though she didn't have the right to do so. At that time, he should have been the only one who could have rented his farm to another farmer because it had not been taken from him. The supervisor had done something that was not legal. Be that as it may, the fact that he hadn't farmed the previous year made him ineligible for a chapter of bankruptcy that Congress had created just for family farmers.

Even though I knew Roger would not qualify for Chapter 12, I took him to a lawyer in Albany who had attended the training that was held on Chapter 12 when it was offered at the Albany Civic Center. I made the appointment while Roger was sitting in my office. When he came back to Albany for the appointment, he was accompanied by his wife, Eloise. They were obviously good, hardworking people, and I could see that they were placing all their faith in me. I explained the situation to them, and the lawyer asked them to bring financial records and other documents for filing Chapter 11 bankruptcy. That was in November 1986. When we left the lawyer's office that day, I felt confident he would work to save the Spooners' farm.

The next time I heard from the Spooners was in May 1987. The USDA injunction had been lifted, and foreclosure notices had been mailed. The Spooners were among a group of thirteen farmers in Georgia who had received a notice. They called me to say that it had arrived and the sale date at the courthouse was the first Tuesday in June. I told them to make an appointment with their lawyer and promised to meet them at his office.

It was not a good meeting. First, the lawyer made us wait for more than an hour, which only increased Roger and Eloise's nervousness. When we were finally admitted, the Spooners gave him the foreclosure documents. The lawyer looked at the documents and then looked at the Spooners and said, "You all are getting old. Why don't you just let the farm go?"

His words shocked me to the core. This couple had paid him since November, and he was advising them to give up! I said, "I can't believe you said that. It is obvious to me that if you cannot use a Chapter 12 to stop the foreclosure, you will have to use Chapter 11." The lawyer looked at me and said, "I will do whatever you say." I told him firmly, "You have to file Chapter 11."

We left his office understanding that he would file Chapter 11 bankruptcy to stop the sale at the courthouse steps. We knew—I should say, *I* knew—that the work to save the farm would be more difficult under Chapter 11, but it was a necessary first step.

On the Thursday before Memorial Day, the Spooners called me, upset, to say their lawyer had not made a filing. They were rightly worried, because we were a little less than two weeks away from the sale date. I told them I would see if I could find someone else to help them.

I began calling everyone I knew. I even called friends who lived in other states. I remember spending hours on the phone reaching out to every person I could think of to assist us with stopping the pending sale on the courthouse steps. When I'd run out of names, I sat pondering at my desk. Suddenly I remembered a lawyer I had visited with a farmer who was located just forty miles away in Americus. His name was Ben Easterlin. I called Ben and explained, "I have a man whose farm is getting ready to be sold on the courthouse steps in two weeks, and his lawyer is not doing anything to stop the sale." I explained the problem with Chapter 12.

Ben listened and then asked, "How soon can you come to the office?"

"You tell me a time, and we'll be there," I said.

To my great relief, he replied, "How's ten o'clock tomorrow morning?"

I called the Spooners and told them that we were going to Americus the next morning and they should bring all their financial documents. We arranged for them to pick me up on the way.

I will never forget how carefully Ben studied each document, with a thoughtful expression on his face. Finally, he looked up and smiled at the Spooners. "We can't file Chapter 12, as you know," he said, "but I will file Chapter 11, and we'll get the same result."

Time was growing short. The following Monday was Memorial Day. Ben made sure the documents were filed in federal court in Columbus, Georgia, that week.

The Spooners were very grateful, and I felt blessed to have had the opportunity to help them. Filing the papers in federal court was only the start of the difficult struggle to save the farm. It took several years, but when Roger and Eloise were finally released from Chapter 11 bankruptcy, they called me to say it was finally over.

It wasn't easy, but the important thing is that they didn't lose the farm. In fact, they're still there. We've stayed in touch over the years, and I'd say we developed a friendly relationship.

The Spooners opened my eyes to the fact that poor farmers, both white and black, needed help and there weren't many resources available for any of them. Until then, I had been completely focused on the plight of black farmers, and although that was a worthy mission, I was beginning to see that the greatest struggle for farmers was poverty, and it didn't matter what color your skin was. I saw my job as creating a bridge from poverty.

One case I remember well was that of a white farmer named Jim Garner who grew flowers. He came to me from Ty Ty, in Tift County, Georgia. What they say about Ty Ty is that it's so small that you enter town on the first Ty of the sign and leave on the second. Jim had been trying to borrow money from the FmHA, but he was having trouble with the county supervisor. "He tells me growing flowers ain't farming," he said. I'd never given a lot of thought to flowers, but now I did. Why wouldn't growing flowers be farming? Flowers were a product.

I called the state office to say that the county supervisor would not accept the application because he had said that Jim was not farming. I was assured that if he was growing flowers, he was a farmer, and the county supervisor was obliged to accept the application. However, after accepting the application, the county supervisor sent a letter denying the loan, saying that Jim was not involved in a *normal* farming operation in Tift County, Georgia. I called the state office again and once again was assured that flower production was a normal farming operation. The county supervisor had to accept that, but he then denied the application again, saying that Jim hired too much labor. Jim had only one full-time employee and used seasonal labor, the same as vegetable growers in the area, but the state office would not override the decision and said we had to appeal it.

I jumped into the bureaucratic standoff with both feet, reflecting—not for the first time—how rigidity and intransigence could make such trouble for people who just wanted to make a decent living.

It took me eighteen months to get Jim his loan. On the positive side, Jim was around a lot, and he saw the work we were doing. He approached me about a cooperative arrangement to grow specialty flowers with black farmers. As I studied Jim's records, I was amazed to learn how lucrative flower growing could be. I'd had no idea. One acre of flowers could net $10,000, while many farmers growing peanuts were lucky to net $1,000 an acre. I believed it could be a real boon to the area. We drew up the plans and incorporated with the name Southern Alternatives. We had many meetings with farmers, and Jim taught them how to grow flowers. That was during a time when many of the farmers were just a hairsbreadth away from failing. They needed the infusion of new capital, and I was feeling pretty proud of myself that I'd started the enterprise. But there was something going on beneath the surface that was stalling the effort. I'd go over to the farms, and I'd see that they were really dragging their feet about getting started. I couldn't figure it out. "What's the problem?" I asked them, frustrated. "You can make so much more money growing flowers."

At last one of the farmers looked at me sadly and shook his head.

"I guess it's that if anybody asked me what I was growing, I just couldn't say 'Flowers.'" So Southern Alternatives didn't work because the farmers had a macho problem with the crop. Imagine that. I couldn't push them, though. Their male pride was greater than their need for cash. I always regretted that one.

Over the years I worked with many poor white families. In the latter part of the 1980s, when there were a huge number of foreclosures by the USDA of farmers all over the country, I heard tragic stories of white farmers committing suicide. Black farmers may have had the added burden of discrimination, and that was no small thing, but the white farmers I dealt with were poor and desperate, too. And nobody was rushing in to rescue them. Sometimes it seemed to me that the USDA's solution to every problem was foreclosure. In my view, the agency lacked a dedication to its purpose, which not only hurt farmers but also had a negative impact on the entire economy. People didn't always get the connection between farmers doing well and families across the nation being able to afford to put food on the table. We were all in it together.

Here's an example of what we faced. Typically, when farmers received delinquency notices, they were allowed forty-five days to submit information in an application so it could be determined whether they should be granted a moratorium or a change in payment plan, or some other relief that would help them stay solvent. Again, the purpose was to open up opportunities, not just close the door and turn off the lights. In 1988, which was a presidential election year (Vice President George Bush versus Michael Dukakis), the Reagan administration held up the delinquency notices, which were supposed to go out in June, until after the election. Maybe they were afraid of the publicity that ninety thousand delinquency notices being sent out to hardworking farmers might generate.

The week after the election, which Bush won, the delinquency notices went out across the country, and there was a desperate scramble to get the applications together over the holidays so they could be submitted by the deadline, which was January 2. My office was packed, because the black farmers in the area knew where they could go for help. But then the word started spreading, and white farmers started showing up at the office from Florida, asking if I could help them. I canceled Christmas that year so I could file dozens of applications. I felt then that I was the only one who could help them, and I was glad to do it. But it showed me just how few resources there were. It was a crying shame that the USDA had no program in place to help farmers go through the overwhelming paperwork. Once again, the government didn't seem to want to help.

I was coming to see that education was a critical component of my advocacy mission. Farmers were so desperate that they were trying everything they could think of, but sometimes their solutions didn't make any sense. Once a group of white farmers in Missouri asked me to come to their conference and speak. I stayed around and sat in on some workshops. In one they were talking about starting a free-range chicken operation, because they'd heard of some farmers in Iowa who were doing a good business that way.

I listened to them talk, and finally I couldn't help myself, I had to speak up. So I said, "Please explain to me why you're sitting here trying to figure out how to market something you're not even producing. Why don't you stick with what you're already doing and figure out a better way to market it. What do you produce?"

They said grain, and they also mentioned hogs. Well, that lit up a bulb in my brain. We'd had great luck with hogs at New Communities. "Why don't you market your hog products directly to the consumers?" I asked. They said no, it couldn't be done. So I told them the story of our operation, how we'd take the hogs to be slaughtered and then bring the products back to the farm and make our own cured ham and bacon and pork chops and sausages. And we'd made a better profit selling these products than we would have made selling the hogs.

They listened to me and started to get excited. I even sent them my sausage recipe when I got back home. A year later, they asked me to come back and see how they were doing. It was a growing operation, with a large mail-order business, and it's operating to this day.

With farmers struggling just to get by year after year, we were always looking for creative solutions. In the early nineties Ben &

Jerry's Ice Cream Company came to us, wanting to support black farmers in the area. Ben & Jerry's was already producing pecan ice cream but had the idea of buying processed pecans from our farmers. It sent a representative down to work with me, and we began going around the area, visiting pecan farms. We also had to locate a facility that we could contract with to process the pecans.

While trying to find a processing plant, we encountered racism. We couldn't find anyone to help us. They all saw an opportunity for themselves but not so much for our farmers. The pecan-processing plants were not interested in entering into a contract with black farmers to process their pecans for them. They basically said, "Tell you what we'll do. We'll buy the pecans from black farmers, and we'll process and sell them to Ben & Jerry's, and they can say the ice cream has pecans from black farmers in it." That was no different from what was already happening—with the exception that the plant would have a big new customer. One of the processing plant managers said straight out to the Ben & Jerry's representative, "If your arrangement doesn't work out with black farmers, will you buy from us?" That was not what anybody had in mind. Eventually, I had to inform Ben & Jerry's that we could not find a plant to process the pecans for black growers, and they had to get one of their major suppliers to do the processing.

Throughout this whole experience it occurred to me that what the farmers needed was their own processing facility. Ben & Jerry's paid market price plus a premium to the farmers, and I encouraged them to save the premium. And they did that and acquired their own facility in 1997. There are between twenty-five and thirty farmers who are a part of the cooperative, called Southern Alternatives Agricultural Cooperative. Its current owners are a group of black women who have taken on the job of growing and processing shelled pecans, which they buy from black farmers. They are members of the Federation of Southern Cooperatives/Land Assistance Fund and the Southern Rural Black Women's Initiative and are a real success story. Their work goes far beyond the pecan business. Many of the women of Southern Alternatives participate in a community advocacy group called Smithies Women on the Move that runs an after-school program, holds voter registration drives, and seeks to prevent injustice by monitoring both courts and council meetings. Other community activities include ministering to the elderly with home visits and field trips and ministering to prisoners through correspondence and by hosting their families. It's a well-rounded effort and a shining example of what an organized group of women can accomplish.

I doubt that Ben & Jerry's would have had the idea of working with black farmers at all if it hadn't been for a Farm Aid concert. That's where they met Ralph Paige, the director of the Federation, and came up with the idea of the pecan project. Those annual concerts, sponsored by Willie Nelson, Neil Young, John Mellencamp, and Dave Matthews, had raised millions of dollars for farmers since beginning in 1985, and they had increased people's awareness of the plight of farmers. They were truly a lifeline.

I was invited to the Farm Aid concert in Irving, Texas, in 1992, and it was an amazing experience. Willie Nelson was an inspiration as he called out to the crowd of tens of thousands of people, "I'm proud to be one of you!" At one point I was pulled into a press conference, along with Tracy Chapman and Neil Young. I was embarrassed at first to be sitting at the table because I wasn't a celebrity, but when a reporter asked me, "Shirley, how does it feel to be sitting between Tracy Chapman and Neil Young?" I grinned. "It feels great," I said.

I was so thankful for the work of Farm Aid, because it did more than anything else to raise consciousness about the plight of farmers. Willie Nelson became a symbol of farmers' survival. The farmers worshipped him. He raised up their self-pride and their economic fortunes at the same time. Every year he stood on the giant stage and called out, "Where's the government? Where are the people from the USDA? I thought they'd be here in force to see what they could do for the American farmer." He and Neil Young wrote a ballad called "The Farmer's Song," which brought roars of response from the crowds every time they sang it. I have attended nearly every Farm Aid concert since 1992, and it is always an experience full of hope and joy.

*   *   *

In 2000, I learned that the school system was building a new school and the building that had housed my segregated elementary and high school was scheduled for demolition. I didn't want to let that happen. Surely we could find some community use for the building. Baker County was still desperately poor and in need of services.

We were having a high school reunion at the time, and at the banquet I stood right up and made an impassioned speech. "They're planning to tear down our school building," I said. "Now, most of you recall what that building, that 'separate but equal' facility, meant to us—hot lunches, indoor plumbing, and for the first time an environment where we could learn. We have to protest them tearing it down and find another purpose for it as a community center. Will you help me?" Nineteen people signed up that night, and we formed a committee.

We didn't have any money to hire advisers, so we got a lawyer to volunteer, and I drew up the tax exemption papers myself. The local officials were actually quite open to the idea of the building becoming a community center. They knew we couldn't afford to buy it, but they agreed to rent it to us for what they paid in insurance, which was $3,400 a year.

We started cleaning out the building, which was a mess and in a terrible state of deterioration, and we had dozens of volunteers showing up with mops and paint buckets. It was an invigorating experience. We were also doing fund-raising, and our first grant was for $10,000, arranged through the state by our local state representative. The first thing we renovated was the girls' restroom, which was unusable. We kept raising money, and we came up with the idea of a $1,000 charter membership, with plaques for those who contributed. I remember vividly one of those people, a ninety-two-year-old lady who paid her charter membership in increments of $20. One night before our meeting started, I heard her holler, "Oh, thank you, Lord." She had just been told by the treasurer that she'd finally finished paying the charter membership and her name would go up on the plaque in gold letters.

One of the centerpieces of the operation was planned as a community commercial kitchen, where folks could cook up their recipes, bottle and package them, and then sell them. We submitted an application to USDA Rural Development, and it took a couple of years for it to come up with the grant that allowed us to buy kitchen equipment. The grant from Rural Development was a reimbursable grant in the amount of $99,999. Four of us guaranteed the loan from the bank to buy the equipment for the kitchen.

We also began to get funding from private and church foundations—$60,000 here, $50,000 there. We got the kitchen up and running and started a boys' and girls' club and a historical library. We also started a sewing cooperative called Southern Journeys. Southern Journeys was created from the Southern Rural Black Women's Initiative for Economic and Social Justice, a three-state project I helped start in 2001.

Today the center is our pride and joy, especially the kitchen. It is beautifully laid out, with state-of-the-art equipment. There are classes in production and marketing. Some of the products made there have become huge sellers, and we get a nutritional analysis on each item done by the University of Georgia, so they all have labels. Enthusiasm runs high. The fish sauce guy was a good example. One day I went to the drugstore, and the druggist told me about a friend who owned a restaurant and made the best fish sauce he'd ever tasted. He wanted help getting it to market.

"Tell him to send me a bottle," I said. The next day a *case* of fish sauce arrived at my office.

We always asked the school board to give the building to us since we were doing things for the community. The school board hadn't thought we would be successful, which is why it had initially told us to rent and keep up with the amount of money we spent on improvement. Its members told us that once the amount we spent equaled or exceeded the value of the building, they would give us the deed. They deeded the property to East Baker in 2010.

The matter of who had owned the previous deed was of great interest to us. One day the school board's attorney, Kenneth Musgrove, called me to his office to show me the original deed for the property where the school is located. It had been owned by the Negro Board of Trustees. In 1951, it had given the property to the school board for $10 to try to get a better educational facility for the black children. He said, "It's only right that it come back to you."

The community center became a bulwark of our economic vision for blacks in our area, but as word spread to other struggling communities, we had frequent visits from city managers and small businesses from across the state, wanting to know how they could launch similar projects, and many of them were white. Poverty, more than race, was the tie that bound us.

CHAPTER 9

————— • ◆ • —————

At Home in the World

I n the early years of the Clinton administration, I was approached about becoming state director of the FmHA. Now, *that* was a job I could sink my teeth into. The FmHA had been the bane of all our existences for so long. I could see the potential. Needless to say, there had never been a person of color in the state director's job. The only reason I felt I had a decent chance of getting the appointment as state director was that Mike Espy was the first African-American secretary of agriculture and the atmosphere for change seemed more positive.

During a review for my appointment, I got to see a little more of the tortured political process than I cared to. Sam Nunn was the senior senator from Georgia at that time, and although he was a Democrat, he hadn't initially supported Clinton, and he opposed my appointment. I had to prove to him that I was capable of doing the job. I agreed to go to Atlanta for an interview, and I felt very confident. I knew the regulations backward and forward. I understood the purpose of the FmHA as if it were imprinted in my DNA. I walked into the meeting to find four white men sitting around a table, waiting to grill me. After a vigorous discussion, which dwelled more on my personal life than on my work and knowledge of the agency, I walked away not having any idea what kind of impression

I'd made. But I kept hearing that Nunn was intent on blocking my nomination and the administration was trying to push it through.

I felt that if the job offer came, I had an obligation to take it. But I had a conflict that was weighing on me. I was in line for a W. K. Kellogg Foundation fellowship. If you think I was amazed to find myself in that position, you'd be right. I never would have expected something like that to come my way.

Here's how it happened. Jerry Pennick, my friend and colleague at the Federation, had been bugging me about applying for a Kellogg fellowship. Finally, just to shut him up, I called for the application, but it seemed kind of crazy to me. When I read the application, it was even crazier. The fellowship was all about taking time out to study and travel and experience the world. I laughed to myself. "Who has time for that kind of luxury?" I thought. I put the application on the credenza behind my desk and didn't fill it in. It didn't seem right for me. I even called a friend who had just lost a congressional election and suggested she come by my office and pick up the application. Maybe it would be right for her. She never came, though, and the deadline was getting closer.

One day, I was having a particularly rough time. I was tired and frustrated, and on a whim I pulled the application off my credenza and started filling it out. It was nearing the deadline by then, and I had to send it by overnight mail. And I thought, "That's the end of that."

But it wasn't. To my surprise I received a letter saying I was one of 134 finalists chosen for a personal interview. The foundation arranged for me to fly to Dallas on Sunday, have the interview Monday, and fly back that same day. When I looked at the ticket and saw that it had cost $1,100, I was horrified. Surely the foundation didn't want to spend that much. I actually called and said, "You can get a cheaper ticket if I stay over Saturday night, and I really don't mind doing it." I could hear the amusement in the woman's voice as she assured me, "No, that's all right, Ms. Sherrod. It doesn't matter."

When I arrived for my interview, I expected my application to be discussed, and I was ready for it. But the six people in the room were smiling and casual, and they made it clear that they just wanted to get to know me as a person. So we started talking, and soon the issue of education came up. I said that I had strong views about education and how it leads to better opportunities. I told them a story about my daughter. "She announced one day that she didn't want to go to college," I related. "I told her, 'Oh, no, you're going to college. Maybe in another life you don't go, but in this one you're going!'" They started laughing, and I felt much more at ease.

Toward the end of our interview, one of the panel members asked me a question that surprised me: "Shirley, is there anything you've always wanted to do that you've never had the opportunity to do?"

I said, "Yes, I've always wanted to go to Africa."

"Where in Africa?"

I started listing Ghana, Kenya, Nigeria, and some other places. They smiled and nodded.

I left the room, thinking how remarkable it was to be in a setting where people talked more about dreams than necessities. But I told myself that it was time to get back down to earth. I still had interviews for the state director's job coming up. I didn't think I had much chance of getting a Kellogg fellowship, but it had been a great experience.

A few weeks after the Kellogg interview, I was scheduled to accompany Ralph Paige to Washington, where I would spend a day making the rounds of elected officials and talk about my qualifications for the state director's job. I returned to my hotel room at the end of the day with sore feet, weary of talking about myself. I sat back and called Charles, eager to hear his warm voice from home.

With a teasing chuckle, Charles said, "You got a letter from Kellogg today."

I said I'd open it when I got home. I assumed it was a letter saying I hadn't gotten the fellowship, and I didn't want to know the contents until I got back. The next day I was flying from Washington to Cleveland to attend a weekend meeting with rural women. I wasn't interested in hearing any bad news while I was on the road.

We kept talking for a while, and then Charles brought up the letter again. Now I sat up a little. "Did you open it?" I asked suspiciously.

"Yeah," he admitted, and I could tell he was grinning.

"Okay, what did it say?"

"You got the fellowship," he announced, and I just sat there in stunned silence. When we hung up the phone, I paced the hotel room for a long time, murmuring "Oh, my goodness. Oh, my goodness."

I didn't know what to think, because I realized that if I got the state director appointment, I would have to take it. I owed it to the farmers. I wondered if anyone had ever turned down a Kellogg fellowship before. It was a pointless fear, because Nunn won out and I didn't get the FmHA appointment.

Nunn's announcement of Georgia appointments, which didn't include my name, came the day after the Senate voted to approve Clinton's pet project, the North American Free Trade Agreement (NAFTA). I always assumed that Nunn's being given the choice of appointments was part of a trade for his favorable vote on NAFTA. Now I was free to embrace the Kellogg opportunity.

The Kellogg fellowship was an unprecedented life experience: three years of growing and learning, with a personal budget attached. Believe me, it wasn't frivolous. The intention was to better prepare motivated people to accomplish more in their real life occupations. I took on the task with great vigor. I was determined to make it count in my work back home.

We began with a weeklong gathering of the fifty selectees at a center near Chicago. They gave us computers and brought in twenty-one psychologists to talk to us individually about our issues and aspirations. One of the bright spots was that if you were currently working with a nonprofit organization—which I was—they would put your designated money into the nonprofit, and you'd draw off that. They also gave money to the nonprofit so you would be released to travel—so that far from abandoning the Federation, which had been a concern of mine, I was enabling it. After a day of work, I would go back to my room and pinch myself. It was unbelievable.

Kellogg had six advisers, and each of us was asked to choose one. I chose Frances Hesselbein, who had been the CEO of the Girl Scouts for fourteen years. She was at that time the president of the Peter F. Drucker Foundation for Nonprofit Management, a truly impressive woman.

I remember that after that week you could have peeled most of us off the ceiling. We were flying with possibilities that we'd never imagined. So the last thing they did was bring us back down to earth. "Just remember," they said, "while you've been here, your families have been dealing with their ordinary stresses, so tone it down a notch when you get home. Don't be princes and princesses. You have a gift in this opportunity. Be humble."

I took that message to heart. Someone told me that there had been a rash of divorces as a result of the fellowship, and you could see where it might be hard for the landlocked folks to not be a bit resentful of us. We felt like the chosen few, but I decided to keep my eye on how I could use the fellowship to improve the plight of poor people. To that end, the program helped me enormously. I had mediation training and conflict management training. I developed skills that I knew would be put to good use.

My first international trip was to Ghana in West Africa. Ghana was the center of the British slave trade for more than 150 years, and many of the sites have been preserved to this day. We toured the slave-trading sites, such as Elmina Castle, where we walked through the slave dungeons and tried to imagine the fear and horror of the men and women chained there. Some of those slaves were eventually shipped to America to work on plantations not far from my home. I could not stop my tears. The emotions welled up in me as I stood at the center of my own brutal history. I was eager to bond with the people in Ghana, because surely we shared so much. They didn't exactly agree. We might have called ourselves African Americans, holding tight to the link with our ancestral homeland. But they called us black Americans, dismissing the brotherhood and sisterhood we wanted to establish.

I became friendly with a Ghanaian woman, and one day she invited me to dinner at her home. She said she would send a driver and asked me to bring two males and a female as part of the group. I had no idea that she was wealthy until the driver pulled up to a beautiful gated estate. He blew the horn, and a gardener appeared to open the gate. The house was lovely, and she had many servants. Her husband was a prominent physician.

The dinner conversation was fascinating and sometimes heated. Her husband had gone to the United States at one point, but he had felt poorly treated by black people. He definitely had a sour opinion of U.S. blacks, and he didn't mind saying so. As the discussion grew more argumentative, I finally broke in to plead that we put our past behind us and become brothers and sisters. I wasn't being naive. I truly believed that was our only hope. We left the dinner with hugs and promises to meet again, but the visit was a wake-up call for me. I had glibly assumed there would be a soul connection with the people of Ghana. However, they were more circumspect. American blacks were cultural strangers to them, and our life experience was different. We could not automatically assume kinship. We had to build it.

I also had the opportunity to travel to China to attend the United Nations' Fourth World Conference on Women in Beijing in 1995. Working with Starry Krueger at the Rural Development Leadership Network (RDLN), we decided to raise money to take a group of rural women to the conference. We raised enough to take fifty women of diverse backgrounds—black, white, Hispanic, and Native American. (The Native American women accompanied us as far as Seoul, Korea, but could not enter China because they had not applied for their visas in time.)

Most of the women had never been outside the country or even their own local communities. And there they were in China, touring the Great Wall. It was something to see. The work and the bonding that occurred on that trip paid off when we got back home. The fellowship period flew by, and I emerged stronger, more confident, and full of renewed purpose.

My life had always been grounded in the rural soil, but over the years—especially after my Kellogg fellowship—I was growing more aware of how interlinked we were with the global economy. At the Federation, we were especially frustrated by the ongoing Cuban embargo, which seemed to have long ago outlived its purpose. There was a knee-jerk attitude about communism, but it was nothing more than a dusty remnant of an old reality. To me it seemed hard to argue that Cuba provided a danger to the United States. What it *did* provide was opportunity in the form of exports. That was a fact U.S. farmers knew all too well. In reality, the tiny nation ninety miles from our shore might have added billions of dollars to the agricultural economy of this country if only we had opened our minds to the possibility. Agricultural experts stated that if the embargo were lifted, U.S. farmers would reap an immediate benefit that would continue. Sadly, the idea that a Cuban embargo was necessary for our security was deeply entrenched.

On my first visit to Cuba, in a group that included former Secretary of Agriculture Mike Espy, we were looking into the possibility of growing black beans for Cubans. We took a convoluted route through the Bahamas. After a seven-hour layover, as we boarded the plane to Cuba, I was nervous, because the plane was a very old Russian model that looked long past its use-by date. As we flew over the water, I looked out the window and prayed that we'd make it to Cuba.

We arrived in Havana late on a warm, humid night and were met by our hosts and taken to a glorious guesthouse across the street from the Chinese Embassy. It was old-fashioned, with a rural feeling that I found quite comfortable, although it had a dining room and bar more like a hotel's. The rural feeling was heightened when I was awoken suddenly at 5:30 AM the following morning by the cacophony of crowing roosters. They were so loud that at first I thought they were inside the guesthouse, but they were next door.

We stayed for nine days, and it was a real eye-opener. We visited many farms, and everywhere we went there were lavish spreads of food laid out for us. We were learning that the Cubans themselves didn't get very much to eat, so it was embarrassing, but they took great pride in providing us with such plenty. It wasn't very sanitary, though. There were flies everywhere, buzzing atop the food spread, and I kept trying to brush them away, without success. Finally, Jerry Pennick, who was with me on the trip, laughed and said, "Just give it up, Shirley."

We visited a medical facility and found that Cubans had medical care from womb to tomb. We talked to doctors and also visited a school where medical students from the United States were studying. We didn't get a chance to meet them but were told that Cuba offered five hundred scholarships a year to students from the United States. We also learned that the literacy rate in Cuba was 97 percent and education was free.

When we began to visit farms, I noticed something that startled me: perhaps from economic necessity or from a commitment to the environment and health, Cuban farmers had long before adopted the techniques of sustainable agriculture—something that was only just being started in parts of the United States. Sustainable agriculture is considered very progressive in our country. In Cuba, it was just the way it was done.

On that trip, I was very interested in the plight of women, and I always wanted to talk with them. I kept asking "Why are there no women in leadership positions?" By the end of the trip, the organizers made sure there were women at the table, because they knew I'd ask.

A few years after my first visit, I had the opportunity to return, representing the Federation on a fact-finding mission facilitated by Oxfam America. Our goal was modest: to promote dialogue between farm cooperatives in the United States and Cuban farmers and in the process to maintain pressure on the government to open up trade between the two countries. Our sponsor in Cuba was the National Association of Small Farmers (ANAP).

Repeatedly, I observed how Cubans were creative and hardworking, in spite of living in conditions that most Americans would not tolerate. Basic supplies such as soap, toilet tissue, paper, and school supplies are hard for the average family to procure. I talked to a few young people who were married and, because of the embargo and lack of building supplies, could not afford to move out of their parents' homes.

Yet in spite of it all—or perhaps because of the creativity required in harsh conditions—the people have become good farmers, mechanics, teachers, and doctors. They've adapted. In some ways the experience of traveling through Cuba took me back to my childhood. We, too, lacked many of the basic essentials that one might think were a requirement for success. Often we didn't even have schoolbooks or heat during the winter. But many of us rose above those hardships and were more driven to succeed than we might have been if we'd had everything handed to us.

I returned home convinced that there was no logical reason for the Cuban embargo. Our farmers were crying out for the opportunity that trade with Cuba provided. And the Cuban people seemed eager to meet us halfway. I prayed that common sense would prevail.

CHAPTER 10

A Place at the Table

A consistent theme of my work with black farmers was the difficulties they had dealing with the FmHA. I heard countless stories of loans delayed or denied, a topic I was intimately acquainted with from our own experience at New Communities. We were constantly challenged by these new, more hidden forms of racism, which were much harder to uncover, prove, and remedy.

The early civil rights movement had been built around reversing measurably intolerable conditions that anyone with eyes to see could observe: whites-only facilities, protesters hosed, beaten, and jailed for peaceful assembly, segregated schools, people lynched in the night, citizens refused the right to vote, cross burnings on lawns, churches bombed, and so forth. But once segregation was no longer an official and lawful daily reality, the movement floundered somewhat. There was no master strategy for rooting out the deeply ingrained racism that still lived in the hearts and minds of many people and was buried in the system itself. The burden of proof for discrimination was high, and it was higher still for the poor. When the Reagan administration closed the USDA's civil rights office in 1983, it was with the tacit understanding that discriminatory practices were a thing of the past. But that was far from the case.

In 1994, the situation got so bad that Secretary Mike Espy commissioned a research study to analyze the treatment of minorities and women in FmHA programs. The study was an eye-opener. It showed that few discrimination claims were ever made because the process was so daunting and the barriers to success were so high. However, it definitively demonstrated that discrimination went on. The study also found that an overwhelming percentage of USDA loans went to corporations and white male farmers.

In 1996, Espy's successor, Daniel Glickman, ordered a suspension of government farm foreclosures while he launched an investigation into racial discrimination. He appointed the USDA Civil Rights Task Force, which ultimately made ninety-two recommendations for corrective action. Those recommendations promised to be a good first step in changing the situation, but they did virtually nothing to accommodate the thousands of farmers who had suffered, and even lost their land, through discrimination in the past. What would be done to give them justice?

Even as that matter was being debated in the administration, there were congressional efforts under way to remove safety nets that had protected poor farmers, including black farmers. Under Speaker of the House Newt Gingrich's "Contract with America," the little guy got squeezed out.

In 1996, Congress passed the Federal Agriculture Improvement and Reform Act, also known as the Freedom to Farm Act, which blatantly favored corporations over family farms. Most disturbing, small farms were in danger of losing even the shaky support that had allowed them to barely get by in previous years. One important program that was being stripped of most of its money was the Outreach and Assistance for Socially Disadvantaged Farmers and Ranchers grant program, created to provide technical assistance to poor farmers, including blacks, Hispanics, Native Americans, and women—the very groups that the commission's report had proved were discriminated against.

Under Gingrich, affirmative action programs were openly targeted, and for the first time the idea of reverse racism gained currency in some circles. No one wanted to talk about the past anymore, and some people were growing impatient with the demands of minorities. A comment I heard often was "How much do you people want?" as if equality were a greedy quest. At the Federation, we waged an uphill battle to protect small farms, but we were seeing an increasing shift to corporate farm power.

Under the auspices of the Federation of Southern Cooperatives/ Land Assistance Fund, the Land Loss Prevention Project, and the Farmers' Legal Action Group (FLAG), we had worked on the issue of a lawsuit for several years. We kept talking about the alarming instances of black farmers' land loss and discrimination against them at the USDA, and we finally decided to start the process of filing a suit. We began with a Freedom of Information Act request for files of discrimination complaints and were initially told by the USDA that there were *none*. When the agency was finally ordered by the court to release the records, it delivered fifty-five boxes. We filed a lawsuit using six farmers, and those cases were eventually won. They would be the precursor of a major class action suit.

A class action suit is one that represents a large group of people with a common claim, and it is named for the lead claimant in the suit. In this case that was a man named Timothy Pigford. Pigford, the son and grandson of farmers in Wilmington, North Carolina, had always dreamed of having his own land. In 1976, he wanted to buy a 175-acre farm. The local FmIIA office would not approve him for ownership, but it gave him an operating loan to work a rental property, with the expectation that he'd get his ownership loan before too long. But year after year, Pigford was denied an ownership loan. Then, in 1984, after eight years of successful farming, he was denied not only an ownership loan but also an operating loan, making it impossible for him to continue farming his rental acreage. The reason given was that he lacked training and experience in farming! Pigford believed it was racism, pure and simple. He'd been farming all his life.

The decision was devastating to Pigford's family. He and his wife had two young children, and they could barely survive. At one point they could not even afford electricity. It took them many years to get back onto their feet.

In 1997, Pigford decided to file a discrimination claim, which was joined by four hundred other black farmers who had faced discrimination between 1981 and 1996 and became the lawsuit *Pigford v. Glickman*. (Dan Glickman was the secretary of agriculture at the time.)

Soon farmers began to come to me for advice about joining the suit and filing their claims. Late one night, I was driving home from Alabama, and I was thinking about some of the farmers I'd met and the work I'd done helping them file. They were sad stories. One man described being kicked off his property right before bulldozers came and turned his farmland into a pit. "We were hurt, and we had to take that hurt and move on," he said softly. But now he was looking for justice.

Driving into the night, I reflected on our own experience with New Communities, and I realized that we had a claim as well. I'd been so busy helping others file that I hadn't given it proper thought, but now the deadline was looming. I had no cell phone then, and I was in the boondocks over by Eufaula, Alabama, with another two and a half hours to go before I reached Albany. I couldn't wait to get home.

I burst into the house and called out, "Charles, we need to file a claim in the Pigford case." I told him about my realization, and although the hour was late, his face lit up with pure excitement, and he was energized like you wouldn't believe. We got an attorney named Rose Sanders, an activist in Selma, Alabama, and began the long process.

When we'd been foreclosed on, we'd had to leave the property so fast that we hadn't had proper storage for all our files and documents. We'd stuck them in an old warehouse by the Flint River that had been flooded during the flood of 1994, so we'd lost a lot. But we still managed to pull together a credible amount of material, and then we went with Rose to the Lee County public archives to get more information. Rose told us that we needed to prove that similarly situated white farms had gotten loans that we hadn't. Until that point, we'd never known that the white farmers had received relief during the drought that had been denied to us. We didn't know that plantations around us had received loans. We'd just figured they'd been rich. But the files at the courthouse told another story. We felt heartsick as we saw the evidence that all the other plantations had received the emergency loans that we couldn't get. The words of the FmHA official spoken so long ago were ringing in my ears: "You'll get a loan over my dead body."

In one sense, though, having the information made us feel vindicated. So many people had blamed us for the failure of New Communities, as if we'd made bad decisions. Seeing the truth so clearly written down lifted some of the emotional pressure that had been weighing us down for twelve years.

So we filed our claim. In the *Pigford* case, there were two classes, a class A and a class B. Class A claimants didn't have to use much to prove discrimination, and they would get awards of $50,000 each. Class B was for people who had more records to prove the discrimination. We filed a class B claim. That also entitled us to a hearing in Washington. Believe me, we didn't sit around twiddling our thumbs and waiting, because our hearing didn't take place until July 30, 2002. In the meantime, I kept working at the Federation, and Charles took a position as a chaplain at the Georgia State Prison, which was a perfect position for him, because he had always been able to lift up people who felt the most hopeless. He also taught at Albany State University. Our children were grown by then, living close by in Albany but following their own paths. The *Pigford* suit was something that was going to happen far in the future, and we were too busy with the present to give it much mind.

In April 1999, Judge Paul Friedman of the U.S. District Court for the District of Columbia issued a consent decree on *Pigford*. A consent decree is a binding order of the court, stipulating that the settlement would go forward. In his decree, Judge Friedman cited the failed covenant between the government and black farmers:

> For decades, despite its promise that "no person in the United States shall, on the grounds of race, color, or national origin, be excluded from participation in, be denied the benefits of, or be otherwise subjected to discrimination under any program or activity of an applicant or recipient receiving Federal

financial assistance from the Department of Agriculture," the Department of Agriculture and the county commissioners discriminated against African American farmers when they denied, delayed or otherwise frustrated the applications of those farmers for farm loans and other credit and benefit programs. Further compounding the problem, in 1983 the Department of Agriculture disbanded its Office of Civil Rights and stopped responding to claims of discrimination. These events were the culmination of a string of broken promises that had been made to African American farmers for well over a century.

Friedman's ruling initially hit a barrier with the fact that there was a two-year statute of limitations in the Equal Credit Opportunity Act. Congress had to pass a measure to waive the statute of limitations on civil rights actions against the USDA for the period between 1981 and 1996. That was done with full bipartisan support.

The consent decree was just the first step. Individually, we still had to have our cases heard and be accepted into the class. In July 2002, we arrived early at the courtroom in Washington with Rose by our side. The only person there was the court reporter, and as she was setting up the room, she asked Charles, "Who's the lawyer from the state?" He told her the woman's name, and she cackled. "Oh, you are lucky, lucky, lucky," she said. We smiled nervously at each other, not sure what she meant. But we soon found out. The state's lawyer was very ineffective, and she didn't seem to know how to present the case properly. When we left the courthouse that day, Rose was ebullient. She kept saying "We won, we won."

But we didn't win. We were totally shocked in October of that year when we received the judge's ruling against us. There just didn't seem to be a legitimate basis.

Incidentally, about two years later I was reading an article in the newspaper about a woman who had been arrested in California for pretending to be a lawyer. The article said she'd handled cases for the Justice Department and the USDA. When I saw the name of the lawyer who had represented the state, I nearly fell off my chair. Sure enough, Rose got a letter from the Justice Department saying that the lawyer hadn't been a real lawyer, but it also said that that fact hadn't had any bearing on the case. Maybe that was true, but it was an awfully strange thing.

Fortunately, Judge Friedman had arranged for a monitor to handle appeals in cases where farmers had been denied by the original hearing officer, and we immediately began working with Rose on an appeal. We could not submit any new information, and the person handling the appeal had to consider the information presented. The process of reviewing the appeal took a long four years, and during that time we were unable to learn anything about our case. All we could do was wait.

After four years, a report was sent to Michael Lewis, the chief arbitrator, and we received a copy. The documentation showed that the original hearing officer had made a number of mistakes that had caused a miscarriage of justice in our case. Lewis sent a letter to us in October 2006 saying that the discoveries of the monitor had merit but our case was extensive and would take some time to review. We continued to wait. During that time we started learning about some of the other farmers who had filed discrimination claims.

There was a man in Yazoo, Mississippi, who reminded me of our experience with the FmHA. Lloyd Shaffer had been active in the civil rights movement, and the white farmers in the area didn't give him much respect. His nickname was "Mr. NAACP," and it wasn't meant kindly.

Lloyd had grown up farming with his father and had been working as a farmer all his life when he applied for a loan to buy two hundred acres of his own. The local FmHA official had given him a dirty look when he had come to the office and thrown his application in the trash right in front of him. That reminded me of Charles's experience.

Lloyd eventually managed to lease some land, but he could not get onto his feet because every loan he needed was denied or delayed. In the end, the lending agency showed up in the middle of a harvest and took all his equipment right off the field.

Another farmer with a heartbreaking story was George Hall over in Greene County, Alabama. George had grown up in a farming family, and after serving his country with distinction in Vietnam, he just wanted to get back and settle down and work the family land. During a terrible statewide drought in 1994, George applied for disaster relief and was rejected. The county officials said he wasn't a good farmer because he didn't properly cultivate and fertilize his land. But white farmers around him cultivated their land the same as George did, and they were given emergency loans.

Story upon story revealed a pattern of racial bias that cut down opportunity for black farmers like a sharpened scythe. I hadn't felt such indignation since my early days in the civil rights movement. It seemed as if we hadn't come so far after all. It was particularly disturbing for me to see that officials of the federal government, whose work was paid for with our hard-earned tax dollars, were the agents of discrimination.

The *Pigford* settlement was slowly grinding its way through the process, but after 1999 it became increasingly clear that it had not even begun to reach thousands of farmers who had filed late claims or who had not had the information or means to file claims at all. Now they wanted their cases heard, too. Various efforts were made by the court to offer brief windows for late filers. But nobody understood the sheer size of that group—more than sixty-five thousand farmers. The term "late filer" was a misnomer, implying that the farmers had been nonresponsive. In fact, most of them had never received timely notification about the lawsuit and didn't even know they qualified, much less have the knowledge of how to proceed. When that many people are left out of a process, you just know something is wrong with the *process*, not with the farmers. One example was that between 2001 and 2008, the Bush administration changed the USDA's approach to handling civil rights claims. It stopped doing field investigations and investigated civil rights cases only over the phone. During that period, the statute of limitations on most of the administrative claims ran out while they were being considered by the USDA.

Finally, after years of dissent and false starts, Congress passed a provision in the 2008 farm bill to assist late filers and set aside money for paying claims. This second round was referred to as *Pigford II*.

There were two sponsors in the Senate. One was Republican Chuck Grassley of Iowa. The other was Barack Obama of Illinois. Obama was only a first-term senator, but he was quite well known. His stirring speech at the 2004 Democratic National Convention had captivated the country and instantly propelled him to national fame. In that speech, he had spoken movingly of the greatness of our nation and what we could do together. His words had an emotional resonance that had become unusual in the calculating formula of modern political life:

Do we participate in a politics of cynicism or a politics of hope? I'm not talking about blind optimism here—the almost willful ignorance that thinks unemployment will go away if we just don't talk about it, or the health care crisis will solve itself if we just ignore it. No, I'm talking about something more substantial. It's the hope of slaves sitting around a fire singing freedom songs; the hope of immigrants setting out for distant shores; the hope of a young naval lieutenant bravely patrolling the Mekong Delta; the hope of a mill worker's son who dares to defy the odds; the hope of a skinny kid with a funny name who believes that America has a place for him, too. The audacity of hope!

From then on Obama was singled out as a man with presidential potential. A lot of people said he should wait a decade or so, as he was young and the country wasn't ready to elect a black man. But Obama saw it differently. Against all odds, he decided that 2008 was the time to make his run.

In the beginning, his opponents wanted to make the issue about race—to portray Obama as a militant black, to characterize him as "the other," all in spite of his obviously centrist political history and mild demeanor. This was a well-worn tactic used against blacks seeking political office. The controversy over Reverend Jeremiah Wright played perfectly into that scenario. Wright was a fiery pastor with a booming, angry approach to social justice. Obama had attended his church and listened to him preach many times. Some people tried to say that Reverend Wright and Obama thought alike, that Obama was secretly a raving radical. It was almost comical, because one thing Obama was not was fiery; he had a more intellectual approach to the issues. Some of us wished he'd be more contentious!

For a long while Reverend Wright's connection to Obama dominated media coverage of the campaign. Eventually Obama decided he had to give a major speech about race—a daring prospect. You rarely heard race discussed overtly in politics. It was too fraught with the potential of insulting people from either side. Obama gave his speech, partly out of necessity and partly out of courage, and he managed to strike just the right tone, telling very frank stories about his upbringing in a mixed-race family and concluding "But I have asserted a firm conviction—a conviction rooted in my faith in God and my faith in the American people—that working together we can move beyond some of our old racial wounds, and that in fact we have no choice if we are to continue on the path of a more perfect union."

Hearing Obama speak, I thought about how long it had been since I'd heard anyone talk openly about race. It's almost a taboo subject, whispered behind closed doors. It's as if we had skipped a step between the days of segregation and today—and that step is talking about it honestly, exploring our prejudices, and seeing what we can do about them. When you think about it, it doesn't make sense that we'd make the leap from a time when black people had to use separate facilities to a unified society as if someone waved a magic wand and everything would be okay. I felt that Obama would provide that critical bridge if only we would let him. But he had to understand—and I wasn't yet sure he did—that racial justice was not just about words but about actions that would create economic equality and progress.

CHAPTER 11

Joining Obama's Team

By 2009, I had been working at the Federation of Southern Cooperatives for almost twenty-five years. I probably knew more about rural development in Georgia than any other human being. I had witnessed the tremendous emotional uplift that the election of the first black president had given to farmers and to all black Americans. Watching Barack Obama being sworn into office, Charles and I felt very positive. We just knew that things were going to change, because his election was something we could never have imagined forty years earlier. Of course, Georgia is a red state, and it went for John McCain. The last time the state had voted Democratic had been in Bill Clinton's election in 1992. But our spirits were still high, because Obama was in the White House.

There was a lot of talk that Obama's presidency signified that we had entered a postracial era. Charles and I knew in our hearts that that wasn't true and maybe never would be. I felt some sympathy for the idea that Obama didn't want his presidency to be defined by racial issues, but because he was black, any racial issue that did come up landed in his lap. It reminded me of having been in meetings over the years as the only black person, and if a question about blacks arose, everyone would swivel in their chairs and look at me for an answer. I once even complained, "Why am I always the only one who can speak to race?"

In Obama's case, an example of this thinking came early in his presidency, after an incident involving the noted Harvard professor Henry Louis Gates, who was arrested after James Crowley, a white police officer, "caught" him breaking into his own house. Obama was immediately pursued by the press for his opinion, and he willingly jumped into the fray, even inviting Gates and Crowley to the White House, where they sat on the Rose Garden patio talking and drinking beer. The so-called beer summit drew more scorn than praise, in part because it seemed contrived and in part because it was naive to think that racial healing could be that simple. After the beer summit, Obama tended to stay silent on racial controversies. He didn't want to be perceived as the president of the black people, nor did he want his initiatives to be mired in old wounds and unresolved conflicts. Many of my colleagues and friends in the movement wondered if important racial issues would be put on the back burner out of Obama's reluctance to be perceived as favoring our community. We feared that we'd be worse off than we'd been before he was elected. These were critical concerns. The economic desperation in black America was growing. The disparity between blacks and whites in terms of wealth, jobs, home ownership, and education was increasing, not declining. It was urgent that those very real concerns be addressed. Yet who would address them?

The highly vocal Tea Party and other voices on the right were determined to keep the Obama administration off message on race by regularly raising the specter of reverse racism and vowing to fight it at every turn. I was amazed at how many people thought that Obama's tenure would create wholesale black favoritism—that the preferential treatment of blacks would doom whites to the same kind of discriminatory practices that blacks had long experienced. The notion of reverse racism was deeply insulting, especially for those of us who had lived through the civil rights era. It was also ludicrous, given Obama's centrist leanings, to think he would ever be a racial revolutionary.

Racial politics always unnerved me. I was a practical person, more interested in programmatic execution, and my focus early in Obama's term was on his commitment to economic solutions. I was pleased with his advocacy for a settlement in *Pigford II* and his promise to put the settlement issues on a fast track.

At the Federation, we were all waiting to hear whom he would tap as secretary of agriculture. When he named Tom Vilsack the day after the inauguration, I immediately started doing research to find out more about the man who held so many farmers' futures in his hands. As the former governor of Iowa, he knew a lot about rural life, and I thought that was a good sign. Still, he had absolutely no experience in farm administration, and that meant he'd be learning on the job.

To my delight, Vilsack came down to Georgia in February to speak at a farmers' conference hosted by the Federation. He was smart and personable, and when I introduced him to the meeting, I was very interested in what he would say. He came across as down to earth, and I could see the audience leaning forward to listen carefully to his personal pledge:

I thought about this when I woke up this morning at about 4:30 a.m. to prepare to fly down here. I thought to myself what if somehow Abe Lincoln could come back for just a few minutes. And then he might wander down to the mall and he might see this rather large building—the United States Department of Agriculture. And he might wonder to himself, "I wonder how they're doing in there? I wonder if they're supporting farmers. I wonder if the People's Department is truly the People's Department?" And then he'd walk in and maybe he'd stop someone in the civil rights area and he'd sort of ask, "How are we doing?" And he'd be told, "Mr. President, some folks refer to USDA as the last plantation." And he'd say, "What do you mean by that?" "Well, it's got a pretty poor history when it comes to taking care of folks of color. It's discriminated against them in programming and it's made it somewhat more difficult for some of color to be hired and promoted. It's not a very good history, Mr. President."

Vilsack followed with a pledge to make civil rights a priority for the agency. And we believed him. I thought silently, God bless you for saying that. He made a very good impression that day. For us, it was significant to have the secretary even acknowledge the problem. It was a baby step, to be sure. I had experienced how the early sprouts of good intentions could be choked by bureaucracy and politics.

It had been years since we'd had any real updates on our claim with the *Pigford* lawsuit. Then, one evening in July 2009, the phone rang and it was Rose. "Shirley, have you heard?" she asked excitedly.

"No." I'd had a long day, and I wasn't thinking about *Pigford*.

"We won!" she cried.

"We did?" I asked dumbly. It wasn't sinking in yet.

"Do you want to guess how much New Communities received?" she asked.

I said, "I hope it was at least a million."

"Shirley, it was twelve million," she said. "Twelve million. And not only that, you and Charles each received $150,000 for mental anguish."

Rose warned me that it would take at least two or three years for the judgment to be finalized, so it wasn't as if we were going to see money anytime soon. But it was a wonderful, blessed feeling.

We certainly hadn't expected a personal amount for mental anguish. That was very unusual. It had come as a result of a judgment by the chief arbitrator for *Pigford*, Michael Lewis, who felt that we had been treated particularly harshly and illegally. Lewis wrote that the USDA taking our timber money "smacked of nothing more than a feudal baron demanding additional crops from his serfs."

When the news leaked out in our local area that New Communities had received a large settlement, there were some people who were disgruntled. One man wrote, "There go the Sherrods again, sucking off the public teat." That was typical of the slurs against us. Many people thought it was a glorified form of slave reparation, which couldn't have been farther from the truth. I saw again how little people understood the crippling effect of discrimination.

Charles gathered a group of New Communities farmers at the house. With a light in his eyes, he told them that our work was not done. "This settlement is our new lease," he said. "One day we will build again." And we all sat there and gave thanks to God that New Communities, which had lived on in our hearts and souls, might once again live in our reality. We just had to be patient, and that was okay. Patience was something we had learned to be very good at.

Only days later, I received a call from a staff person at the White House telling me the new administration wanted to appoint me to the position of Georgia director of rural development. It was an incredible opportunity, and I was happy to accept. It was the first time the USDA had selected a black person for the job. In fact, many of the administrators were people who had been around for a while and who had started at FmHA. Among them were those I'd had to nudge and confront over the years. Now I would be their boss.

I felt I was uniquely suited for the job, and I was excited about the idea of expanding my reach across the state and also becoming involved in economic programs beyond farming. USDA Rural Development administers more than forty housing, business, and community infrastructure and facilities programs nationwide and has more than $100 billion available in loans and loan guarantees. In Georgia alone, the budget is between $1.2 billion and $1.3 billion. The scope of the agency touches every area from agriculture to housing to health facilities to broadband accessibility. Its mission is to bring rural communities, which often lag behind in basic services and conditions, fully into the twenty-first century.

My office would be in Athens, Georgia, two hundred miles from Albany, but I didn't want to move to Athens, since it was a political appointment, subject to change with a new administration. I rented a small apartment less than a mile from the office, although I didn't expect to spend much time there as I would be on the road so much, traveling across the state. I devised a schedule that would take me to Athens and other areas during the week and back home to Albany on weekends. I got ready to live out of a suitcase. At 57,906 square miles, Georgia was a big state with a lot of territory to cover. I wasn't planning to be the kind of director who sat in my office shuffling paper. I would be a hands-on leader.

The first thing the White House staffer asked me was "How soon can you start?" The administration had left the appointment open for so long that it was desperate to get me into position. But I had a lot to do to make sure my work at the Federation would be handled. I had to resign from various boards. I thought I was being generous when I said I could start in a month, on August 30.

He laughed and said, "We were thinking August 17." I took a deep breath and agreed, not quite knowing how it would be possible. I had seventeen days.

The weekend of August 15, I attended the Federation's annual meeting in Epes, Alabama. Dallas Tonsager, the federal undersecretary of rural development, was there. His deputy, Cheryl Cook, would be my direct supervisor. I came back from Epes that Saturday night and drove to Athens on Sunday so that I could be on the job at 7:30 Monday morning.

As an administrator, I was very conscious of the need to get my agency in order. We could not really help people unless we were of a common commitment. It's always the case in any organization that there are some people who want to do the right thing and some who don't and others who are willing but need to be pushed. On my first day, I told people that we weren't going to sit around. Our primary job was to do outreach. Many people thrived on being encouraged, for the first time, to get out into the communities. And I would be right there with them. I let them know if they set up meetings, I'd join them. They'd never experienced that before.

I said, "If I don't do anything else while I'm here, there are two things I want to accomplish. I want people to know about this agency and what it does. And I want them to know that they have equal access to the program." I felt when I arrived that things had grown kind of complacent. And I was determined to change that. I know they probably thought, "Oh, my goodness, here she comes"— and not in a good way. A lot of them knew me already as someone who had been pressuring them to do the right thing from the outside. But my intention was not to beat people up but to inspire them, train them, and treat them with the respect they deserved. I've always decided that I will treat people the way I want to be treated, and it was no different now that I was in charge.

I would be overseeing more than 120 people spread across the state, six area offices, ten suboffices, and twenty-three rural development offices. One of the first things I did was hold staff appreciation days in each region. It was a chance to meet everyone and to praise them for the good job they had been doing. I understood that people need support and motivation to do their best. I asked the six area offices to combine into three groups to plan the events. I met with areas one and two together, three and four together, and five and six together. At each site, the staffs laid out wonderful spreads of food, and I contributed a small gift for each person: a nice binder with the Rural Development logo.

After one of the meetings, I received a note from one of the old hands. He wrote that in almost thirty years working in the agency, he'd never had a state director say "Thank you."

Those meetings helped create goodwill and inspire teamwork. It was so simple and obvious, but it worked. I was also conscious of rooting out hidden issues of race in the state. In one location, I'd heard some rumblings because the manager was black and the white people in the office did not want to be managed by a black person. They were disrespectful of him and frequently bypassed his decisions. Every time I turned around, I was getting complaints from the office about this black manager. There were also frequent complaints from citizens about the office.

I went down and had a special meeting with them, and I immediately noticed the attitude at the place—a visceral sense of insolence and unhappiness. I thought, "Uh-oh." This could not go on. I immediately arranged for a civil rights trainer and a customer service trainer to hold a session with the staff. Things improved after that. Later, I arranged to have all the staff in Georgia have civil rights and customer service training at a nice conference center, where they could relax a little between meetings. Unfortunately, I was gone from the agency before that could occur.

My early months as director were nonstop. I wanted to get the word out to the people in our rural communities that we were there to support them. Folks just didn't know what the opportunities were. For the first time, our offices were truly open, and I encouraged everyone to go to their local office for help. I'd tell people, "You don't have to wait until you have a full-blown plan. Come on up, and we'll bring in the housing program director, the water and sewer program director, the business director to sit around the table and talk with you." I told them that they shouldn't have to go forward with their applications in the dark. First they could talk to the people who were actually going to review the applications and knew the regulations. It was an innovative and very practical approach. I also encouraged elected officials in the towns and community-based groups to come to the state office, where I would bring a team in to discuss their issues and help them fine-tune their requests.

I knew from long experience that rural poverty was a pressing matter in Georgia and indeed throughout the Southeast. There was a stark and disturbing difference between the burgeoning urban centers and the plight of people spread out in the small towns throughout our state. Atlanta was the jewel of the South—a vibrant, prosperous, diverse, modern city, with businesses vying for a place at its opportunity-laden table. But Atlanta's wealth did not trickle out to other parts of the state, where the constant struggle for survival was a gripping daily story. When I was at Rural Development, the average per capita income of rural Georgians was $27,136, with a poverty rate of 22.7 percent. Unemployment was over 11 percent.

There were nine counties in the state that had median household incomes of $20,000 or less, and I decided to concentrate our efforts there. Those poor counties didn't have the staff to help people prepare the paperwork. They needed special help, and until then they had not been receiving it. It was hard to even find statistics for those lost communities. I made them a priority.

When the American Recovery and Reinvestment Act stimulus money was approved in 2009, I was eager to see what we could do with our share. I was initially concerned, because many Republican governors were announcing that they would reject the stimulus money. I hoped that wouldn't be the case in Georgia, and our governor, Sonny Perdue, made an ominous statement at the National Governors Association meeting that he wasn't sure that he'd accept all the money; he'd have to review it. That put us on pins and needles.

Privately, I hoped for the best but feared the worst. Perdue, who'd been in office since 2003, had alienated many people over the years for his vocal praise of the Confederacy. There was some tension in the black community. However, most people were focused on economic necessity, and the stimulus money was a golden opportunity to improve the desperate plight of rural communities. In the end the state was allocated $3.2 billion and Perdue accepted it, although he was very slow to spend it.

My office was busy finding worthy recipients on both large-scale and micro levels. But it wasn't just the stimulus money that was important, it was also the opportunity Rural Development provided for worthy businesses and individuals to secure loans that in some cases transformed their lives. The grants were diverse, and it never ceased to amaze me that very modest amounts of money could make such a big difference. Among the grants and loans we arranged in the early period of my tenure were $140,000 to the Cornelia Police Department for five police cars, as well as $62,700 to purchase a Jaws of Life for the fire department; $9,000 to the city of Maysville for police equipment, including police vests, radios, and a metal detector for the courtroom; $98,525 for three patient simulation dummies—an adult, a child, and an infant—for the Heart of Georgia Technical College in Dublin; and $150,000 for a new ambulance for Franklin County.

The stimulus money also provided food programs for those most in need, including funds for the National School Lunch Program, Special Supplemental Nutrition Program for Women, Infants, and Children, and the Food Distribution Program on Indian Reservations. That was a huge benefit for the poorest people. You can't advance in life if you're hungry.

We also worked on large-scale projects, such as a new sewer treatment facility in Port Wentworth. It was desperately needed. The old facility had been repeatedly cited by the EPA for being over capacity and exceeding fecal coliform limits. Another large project helped Georgia forest landowners better manage their property through the use of prescribed fire. Prescribed fire is a forest management tool used to prepare land for planting, attract wildlife, improve aesthetics, and reduce the risk of catastrophic wildfire. All those projects had the added benefit of creating new jobs.

When we were dealing with the stimulus money and guaranteed loans, I noticed that most of the loans for housing were not in southwest Georgia. People there didn't even know about them. You'd drive through those areas, and they were filled with mobile homes. I explained to people that they could borrow money from Rural Development to buy land and build homes, and they looked at me in astonishment. They couldn't believe it. It made economic sense for them, because by the time they got done paying for those mobile homes, they were worthless.

My attitude as director was that I would do anything I could to help. I'd move mountains or in some cases just boulders, but I'd go to sleep every night knowing I'd made some kind of difference.

I had been focused on southwest Georgia for my entire career. Now I had the entire state to take care of. For the next year, my feet never seemed to touch the ground. I was always on the run across the state. There were plenty of moments when I shared black-white encounters with people who hadn't ever seen a black person in charge. But they always ended in an uplifting way. I believed we were learning to come together.

My federal position gave me more opportunities for public speaking. I always emphasized the importance of looking beyond racial divisions to solve the economic challenges facing rural communities, farmers, and small businesses. On some occasions I got more personal, going beyond the usual themes and talking from the heart about where I had come from and the journey I had taken. The message I would convey was that we had to lay down the burden and the bitterness of the past and work together for a better world. I wanted to reveal something of my own personal struggle—with a message of love and conciliation, not of hate. I gave that speech on several occasions, including at my alma mater, Albany State University.

In March 2010, I was invited to give a speech to the Coffee County NAACP Annual Freedom Fund banquet, which was taking place in the south-central part of the state. I was also to receive an award at the banquet in recognition of my lifetime in public service. I decided to give my personal speech as a way of testifying to the distance we'd come and the road we still needed to travel.

Fifty years after the marches and the jailings and the hardships of segregation, there was still much work to do, but I wanted my message to be positive and heartfelt, especially since the date of my speech held such significance for me: it was the forty-fifth anniversary of the day we had buried my father. My heart was always heavy around that time of year. So I began my speech to a packed audience by telling them about my father's death and about life growing up in Baker County. I described Sheriff Claude Screws, who had lynched Bobby Hall, and recalled the days under the regime of the Gator, which were still so fresh in my mind that they might have happened the day before. And I talked about my dream of leaving—of fleeing segregation for good:

> I wanted to leave the farm and Baker County. It was—life was—the older folk know what I'm talking about—the segregation and the discrimination and the racist acts that we had to endure during those years made me just want to leave. And you know, we used to have people who'd leave and go north. You all know how they come back talking and they come back looking. I learned later that some of those cars they drove home were rented. But it made you want to go north, 'cause you thought they were free up there and you thought everybody was free in the North. So, my goal was not to even go to college in the South 'cause . . . I was always told you find your husband at college. So, I didn't want to find one living in the

South. I wanted to go to college in the North so I could get
a husband from the North, and never ever come back down
here and live again. But, you know, you can never say what
you'll never do.

There was a lot of nodding and murmurs of assent. Many people in the audience had experienced similar things. Those who had
grown up in Coffee County no doubt remembered the struggle
for school integration, which had received national attention when
Governor Maddox had gotten into the act, visiting the county and
declaring "If we don't protect our interests at home, soon we'll have
no home." Those "interests" were segregation. Schools in Coffee
County didn't begin integrating until 1969.

I talked about how Charles and I had stayed in Georgia our
whole lives and always believed we were in the movement, both in
fact and in spirit. Then I talked about my appointment as Georgia
state director of rural development, including the story that became
the spark of an enormous controversy:

You know God is so good 'cause people like me don't get
appointed to positions like State Director of Rural Development. They just don't get these kinds of positions 'cause I've
been out there at every grassroots level and I've paid some
dues.

When I made that commitment [after my father's death],
I was making that commitment to black people—and to black
people only. But, you know, God will show you things and
He'll put things in your path so that . . . you realize that the
struggle is really about poor people, you know.

The first time I was faced with having to help a white
farmer save his farm, he took a long time talking, but he was
trying to show me he was superior to me. I know what he
was doing. But he had come to me for help. What he didn't
know—while he was taking all that time trying to show me
he was superior to me—was I was trying to decide just how
much help I was going to give him.

I was struggling with the fact that so many black people have lost their farmland, and here I was faced with having to help a white person save their land. [I went on to describe how I had ultimately helped the Spooners save their farm.]

Well, working with him made me see that it's really about those who have versus those who don't, you know. And they could be black; they could be white; they could be Hispanic. And it made me realize then that I needed to work to help poor people—those who don't have access the way others have. . . .

But where am I going with this? You know, I couldn't say forty-five years ago—I couldn't stand here and say what I'm saying—what I will say to you tonight. Like I told you, God helped me to see that it's not just about black people—it's about poor people. . . . I've come to realize that we have to work together and—you know, it's sad that we don't have a room full of whites and blacks here tonight, 'cause we have to overcome the divisions that we have. We have to get to the point where, as Toni Morrison said, "Race exists but it doesn't matter." We have to work just as hard. I know it's—you know, that division is still here, but our communities are not going to thrive—you know, our children won't have the—the communities that they need to be able to stay in and live in and—and have a good life if we can't figure this out, you all. White people, black people, Hispanic people, we all have to do our part to make our communities a safe place, a healthy place, a good environment.

I ended with a line that had become meaningful for me: "Life is a grindstone, but whether it grinds us down or polishes us up depends on us."

I could see that the audience was moved by my speech. And I hope they were motivated. But you have to know that this was not considered a controversial speech by anybody. What could possibly be controversial about saying we have to work together to help our communities thrive? Not only had I delivered the same speech on other occasions, but it was videotaped by the NAACP. Afterward, it was repeatedly broadcast on DCTV3, a leased-access television channel dedicated to providing public, educational, and government programming for the communities of Douglas and Coffee counties. It was out there, available to be viewed by anyone who cared to see it.

Andrew Breitbart did not just stumble on the speech. It was sent to him by someone in the South, whose identity remains unknown, in response to Breitbart's call for examples of reverse racism. That had become a new obsession of the Right, as if all the years of civil rights struggle meant nothing. Breitbart, born almost a year after Martin Luther King's assassination, had not even been alive when Jim Crow law was practiced throughout the South. But he was scathing in his criticism of what he perceived to be reverse racism practiced by blacks. He chose to make me an example, and the USDA and the White House took the bait and got tangled up in a real mess. The tremendous national attention that accompanied my removal from Rural Development catapulted me from an unknown worker in the fields to a public figure. I'd never sought that role, and I was uncomfortable in my new public shoes. Still, I wondered if my story would provide one of those lauded teachable moments people are always talking about. I wasn't sure. It would depend on what I said and did next.

Walking into the Light

Three weeks after my forced resignation from the Department of Agriculture, I was on a plane headed for Washington, D.C., to meet with Secretary Vilsack. The fury had not died down as I had expected it would. There was still a lot of media coverage, and I had received thousands of letters and e-mails, including dozens of requests to speak at a variety of venues across the country. I didn't mind the idea of speaking to groups, but I didn't want to be known only as the woman at the center of this particular controversy. I wanted to be able to offer more in terms of a thoughtful dialogue on race, community building, and economic opportunity.

Meanwhile, though, Vilsack was sending very strong signals that he wanted me to consider the job of deputy director of the Office of Advocacy and Outreach, a department that had been established the previous year.

I think the media, which was following my every move, would have liked to see me accept so they could say, "It's a wrap," and tie everything into a neat conclusion. But I knew it was a critical moment for me, and I had to think calmly and clearly about what would be the right thing to do.

I checked into a hotel the evening before my meeting with Vilsack and was taken to dinner by three people from the agency. They warned me that there would be a crowd of media waiting the next day and that Vilsack's office had scheduled a press conference after our meeting. I was uneasy.

I got little sleep that night. Someone posing as a reporter had found out where I was staying and called my hotel room directly, badgering me for an interview. It made me nervous that people knew where I was. I didn't hear from the man again until I walked into the lobby the next morning and he jumped at me. There was a scuffle as hotel security tried to keep him away. Finally my car arrived with a fanfare that embarrassed me. There was so much security you'd have thought I was a visiting dignitary. Any hope that I would be able to sneak into and out of Washington was completely dashed. Fortunately, there's a ramp to the underground parking at the Department of Agriculture, so I didn't have to face the press that were gathered out front. We walked through a tunnel into the building, and suddenly I was being ushered into the secretary's office. He came toward me, smiling and eager, and grasped my hand in a warm shake. There were two staff members there prepared to participate in the meeting, but I asked that Vilsack and I be allowed to meet alone.

As we sat across from each other at a large oblong blond table, Vilsack began to tell me about the progress that had been made on the *Pigford II* settlement. I appreciated his comments, but I didn't say much. I was waiting for him to address the elephant in the room.

Tom Vilsack was a very caring man. I'd had that impression of him before, when he'd come down to Georgia, and I hadn't changed my mind. Of all the people involved in this fiasco, he seemed the most genuinely sorry. Now he was trying to make amends, and I had the feeling that he was pretty confident that he could talk me into this newly created job he wanted me to fill.

Vilsack was extremely graceful and convincing. "You know, Shirley," he said, "because of your experience, and because of what's happened to you, you're the one person in this country who can take this position and do something with it." He went on in that vein for some time, and I listened politely. In spite of his entreaties, I told him that I had decided not to accept his offer.

He kept on for a while trying to convince me, but when it became obvious that I wasn't going to take the position, he sighed and said, "There are eighty reporters out there waiting to hear from us."

"I don't have a problem having a joint press conference with you," I said. "But before doing that, Mr. Secretary, this whole country wants to know why you didn't offer me my old position at Rural Development."

Vilsack immediately extended both his arms in an expansive gesture and replied, "You can have it."

It was the last thing I expected, but it didn't seem like a genuine offer, more like a spontaneous reaction to my question. I was awash in regret that we had come to that point, that I'd been forced to resign in the first place. Suddenly I had a decision to make, but almost immediately I realized it was too late. I was reluctant to go back to the agency in any capacity at that point because I still had such deep feelings of mistrust. Vilsack might have been sincere, but I knew that the force of politics was overwhelming, and I was aware of how bright promises dangled one day might become tarnished the next by the constant grind. I feared that I would always be known in the agency as racist, that the bureaucracy would swallow me up and force me into silence. I'd been in the work a long, long time at that point, and I had a good sense of what would happen. I wasn't naive. I could probably not have spoken anywhere without having to get my speech approved. And certainly any discussions of racial issues, which were so important for us to talk about, would be out of bounds. I would have felt muzzled.

I also couldn't get Vilsack's own words out of my mind. They had been spoken only three weeks earlier. Even as he'd publicly apologized to me, he'd told the press that I couldn't be rehired in my old position because people might have trouble feeling that they would be fairly treated. How could I look him in the eye now and pretend he hadn't said that? I also believed that I had yet to hear the real story of how I had come to be fired, and that troubled me.

I told Vilsack that it was too late to go back to the way things had been, and he began pressing me harder about taking the new position. The meeting was scheduled to last an hour, but an hour and a half later we were still talking. Finally it was time to meet the press.

"I did my best, I think it's fair to say," Vilsack told them. "I did my best to try to get her to come to USDA, to stay at USDA on a full-time basis. We talked about the Office of Advocacy and Outreach and what her unique skills could bring to that office. We also talked about the opportunity that would be made available, if that was not something she was interested in doing, to return to Georgia in her position as the state director. For reasons that Shirley will get into, that doesn't fit what she needs, what she wants, and what she deserves."

He went on, and I stood there in the glare, thinking about how I would explain my decision. Finally, when asked about it, I told the reporters that I didn't really know what the Office of Advocacy and Outreach did, but it was a new program and I didn't really want to be the one to test it. I was very respectful of Vilsack's obvious efforts to accommodate me, but I felt I needed a break to think about my next steps, and that's what I told them. I didn't close the door completely. "I've had many, many thousands of pieces of mail," I said. "Many of those I would like to answer. I need a little time to be able to deal with that, to sort of take a break from some of all that I've had to deal with over the last few weeks, and I look forward to some type of relationship with the department in the future."

What I didn't say was how completely exhausted I was, both emotionally and physically. Perhaps they could see it in my face. Most of all, I needed a mental rest—time to figure out where I could best use my abilities. I didn't want a post in Washington, D.C., far away from my family and friends, where I would be stuck in the bureaucracy. Nor could I face returning to my old job as if nothing had happened and tolerate the agency and the media watching my every move, looking for trouble. I needed to think.

I was very happy to board the plane out of Washington that afternoon, but if I expected rest, it was not to be. In the coming days I was overwhelmed with requests to speak about my experiences. At first the idea didn't especially appeal to me. I didn't want to talk about it anymore. But then I realized that what people really wanted was an inspirational talk about the need to get past the racial hurts and work together, and my life story was an entrée to that new possibility. So I began accepting speaking engagements, and before I knew it I was crossing the country every week.

After the firing, Don Lemon of CNN had done a documentary about my life, and he asked if I would be willing to be on a program for the convention of the National Association of Black Journalists, which would be meeting in San Diego. Charles and I flew out. At the time no one was handling my growing list of engagements. I was on my own.

Someone suggested that I could use an agent, and I was surprised. "Agent? Me?" I really didn't see it. But I was told that a man named Drew Berry wanted to talk to me at the convention. I might have declined to speak to him, except for a very important piece of information: Drew was married to Brenda Fowler, who had lived across the street when she was growing up. I invited Drew and Brenda to my hotel room, and Brenda and I had a great time reminiscing. I liked Drew, too. He had a lively personality and great warmth. When he began to talk about representing me, I listened intently, and what he said made sense, but I still wasn't sure. I told him I'd think about it. The truth is, I figured that if I had to get an agent, it would be Drew. I trusted him because of Brenda. After Charles and I talked it over, I decided to hire Drew, and that was the best decision I could have made. Drew has coordinated my publicity and speaking engagements ever since, and either he or an associate always accompanies me.

I quickly found out how valuable it was to have someone running interference at the speeches. Before, people would want to stand there forever and talk, and I didn't know how to pull myself away. Drew would say firmly, "Last question," and off we'd go.

I was meeting so many great people, and I have to say that the constant bookings surprised me. I realized that something about my experience had struck a chord with people both black and white. On so many occasions they would just come up to me and say thank you or tell me they were praying for me.

I don't like to say it, but it's true, that before this incident it was unusual for a white person in the South to come up to me on the street or in a store and say hello. That's just the way it's been; there's still a silent separation and maybe a fear. But because of my notoriety, all that changed. Now people viewed me as more approachable, and they had no trouble coming up to me—when they could have done so all along.

I had vowed to move on and not be stuck in thinking about what had happened to me, but I also recognized that it would be hard to do while there were so many unanswered questions. I still could not get my mind around exactly how my firing had taken place so rapidly. I recounted the events of that Monday in July over and over in my head, and the official story just didn't make sense. I was the one who had alerted Cheryl Cook to the problem well before Monday. The agency had not been blindsided. I had asked Cheryl to be sure to view the entire tape. I had assured her that Breitbart's two-and-a-half-minute clip was meant to depict the exact opposite of what I was trying to say. But suddenly I was tossed aside, and it didn't seem to me that anybody had looked at the whole tape until later. Vilsack had admitted as much. As for the White House involvement, that had also been kept in the shadows, although Cheryl had told me it was the White House that wanted me out. Vilsack always took full responsibility, but that didn't satisfy me, because surely there was more to the story.

I remember thinking during the episode, "This is what political fear looks like." I had always known that my firing had been hasty and cowardly. What I hadn't realized was how strong and steady the calls for my dismissal were during the critical hours of July 19. In October, several hundred pages of e-mails became publicly available through a Freedom of Information Act request made by the *Los Angeles Times*. They provide a fascinating portrait of political fear. Across the Department of Agriculture and from the White House, staffers were rushing to judgment and then expressing relief when I resigned. Meanwhile, no one ever thought to get off the computer and watch the video of my speech.

When East Baker High and Elementary School—our "separate but equal" blacks-only facility—opened in 1957, we were excited to finally have indoor plumbing and central heating. But our supplies were still inadequate hand-me-downs from the white schools. *(Personal photo)*

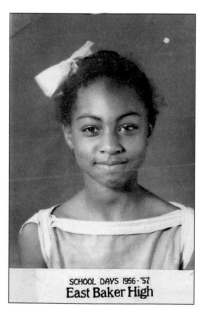

SCHOOL DAYS 1956-'57
East Baker High

This picture was taken shortly after we moved to the new school. I was nine years old. *(Miller family collection)*

My parents, Hosie and Grace Miller. *(Miller family collection)*

Only months before I graduated from high school, I had planned to move north, where there were more opportunities for blacks. Then my father was murdered, and I made a commitment to stay and work in Georgia. *(Miller family collection)*

The old rough-hewn wall is still standing outside the courthouse in Newton. After he shot my father, Cal Hall used to sit there often, with his rifle by his side, in a manner we found taunting. He was never prosecuted for the murder. *(Personal photo)*

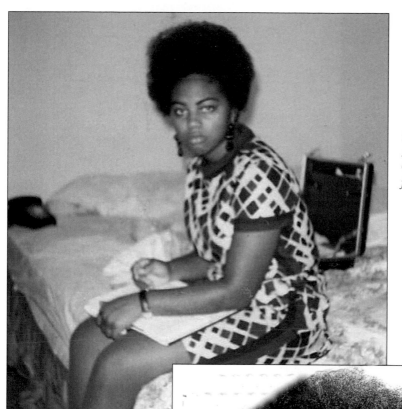

Studying at
Albany State
College. *(Sherrod
family collection)*

I was a serious
young woman,
committed to the
movement and
learning to love the
land again. *(Sherrod
family collection)*

Charles and I out canvassing in 1967. *(Sherrod family collection)*

Our young family— Charles and I with Russia and Ken. Those were happy years at New Communities. *(Sherrod family collection)*

I was so proud of my bright little girl, Russia. *(Sherrod family collection)*

A meeting at New Communities. Charles is at the front left, turned toward the camera. I am at the back left. *(Sherrod family collection)*

At work in the New Communities office. *(Sherrod family collection)*

During a trip to Ghana, Mozzie Johnson, Billie Jean Young, and I visit Elmina Castle and walk through the former female slave exit. It sent chills down my spine to think of the women who had walked this path so long ago. *(Personal photo)*

Working with farmers in the Dominican Republic, under the auspices of the Federation of Southern Cooperatives. *(Personal photo)*

Visiting farms in Cuba during a fact-finding mission there, I was impressed with their commitment to sustainable agriculture. We have much to learn from each other—if only the political barriers that prevent open trade and communication would finally be lifted. *(Personal photo)*

I was delighted to be reunited with the Spooners. It was one of the positive things to come out of the controversy. (© *Carol Heard,* The Post-Searchlight *by permission*)

Roland Martin had criticized me harshly on the air after Breitbart's piece came out. He later apologized when we met at the National Association of Black Journalists meeting. *(Courtesy of Jason Miccolo Johnson/NABJ)*

Ralph Paige, the executive director of the Federation of Southern Cooperatives, has spent his life dedicated to the cause of economic opportunity for poor farmers. Here he is pictured with Charles and me. *(Courtesy of Federation of Southern Cooperatives)*

After I left Rural Development, I received countless invitations to speak, and I was determined to spread my message of racial healing across the nation. This is me speaking at Old Dominion University, with Martin Luther King, Jr.'s, image on the screen behind me. *(Courtesy of Old Dominion University)*

Ben Jealous, the progressive young head of the NAACP, is a dynamic figure who has breathed new life into an old organization. Here we are with Ralph Paige at a Federation of Southern Cooperatives event. *(Courtesy of the Federation of Southern Cooperatives)*

I had the honor to speak with Christine King Farris, now eighty-four, the elder sister of Martin Luther King, Jr. Ms. Farris is a teacher, author, and advocate for educational policies. She is a woman of great achievement who has shunned the spotlight and still grieves for her brother. *(Courtesy of Phil McCollum)*

Reading the e-mails from my colleagues at the USDA was an especially disheartening experience. I just couldn't believe it. The whole time I was assuming that Cheryl was handling the problem, nothing was being done. It didn't appear that Cheryl had alerted anyone to the situation or gotten hold of the full tape, because at 2:00 PM that Monday, Wayne Maloney, a press aide to the USDA public affairs director, Chris Mather, sent his boss an e-mail:

> I was just informed of a video of the Georgia State Director that was posted on the Internet earlier this afternoon. It speaks for itself and you need to watch it right away.

A half hour later, Mather e-mailed Vilsack's chief of staff, Karen Ross, with a link to the video clip, writing:

> THIS IS HORRIBLE.

Another half hour later, deputy chief of staff Carole Jett e-mailed Cheryl and others:

> Shirley Sherrod is on tape and you need to see/hear immediately. We need to take immediate action.

That was the point when Cheryl might have stepped in and explained what was going on. She might have asked that the full tape be reviewed before any rash conclusions were drawn. But she did not. She allowed the frenzy to build. Vilsack, who was out of the office, was notified, and at 3:32 PM, Krysta Harden, the congressional liaison to the USDA, e-mailed:

> The S[ecretary] is absolutely sick and mad over the Sherrod issue. He wants her immediately on administrative leave.

Cheryl replied with one word: "Done." She then called me at the office in West Point and I started my long journey home.

At 4:00, Undersecretary Tonsager e-mailed Vilsack:

We have just seen the video of Georgia State Director Shirley Sherrod and
are deeply disturbed. Cheryl has put her on administrative leave pending
a full investigation.

But there was never a "full investigation," and that didn't make
sense. Why the terrible rush? I was already on administrative leave.
Why couldn't they take a day or two to figure out what was going
on? I have never understood that, except that the drumbeat from the
right was just getting too strong. By 4:15 PM, a little more than two
hours after they first heard about it, Harden was e-mailing:

This is awful. If he can right out fire her he will or ask for her resignation.

Less than half an hour after that, Cheryl began calling me, urging me to resign, and at 6:55 PM. I did. An hour after I resigned,
as I was driving home, my still shaking hands on the wheel, Kevin
Washo, the USDA's White House liaison, e-mailed Cheryl:

Did we ever get the full copy of the speech?

Cheryl replied that they had not. That was the end of the discussion. They obviously felt they'd dodged a bullet and handled
everything with speed and efficiency. The following morning Chris-
topher Lu, the White House liaison to the cabinet, sent an e-mail to
USDA officials:

Just wanted you to know that this dismissal came up at our morning
senior staff meeting today. Everyone complimented USDA on how quickly
you took this action. . . . Thanks for the great effort.

That final e-mail upset me the most. They were *congratulating*
themselves for the way they had handled me. It had been a "great
effort." I found that hard to stomach. They were happy they'd gotten out in front of an embarrassing situation—although, of course,
they hadn't.

Reading them in the aftermath of events, the e-mails seemed

unprofessional and thoughtless to me. They made me sad. But again, political fear can cause people to behave that way. I know that if I had just stayed silent, that would have been the end of it, because no one at the USDA had any intention of reviewing the full tape. It was interesting that everywhere I went around the country, people said, "I'm so glad you didn't take that job. We were praying that you wouldn't." Now I knew I had made the right decision.

Incidentally, Dallas never called me throughout the entire ordeal, even when Vilsack was proposing my return to the USDA and my old job. I thought it was strange that he alone would not talk to me. I mentioned it to Ralph Paige one day in early October, and I think Ralph contacted him, because he finally called me on October 4, two and a half months after I left the department. I guess he thought he was doing his duty, but he was clearly uncomfortable speaking to me. We had nothing to say to each other at that point.

I did, however, have a chance to come together with the Spooners. I had been asked to give an address at the Albany State University commencement, and it occurred to me that I should ask the Spooners to come to the graduation. I called them and spoke with Eloise. I was concerned that the trip would present a hardship for the aging couple, but she just laughed. "Oh, Roger is always making trips," she said. "At eighty-eight, he's still driving that eighteen-wheeler. So we'll be there." I loved those people!

They sat in the VIP section with my mother, my brother, Hosie, my sister Sandra, and a few cousins and friends. Afterward, the president took us all out to lunch. It was a wonderful day. I could not get over how strong and principled Roger and Eloise were. My mother was delighted to meet them for the first time.

Back in May 2010, when I was still working for Rural Development, Secretary Vilsack had announced that the USDA had received the results of an exhaustive $8 million study conducted by Jackson Lewis, a firm that specialized in affirmative action and workplace law issues. The firm had come up with more than two hundred recommendations, including ways to make Rural Development resources more accessible to women and minorities and to correct the inequities that had led to *Pigford*. They also tackled issues of diversity within the department.

The subject of the study had come up during my meeting with Vilsack. He wanted to know if I would consider working on the implementation phase, and I told him I would be open to that. A few months later, I found out that the USDA, looking at the report, had felt it was already implementing many of the suggested changes. There were about ninety-five that still needed to be done. Originally, Jackson Lewis had been going to oversee the implementation part, but the agency didn't want to pay $8 million for another year and decided to coordinate the implementation itself.

The project was being supervised by Pearlie Reed, the assistant secretary of administration. Pearlie was a rare black in the USDA's top echelon. He had worked for the agency with distinction his entire career, and Secretary Vilsack had asked him to come back from retirement for this important job. I knew Pearlie was committed to resolving the civil rights claims and also to ending discrimination within the agency. I wasn't surprised when he called me about working on the implementation of the Jackson Lewis recommendations, and I was certainly willing to talk about it. I could see myself doing good work on the project. I'd read the report, and I knew what to do. So I was friendly and open on that call, but when we hung up we hadn't settled on any details. We just agreed to have another talk.

Shortly after this conversation, I was traveling in Ohio for a speaking engagement when a reporter called me, saying "I hear you're back with the USDA." I was startled. "That's not true," I replied. But within a day the news articles started to appear, sourced to the website Politico, that I had rejoined the USDA to help it with its civil rights record.

It was clear to me that the leak had come from someone at the USDA, but it was Friday night and I had no luck reaching Pearlie. On Monday morning, I called around and finally spoke with someone in his office. I explained what had happened and said that I was very unhappy about it. Soon after, Pearlie called.

"How are you doing?" he asked.

"I'm okay. How are you?" I replied.

"I'm not doing so well," he admitted. At first I thought he was sick, but he told me that he was having problems over the latest flap. I understood, but I was quietly angry. How had it happened? I felt as if I was being played.

Pearlie arranged a call with some of his media people, and we talked about how the press reports had happened. No one wanted to take responsibility, but one person said—I thought flippantly—that it was just one of those things. "Shirley, if you Google civil rights and USDA, your name is going to pop up. It's always going to happen." I wasn't buying that explanation.

But they did want to go ahead with the idea of contracting me. That afternoon a draft of a contract came outlining all the work, with a fee of $60,000. On closer inspection I noticed that the agency was proposing a cooperative agreement with the Southwest Georgia Project. So my fee was actually only $35,000. There was no starting or ending date, but I figured it wanted me to work for at least a year. Obviously, I balked at the arrangement. Then the people there said they didn't mean for me to work for a year, they just wanted to pick my brain for three months. I have to say that that didn't sit right with me. I was a worker, an implementer. I didn't even know what they meant by picking my brain. So at that point I wasn't willing to commit.

The media was still calling me, and one reporter, April Ryan, the White House correspondent for American Urban Radio Networks, asked me about the $35,000 contract. So that word was out. April wondered if I was going to sign, and I said I didn't know.

Then Emanuel Cleaver II, the chairman of the Congressional Black Caucus, called me. It appeared that April had spoken to him. "Is it true?" he asked, referring to the $35,000 contract. I told him yes.

"That's a slap in the face," he declared. The CBC had wanted me to be involved in the implementation of the Jackson Lewis recommendations—I knew that—but neither Cleaver nor I liked that "pick your brains" stuff. We wanted a real commitment and real action. Sixty thousand dollars to implement an entire program did seem insulting and unserious to me. It was a glimpse of what I might have found had I joined the new Office of Advocacy and Outreach. It was typical of the bureaucratic mind-set: spend $8 million for a study, and then quibble about executing the recommendations. Let's face it, studies are easy; it's the implementation that's hard. I believed that the USDA was serious, but it remained to be seen if it would embrace a full-out effort. My reluctance was less about the money it was proposing than about the structure of the project. Those discussions are ongoing.

One afternoon, Ben Jealous visited me in Albany. Since the events of July 2010 we had become very good friends. He hadn't known me before, nor had he been aware of my and Charles's civil rights journey. Once he realized he'd been "snookered" by Breitbart, he set about getting to know us.

We spent the afternoon deep in conversation about the future of the NAACP and the movement. So many people confronted by racism and poverty rely on the NAACP to be there for them. Ben represented the new generation of the organization. Only thirty-eight years old, he was the son of a black mother and a white father, raised in a new era of civil rights. His parents had been active in the movement, but Ben was a post–baby boomer who had grown up after Martin Luther King and Black Power. A highly educated, energetic man, Ben's focus was on education and economic reform. Blacks might have become more equal, but the statistics didn't lie. Studies showed that the wealth gap was greater than it had been for twenty-five years. Blacks ranked at the bottom on virtually every measure of success, and Ben's passion was finding a way forward. He felt that the NAACP had become stodgy and was still mired in the past. He and I agreed that finding a way forward required new strategies. But we had to be clear about the realities we were facing. It was an illusion to think that Obama had carried us into a postracial society. Obama had once said of the economy, "A rising tide will lift all boats." But we were also seeing that some of those boats, leaky and not built to withstand the tide, were sinking to the bottom.

CHAPTER 13

Seeking Justice

I had put off watching Andrew Breitbart's video clip for as long as possible. I hadn't realized until I forced myself to play the tape that he had not just run a piece of my speech. The video was embedded into a blog post titled "Video Proof: The NAACP Awards Racism—2010." The post was decorated by a cartoon depiction of a playing card, with Black Power fists instead of hearts, diamonds, clubs, or spades, and the word "Race" in the center, intending to represent a "race card." Accompanying the tape was a headline-style narration—just in case the message wasn't clear. One frame read, "Mrs. Sherrod admits that in her federally appointed position, overseeing over a billion dollars, she discriminated against people due to their race." (Breitbart later added a correction, noting that I had not been a federal employee at the time of the incident I described. However, I don't think the correction was enough to unring that bell.)

In the accompanying blog, Breitbart presented the video as an important discovery:

We are in possession of a video in which Shirley Sherrod, USDA Georgia Director of Rural Development, speaks at the NAACP Freedom Fund dinner in Georgia. In her meandering speech to what appears to be an all-black audience, this federally appointed executive bureaucrat lays out in stark detail, that her federal duties are managed through the prism of race and class distinctions. . . .

Sherrod's racist tale is received by the NAACP audience with nodding approval and murmurs of recognition and agreement. Hardly the behavior of the group now holding itself up as the supreme judge of another group's racial tolerance.

It was clear that this was all about the Tea Party versus the NAACP and my speech was the tool Breitbart used to rage against an organization that would dare accuse others of racism, even when some Tea Party supporters were carrying blatantly racist signs and exhibiting racist behaviors.

Breitbart disputed accounts of an incident that had occurred outside the Capitol between a Tea Party crowd and black congressmen who were on the Hill to consider Obama's health care bill, suggesting that it was propaganda. That day, according to those involved, protesters spat on Emanuel Cleaver, chanted "Nigger" at John Lewis, and called Barney Frank a "faggot." It was extremely ugly and upsetting to anyone who observed it. Breitbart described the congressmen's walk through the crowd, "in and of itself," as an "act of racism meant to create a contrast between the Tea Party crowd and themselves." His intention was not only to absolve the Tea Party—or, I should say, people within the Tea Party, because we can't paint the entire group with such a broad brush—but to say that it was the Tea Party critics who were really practicing racism. That was a favorite tactic of the Right: when minorities cited racism, they were then called racists.

Breitbart wrote, "It's time for the allegedly pristine character of Rep. John Lewis to put up or shut up. *If* you provide verifiable video evidence showing that a single racist epithet was hurled as you walked among the Tea Partiers, or you pass a simple lie detector test, I will provide a $10K check to the United Negro College Fund."

On July 13, 2010, two thousand NAACP delegates at the annual convention unanimously passed a resolution calling for repudiation of racist elements within the Tea Party. "We take no issue with the Tea Party movement," Ben Jealous clarified. "We believe in freedom of assembly and people raising their voices in a democracy. What we take issue with is the Tea Party's continued tolerance for bigotry and bigoted statements. The time has come for them to accept the responsibility that comes with influence and make clear there is no place for racism and anti-Semitism, homophobia and other forms of bigotry in their movement."

The resolution created a firestorm, including an angry reply from Breitbart on talk radio. "Let me say something a tad newsworthy to the president of the NAACP: You can go to hell," Breitbart said. "I have tapes, a tape, of racism, and it's an NAACP dinner. You want to play with fire? I have evidence of racism, and it's coming from the NAACP." We now see that he was referring to my speech. On July 19, he released the clip, and we all know what happened then.

As the weeks went by after my firing, the story gained a strange kind of momentum. If I had hoped the whole affair would be over, I was out of luck. I was still getting used to Breitbart's particular brand of attack journalism. I was surprised and dismayed to find, as time passed, that he continued to post the video.

Very shortly, however, Breitbart shifted his focus away from the racist line to declare that the USDA and the Obama administration wanted me fired because of the *Pigford* settlement, which didn't make any sense at all. If the administration had wanted to keep *Pigford* out of the press, why had Vilsack himself brought it up? I couldn't keep Breitbart's narrative straight. One day he was saying I had been fired for being a racist, the next he was saying I had been fired because Obama didn't want people looking into *Pigford*. Later he would admit that *Pigford* had become an obsession for him.

In fact, *Pigford* was a pretty open secret. There had been volumes written on the black farmer settlement, with congressional hearings going back many years. However, a new interest in the matter was being driven by the Tea Party and conservative Republicans, who didn't want to pay the bill. The original 2008 appropriation for *Pigford II* had been $100 million, which hadn't even begun to cover the claims. In 2010, the administration was seeking an additional $1.5 billion. The debate in Congress was contentious, but both houses passed the appropriation in November 2010. After that, the right-wing media, including Breitbart, kept the story alive by asserting that there was rampant fraud in the program. Before Obama even signed the bill, they wanted to take it back.

Vilsack was angry about the charges of fraud. In a tense news conference, he stated that there had been no cover-up of fraud, and he explained that every allegation of fraud was forwarded to the USDA's inspector general and then to the FBI. Out of a total of twenty thousand claimants, only three cases of fraud had been found. Vilsack said that the Obama administration was "committed to ensuring that anyone receiving a payment under *Pigford II* was the victim of discrimination and has a valid claim that deserves compensation by following the very specific criteria outlined in the 2008 farm bill."

When President Obama signed the bill on December 8, that should finally have ended the long effort to get justice for black farmers through *Pigford* and *Pigford II*. But in 2011, the fraud conspiracists kept up the pressure. Leading the charge against the appropriation was Representative Steve King of Iowa, a member of the House Agriculture Committee, who called *Pigford* nothing more than "modern-day slavery reparations programs." I don't think he knew or cared what an insult that was to the black community. Thousands of black farmers had been denied their rights under a federal program paid for with their tax dollars, and King was accusing them of seeking slave reparations. It was unconscionable. There had been various proposals for slave reparations over the years, but none had gone very far. President Obama was even on record saying he didn't support the idea. In any case, whether reparations should be made for slavery was a separate issue from the class action lawsuits by present-day farmers. In my opinion, to raise the notion of slave reparations was a way of spiking the process and instigating further racial tensions.

Appearing on *Anderson Cooper 360*, King also asserted that at least 75 percent of the claims were fraudulent. When Cooper asked him for evidence, he cited a single anonymous source that he alleged had been involved in administering the *Pigford* settlement. For a legislator to base policy decisions on the statement of one person—if that person really existed—strains the democratic process. As Iowa Republican Senator Grassley, an early sponsor of *Pigford II*, pointed out, Congress had made a substantial effort to create a rigorous system that would expose any attempts at fraud. It included the appointment of a neutral adjudicator to review cases, the close supervision of the comptroller general, who was required to report to Congress throughout the process, and a required audit by the inspector general of the USDA.

Well into 2011, King and others refused to let go of the issue, and it became a drumbeat in the Republican-led Congress. In June, King filed an amendment to block *Pigford II* funds. "The new majority in the House of Representatives should not ratify the lame-duck Congress's decision to increase American taxpayers' exposure to *Pigford II* fraud," he said. "I believe that an investigation into the program will reveal that the majority of the claims that have been filed are fraudulent, and Congress should not turn a blind eye to the real possibility that the money is being used primarily to build political goodwill for the president instead of being used to properly redress the much smaller universe of people who have actually suffered harm. If passed, my amendment would put the brakes on *Pigford II* funding, and it would prevent the secretary of agriculture from paying fraudulent claims one $50,000 check at a time."

In July, King was joined by Congresswoman Michele Bachmann, who had just announced that she was running for president. They held a press conference citing the needs of midwestern farmers after floods from the Missouri River damaged their crops. Bachmann said, "When money is diverted to inefficient projects like the *Pigford* project . . . we can't afford $2 billion in potentially fraudulent claims when that money can be used to benefit the people along the Mississippi River and the Missouri River."

That was yet one more in a long trail of divisive statements meant to pit struggling farmers against one another and foster a sense of resentment based on race. It was now common for the word "fraudulent" to be attached to any mention of *Pigford*, and there was no doubt that it would begin to stick in the minds of many people that it was the case. It didn't matter that no evidence had ever been produced that showed the program to be rife with fraud. It didn't matter that there *was* evidence that the legal process leading to the settlement in *Pigford* and *Pigford II* had been lengthy and thorough, advanced under the careful scrutiny of three administrations—Clinton, Bush, and Obama—and had received bipartisan congressional support at every stage. Those who have stated that *Pigford* is a political conspiracy by the Obama administration to win votes lack any sense of history, and I believe they do so deliberately.

One big question on people's minds was whether I was going to sue Andrew Breitbart. It was not something I particularly relished doing. Who wants to be engaged in a lawsuit? But there was more at stake than my personal feelings.

Breitbart made a choice to keep targeting me, to refuse to admit error or deception, and to use my circumstances to launch a bigger platform for himself.

What is justice for a man who makes it his business to shade the truth to advance a political agenda? Does the truth matter? In my life I have experienced unfairness on many occasions. Segregation was the ultimate example of unfairness. But I came away from those times stronger. In deciding whether I would sue Breitbart, I had to ask myself whether I had a duty and if it would serve a higher purpose. He had chosen me; I hadn't chosen him.

My decision to launch a lawsuit would open a new chapter in my lifelong effort to face obstacles head-on. One thing I learned growing up as an outsider was that I would use the gift of power when I had it in my hands.

On February 11, 2011, my attorneys filed a lawsuit in the Superior Court of the District of Columbia against Andrew Breitbart, Larry O'Connor, a Breitbart employee who had posted the excerpted video on YouTube, and "John Doe," a person whose identity was concealed by Breitbart and O'Connor and who Breitbart has publicly credited with providing him the video footage. The complaint began:

> This is an action brought by Shirley Sherrod, a former Presidential appointee and former Georgia State Director for Rural Development for the United States Department of Agriculture ("USDA") for defamation, false light and intentional infliction of emotional distress. Mrs. Sherrod was forced to resign from her job after Defendants ignited a media firestorm by publishing false and defamatory statements that Mrs. Sherrod "discriminates" against people due to their race in performing her official federal duties. Defendants drew false support for their claims from a speech given by Mrs. Sherrod that they edited, deceptively, to create the appearance that Mrs. Sherrod was admitting present-day racism. In fact, Mrs. Sherrod was describing events that occurred ***twenty-three years before*** she held her federal position and, in fact, was encouraging people ***not*** to discriminate on the basis of race.

The complaint went on to explicitly detail the grounds for the defamation, false light, and intentional infliction of emotional distress claims.

Breitbart's initial reaction to the lawsuit was to talk about *Pigford* and his belief that the two were was linked. Later, he and O'Connor filed a motion to dismiss the suit on First Amendment grounds and, when that was denied, asked for a change of venue to the District Court in California. Both of these motions were denied by Judge Richard J. Leon.

On March 1, 2012, Breitbart died suddenly at his home in California. He was only forty-three. I received many calls asking for my reaction. I said the only thing I could, which was that my prayers went out to his family. The fate of the lawsuit will be determined, but my focus is to continue to reach out and build coalitions.

Charles, as always, has been by my side, centering me with his well-defined sense of morality and calming matter. Charles's position is quite pure and completely clear in his own mind. He believes we must move forward, away from past injuries, but always with an acknowledgment that we carry our pasts with us. He shared this perspective in a poetic, candid way with a reporter from the National Newspaper Publishers Association, and it sums up the heart of the struggle and the light we seek:

> . . . we are a confused bunch because of racism in our society in the way that we've been brought up. So, we are messed up. All of us, we are messed up. I can't forget all of the things that have happened to me. I forgive. I can forgive. I can say I'm not holding this in my heart against anybody. I wouldn't hurt anybody because of the wrong that they've done to me all my life. But, I've got to accept that there's something wrong inside of me that hurts—that's suffering, that begs for release. But, I'm not going to have it released in front of you to hurt you.
>
> Some of those things I've got to deal with for the rest of my life. Things that white people have done to me; how they've hurt me. Things they've said to me face to face; the beatings that I've taken; the jailings that I've taken in five states. All of this is inside of me. I can't just put it aside but I can decide who I want to be. Despite all the hurt that I have, I'm not going to hurt another brother.

Grounded in a deep Christian faith, Charles sees that although others may cause us injury, Christ urges that we forgive and embrace them. The lesson of the civil rights movement is that we have an obligation to seek harmony, even though no one ever said it would be easy.

In the blink of an eye our nation went from a land tolerant of racial oppression to one whose laws forbade it. But in many cases, the hearts and minds of the population were left behind. The so-called political correctness of the decades following the 1960s had the unintended consequence of masking the true feelings of those who held deep-seated prejudices. The election of Barack Obama seemed to wash away the fragile membrane covering those prejudices and gave them new life out in the open. Emboldened by having a black president, some people have become freer about expressing their darkest thoughts. It requires an uncomfortable but necessary reality check for all of us.

Have we faced our racism? The question probes at the dark corners of our history and challenges us anew. There are those who believe that racism is embedded in our national soul, that even as we glorify our founding fathers, we ignore the fact that they forged a nation that accepted slavery. Today we have the tools, both legal and legislative, to overcome institutional racism. However, it is far more difficult to address ignorance and prejudice in everyday life.

Not long ago, Haley Barbour, the governor of Mississippi and a Republican Party power broker, said of growing up in Yazoo City, "I don't remember it [segregation and the civil rights movement] being that bad." Barbour spoke glowingly of the White Citizens Council, which had helped keep the peace and drive out the Ku Klux Klan. He neglected to mention that although the Citizens Councils, formed in communities throughout the South, might have lacked the murderous instincts of the KKK, they still had the mission of halting integration.

According to the author David Halberstam, who wrote about Yazoo City's White Citizens Council in 1956, the council members "fired signers of the integration petition, or prevailed upon other white employers to get them fired. But the WCC continues to deny that it uses economic force: all the Council did in Yazoo City was to provide information (a full-page ad in the local weekly listing the 'offenders'); spontaneous public feeling did the rest."

In interviews with Citizens Council members, Halberstam found the same kind of dissembling that was a pattern in Albany, Georgia. As one interviewee said, "If a man works for you, and you believe in something, and that man is working against it and undermining it, why, you don't want him working for you." In case there's any doubt, he was talking about a black man who believed in integration working for a white man who believed in segregation. It was a polite comment with a violent underpinning. There is no question that Citizens Councils were made up of white supremacists without the robes. Their weapon was economic punishment for anyone who stepped out of line. Yet Barbour thinks they were the progressives in Mississippi.

Barbour's rosy view of Citizens Councils is a plain denial of the reality of life in Mississippi during the 1950s and 1960s. The fact that he was a young boy then, who might not have understood what was happening, does not excuse his depictions now as a sixty-three-year-old.

As I write this, in the early stages of the 2012 presidential election, it is impossible to ignore the trend of some Republican candidates flirting with racism well beyond the old wink-and-a-nod codes. I was shocked when I learned that both Michele Bachmann and Rick Santorum had signed a pledge by the Iowa-based Family Leader group, which stated, "Slavery had a disastrous impact on African-American families, yet sadly a child born into slavery in 1860 was more likely to be raised by his mother and father in a two-parent household than was an African-American baby born after the election of the USA's first African-American President."

My first reaction when I read this was "Send these people back to the fifth grade!" It hardly bears repeating that slave families had no rights whatsoever and men, women, and children were sold at will, with little consideration of the family unit. It is obscene to compare slavery favorably with our current situation—not to mention insulting to blacks, who struggle just like anyone else to get by and raise their families.

As for the Tea Party, I've already given examples of clear racism on the part of individuals. The 2010 Multi-State Survey of Race and Politics, conducted by the Institute for the Study of Ethnicity, Race & Sexuality at the University of Washington, using questions to measure racial hostility, found that Tea Party supporters expressed more resentment toward blacks than the rest of the population. For example, when reading the statement "It's really a matter of some people not trying hard enough; if blacks would only try harder they could be just as well off as whites," 73 percent of Tea Party "true believers" agreed. We can push that result under the rug, but there is a disturbing racial undertone to the Tea Party that is hard to ignore. I have often wondered what it would be like to see a Tea Party movement that was not based on anger. Anger is an engine filled with sugar: it stalls on you before you can get very far down the road.

Evil flourishes when the unacceptable becomes acceptable. Even when racism is not overtly expressed, it is easily recognizable in the words that are used—everything from talking about affirmative action babies to calling First Lady Michelle Obama "angry." The so-called Birther Movement, which denies Obama's U.S. citizenship and thus his legitimacy as president, is all about creating the visage of otherness, of one who does not belong. Even when seeing an official copy of the birth certificate, these people refuse to accept it, saying it was forged. They want to believe what they want to believe.

The irony of what happened to me is that I have always been willing, and even eager, to put race behind me. Most of the people I've met in my work feel the same way. They are tired of it. White and black, they want to lay the burden down. That does not mean, however, that we are entering a postracial, or "color-blind," era. When Obama was elected president, the media was full of articles announcing that we had entered a postracial era. Now we're seeing that it wasn't that easy. In fact, the myth of color blindness has actually been a regressive force in race relations. As Tim Wise pointed out in *Colorblind: The Rise of Post-racial Politics and the Retreat from Racial Equity*, by acting above the fray President Obama and other race-transcendent politicians have ceded the field to destructive right-wing racial narratives. Thus we have Rush Limbaugh broadcasting the gleeful singing of "Barack the Magic Negro," even as postracial liberals pretend that racism is a thing of the past. Today, when people talk about being postracial, it is often a code for being opposed to affirmative action. It is more productive and realistic to acknowledge that race is a factor in our history and our common life and that we have a long way to go to relieve all the tensions but can work toward that goal.

That leaves the question at the heart of the charges against me: does reverse racism exist? Setting aside the fact that historically whites and blacks have no parity of experience and whites were never enslaved or denied their rights as a population, in my opinion racism is racism. There's no "reverse" in the equation.

There have been many definitions of racism, but I think the most meaningful distinction is about power. For centuries in this country the racism practiced against blacks destroyed their dignity, opportunity, livelihoods, and even lives. That is an unassailable fact. To this day, even with a black man in the White House, there is no equivalent power to oppress in the black community—nor should there be. Right-thinking people understand that the only way forward is together.

It seems to me that the loudest complaints about reverse racism come from people who don't want minorities to have an equal footing or who don't understand the troubled history of race relations in this country. I was very interested in something that occurred when Supreme Court Justice Sonia Sotomayor was going through her confirmation hearing. People got all upset about a comment she made in a speech that "I would hope that a wise Latina woman with the richness of her experiences would more often than not reach a better conclusion than a white male who hasn't lived that life." I think most of us understand that Sotomayor was expressing Latina and female pride and also pointing out the importance of diversity. But Rush Limbaugh, Newt Gingrich, and even some senators who questioned her at the hearings called it reverse racism. Gingrich remarked that if a white man had made the comment, he would have been forced to withdraw. Maybe that's true, for the obvious reason of white men's historical place in the power structure. Overall, I thought the incident was a new height in reverse reasoning. But it's a sign of the times when no comment about ethnic pride is accepted at face value. It's fair to say that most people would like this silliness to stop.

There is still much work to be done. I don't understand how people can hate so much, any more than I understood it growing up in a segregated community. But I do know that we need to commit ourselves to the struggle all over again. We have to work together to be sure that the next time we bury evil, it's buried deep enough to stay down. We must be brave and have the courage of our convictions, even when elections and livelihoods are at stake. As Obama said recently, reflecting on the legacy of Martin Luther

King, "I think that we forget when he was alive there was nobody who was more vilified, nobody who was more controversial, nobody who was more despairing at times. There was a decade that followed the great successes of Birmingham and Selma in which he was just struggling, fighting the good fight, and scorned, and many folks angry. But what he understood, what kept him going, was that the arc of moral universe is long but it bends towards justice. But it doesn't bend on its own. It bends because all of us are putting our hand on the arc and we are bending it in that direction. And it takes time. And it's hard work. And there are frustrations."

In the end, I turn to my Christian faith to lead me. It requires that we forgive and love one another. A white man murdered my father in the Deep South during an era of racial violence. Had I chosen to hate all white men as a result, I would have been a very different woman than I am today—a woman who could not look her own children in the eyes. Instead, I understand that salvation, in this life and the next, comes from love and understanding. I pray every day that our country will set aside the emotions that drive us apart and devote our energies to the pursuit of happiness and peace.

CHAPTER 14

Planting Hope

On a hot, dry afternoon in late June 2011, Charles and I drive a few miles from our home in Albany, along a pretty country road. Soon we come to a large property, bordered by a lovely white fence, and turn in at the gate. We continue down a long, winding road, shaded by a grove of pecan and longleaf pine trees, until we approach a stately antebellum mansion with a wide front porch where you can almost picture women shading themselves on hot summer days. We stop in front of the porch and sit there for a moment, two older black people who have survived segregation, coming home to a plantation that our organization would soon own.

The property, called Cypress Pond, is a historic 1,638-acre plantation built in 1851, which still retains the architectural details of a long-ago period. Exterior columns provide a grand entrance to an interior whose fifteen-foot ceilings showcase ornate plaster moldings, and antique marble mantels frame the fireplaces. Burnished heart-pine floors shine in the sunlight coming through richly curtained windows, some of them in stained glass.

The mansion, empty now, was previously filled with beautiful Edwardian antique pieces. In the parlor stood a billiard table that had been owned by England's King Edward VII. Now, walking through the bare rooms, it is easy to conjure up the cotillions and family gatherings. Historical photographs show women in long gowns relaxing in large rockers on the front porch. The ghosts of the past bristle in the trees and in the squeaks of the wide plank porch. To the side of the house, in the shadows, stands a shabby wooden shack, which we believe once housed slaves. Their lives, too, can be imagined. Beside the shack stands a large bell tower, whose bell was used to summon the laborers.

Once a cotton, pecan, and vegetable farm, in recent times Cypress Pond has been managed primarily for game and wildlife, using prescribed burns, irrigation, and food plots to enhance the resident populations of quail, dove, white-tailed deer, and wild turkey. The wetlands support healthy populations of waterfowl, including wood ducks, mallards, and ring-necked ducks. Bass, bream, and crappie reside in the three ponds on the plantation. It is a gorgeous, fertile landscape.

Charles and I experience a combination of unease and expectation as we survey the plantation. What can we make of it? We feel a weight of responsibility to do the right thing and the best thing. But we also feel joyful in the belief that God always finds a purpose. The pain of closing New Communities more than twenty-five years ago has led us to this miracle.

When the *Pigford* settlement for New Communities was announced, we gathered together the families and began to talk about how we would use the money to re-create our earlier vision and also to expand on that vision by building a conference center for racial education and healing. We wanted a property where we could both farm the land and also nurture the minds of people across the nation. Our land would become a home for progressive thought and action. Cypress Pond was the ideal setting, and we were mindful that there was a certain moral justice to acquiring a former slave plantation to promote economic opportunity for farmers and dialogue among the races.

As we investigated the history of the plantation, we discovered that it had been built by General Hartwell Hill Tarver, one of the

150 NEGROES FOR SALE
At Public Out-Cry, In The
City of Albany.

IN pursuance of the last will and testament of Paul E. Tarver, late of Dougherty county, dec'd, we will expose for sale, at public out-cry, to the highest bidder, on

THURSDAY, THE 29th DAY OF DEC., 1859,

and from day to day until the sale is completed, before the Court House door in the city of Albany—One Hundred and Fifty likely Negroes—valuable plantation hands, belonging to the estate of the said Paul E. Tarver. Also, at the PLANTATION of the said Estate, five miles west of Albany, all the farm stock of said Estate, consisting of a large lot of Horses and Mules, Cattle, Hogs, Corn, Fodder, Wagons, and farming stock of every description. The sale of the Negroes at Albany, will take place on the 28th, and then the other property at the plantation. Terms liberal, and made known on the day of the sale.

HENRY TARVER, Ex'r
C. C. TARVER, Exr'x

After Emancipation, Cypress Pond continued as a southern estate and probably housed many sharecroppers on its vast property, although its purpose eventually turned to sport and gaming. Its most recent owner was Gerald Lawhorn, who started the Griffin-based PetroSouth chain in 1969. He also invented the system of purchasing gas at the pump with credit and debit cards. Lawhorn had always planned to retire to Cypress Pond. But in 2005, he was diagnosed with amyotrophic lateral sclerosis, commonly called Lou Gehrig's disease. He died in 2008 at the age of sixty-two, and the property went up for sale.

As we began to prepare the property, the young folks were drawn to the place. Everybody was eager to volunteer. My brother Hosie, who was born after Daddy's death and had never farmed a day in his life, fell in love with it and now spends long hours on the tractor mowing. He has found new purpose in the land.

Russia, who was a child of New Communities, is also out at the property whenever she can manage it, cleaning, mowing, and just walking the land. She is truly a daughter of the movement, strong and kind and filled with a bright spirit. She has a talent for finding the outcasts of society and bringing them back into the fold. She is excited about the new chance we have to do good.

Ken and his wife and four children now live in Montreal and won't be here to see Cypress Pond come back to life, but I know my grandchildren will be regular visitors, and they'll learn as their parents did what it means to have a purpose in life beyond themselves.

Seeing the way the young people have embraced the property and the vision, I have renewed hope that the next generation will free itself from the bondage of racial prejudice. I can picture a time when this will be a place where black, white, brown, red, and yellow work together for a higher purpose.

Since my resignation I have seen the United States from every perspective. I have traveled to the mountains of Colorado, the shores of California, the plains of Kansas, and the eastern seaboard. Looking ahead, I can say with certainty that my task until the end of my days is to plant hope—not as an ethereal ideal but as a practical intention. I can never lose sight of the poor folks scattered in farms and towns across this nation, who don't care about rhetoric or taking sides. They're too busy trying to feed their families and stake a claim to the American dream. As a country, during these tough times, we have to ask ourselves if we have the courage it takes to hope.

When I walk the shaded paths of Cypress Pond, my heart is filled with bittersweet emotions. I know that my ancestors, shackled in slavery, could not have dreamed of a time when their people would be standing on this ground holding the keys. For them, freedom was enough. We ourselves, growing up in segregation, could not have imagined this. For us, equality was enough. But we've now come to a time when we have a new dream and a more difficult challenge. For freedom and equality to survive, we must also have reconciliation.

During the civil rights struggles, Charles often told his charges that there were worse chains than jail, and that remains true of the stranglehold of hate on the heart. All the efforts of the past will be as nothing if they only lead to a brewing resentment that is passed down to future generations. Reconciliation is the only way to freedom.

The late Spencer Perkins, a leader in the racial reconciliation movement, once wrote about an automatic mental process that sometimes takes place when a black person meets a white person for the first time. There's a wariness while they determine, Is he for real? Is he a good white? "It is part life experience, part self-preservation, and part projection," he concluded. He also noted that a similar process occurs for many whites when they meet a black person: Is he someone I can respect as a peer? Perkins didn't shy away from acknowledging this reality, but he also said that it presents a challenge, given the Christian call for racial reconciliation. For that, he said, we need the light of God's grace to help us transcend the hard feelings and injuries, to bridge the resentments on both sides of the racial line, to let go of the idea that we have been treated unfairly.

"No, it ain't fair, but it's right," Perkins wrote. "And God understands that there will be slip-ups and wrong turns, moments of anger and unforgiveness. But as we grow in our discipleship of grace, each day will bring more victories. And when we fail, our God, who is full of grace, is eager to forgive. The more I have come to know this divine quality, the dearer he becomes to me, and the more I want to demonstrate this quality to others."

Meditating on this idea, so profound yet so simple, my mind travels back to the tune of an old Negro spiritual. The people of the civil rights movement rewrote the lyrics and sang, "Woke up this morning with my mind stayed on freedom."

Now, perhaps, we can rewrite it once again and let our voices rise with a new awakening: "Woke up this morning with my mind stayed on reconciliation."

Acknowledgments

I could not have written this book without the help and support of many people—both those whose direct involvement made it possible and those who have been instrumental in my life and work. First, among all of these, is my husband Charles, whose steady dedication and courageous actions have been the force behind our lives and those of countless others. This is his story as well as mine. The day I met the brave and brilliant young SNCC worker I set out on a movement path and neither Charles nor I has ever wavered.

I am grateful to all of those who had confidence in this story and helped me bring it to light. Drew Berry has been an active and enthusiastic supporter for getting the word out. Jane Dystel believed my story should be told, and she pushed hard to find the right home with Malaika Adero and Atria Books. Catherine Whitney has faithfully enabled me to bring my words to life on the page.

There are so many people who deserve acknowledgment for the work they do that gives hope to others. Among them are my former colleagues at the Federation of Southern Cooperatives/Land Assistance Fund, particularly Ralph Paige and Jerry Pennick; Starry Krueger at the Rural Development Leadership Network; my colleagues at the Southern Rural Black Women's Initiative (SRBWI), particularly Oleta Garrett Fitzgerald, Sophia Bracy-Harris, Sarah

Bobrow Williams, Winifred Green, and Carol Blackmon; the hard-working folks at the Baker County community center who have staked a claim on the future through the commercial kitchen, the Southern Journeys sewing cooperative, and other activities; the farmers and supporters from New Communities who never gave up hope; Farm Aid, particularly Willie Nelson, who has been a shining light on behalf of rural farmers for decades; and Ben Jealous, Rosalyn Brock, and their organization the NAACP. I also write this book in memory of C.B. and Slater King, who were instrumental in the Movement and gave us help when things looked the most dire.

I want to offer special thanks to Roger and Eloise Spooner, ordinary farmers who made an extraordinary impact on my life.

I want to also thank my children, Russia and Kenyatta, for persevering through both good and hard times associated with the Movement struggle. You have made both of us proud.

Finally, if I have managed to walk even partially in the shadow of my remarkable mother, Grace Miller, I will be satisfied. She and my late father, Hosie Miller, have been with me every day of my life. And my siblings, Nannie, Sandra, Rubertha, Deborah, and Hosea. We struggled to survive after the death of our father but never strayed from his lessons about life and people and giving back.

Appendix: The Speech

March 27, 2010
Coffee County, Georgia, NAACP

G ood evening.

Olivia, I want to thank you for those kind words. You know, it's been a pleasure working with her over the last ten years. I've missed the work. [I] had to move on to some . . . other work, and I'll talk to you more about that.

To the president of the NAACP, here, and the board of directors, and members, and all the others here, it is indeed a pleasure for me to be with you this evening. And I want to say to you, I am very proud to be working with the Obama administration to help rural America's welfare. I want to do all I can to help rural communities such as yours to be a place where we can have a quality life and a comfortable life for our families and our friends.

But before I . . . go into what I have here, I want to—I want to second something that Olivia said. You know, I grew up on the farm and I didn't want to have anything to do with agriculture, but she was right. There are jobs at USDA, and many times there are no people of color to fill those jobs 'cause we shy away from agriculture. We hear the word "agriculture" and think only of working in the fields.

And you've heard of a lot of layoffs. Have you heard of anybody in the federal government losing their job? That's all that I need to say, okay? And I—I might say a little bit more to the young people. It's good to have you all here.

I want to share something with you this evening, something that's always heavy on my heart each day, but especially at this time of the year.

It was forty-five years ago today that my father's funeral was held. I was a young girl at the age of seventeen when my father was murdered by a white man in Baker County. In Baker County, the murder of black people occurred periodically, and in every case the white men who murdered them were never punished. It was no different in my father's case. There were three witnesses to his murder, but the grand jury refused to indict the white man who murdered him.

I should tell you a little about Baker County. In case you don't know where it is, it's located less than twenty miles southwest of Albany. Now, there were two sheriffs from Baker County that—whose names you probably never heard but I know in the case of one, the thing he did many, many years ago still affects us today. And that sheriff was Claude Screws. Claude Screws lynched a black man. And this was at the beginning of the forties. And the strange thing back then was an all-white federal jury convicted him not of murder but of depriving Bobby Hall—and I should say that Bobby Hall was a relative—depriving him of his civil rights.

So, in the opinion, when the justice wrote his opinion justifying overturning the conviction, he said you had to prove that as the sheriff was murdering Bobby Hall, he was *thinking* of depriving him of his civil rights. That's where the whole issue of proving *intent* came from and you heard it a lot. It was used a lot during the civil rights movement. What you also heard a lot when Rodney King was beaten out in California. Y'all might remember that. They kept saying you had to prove intent—and that came from Screws versus the U.S. government. I'm told that case is studied by every law student. And usually when we have people coming into southwest Georgia and wanting to take some tours of—of things where some events happened during the civil rights movement, I usually take them to the courthouse in Newton to show where Bobby Hall's body was displayed.

During my years of growing up, the sheriff was L. Warren Johnson. He wanted to be called "the Gator," and that's how people referred to him 'cause he had a holler that would make you want to tremble. He also killed a lot of black people—and Gator Johnson was *the law* in Baker County. And when I say that I mean no one, black or white, could ride through the county with an out-of-county tag. That means you could have a tag from anywhere else in Georgia—you couldn't ride through Baker County without being stopped. And *The Atlanta Constitution* reported at one point that his take on the road was at least $150,000 a year—and that was during the sixties.

My father was a farmer. And growing up on the farm, my dream was to get as far away from the farm and Baker County as I could get. And picking cotton, picking cucumbers, shaking peanuts for a little while before they—you know, the older folk know what I'm talking about, when you had to shake them and take them up to the pole and . . . put them around that, you know—doing all that work on the farm, it will make you get an education more than anything else.

But I didn't want to just get an education. I wanted to leave the farm and Baker County. It was—life was—the older folk know what I'm talking about—the segregation and the discrimination and the racist acts that we had to endure during those years made me just want to leave. And you know, we used to have people who'd leave and go north. You all know how they come back talking and they come back looking. I learned later that some of those cars they drove home were rented. But it made you want to go north, 'cause you thought they were free up there and you thought everybody was free in the North. So, my goal was not to even go to college in the South 'cause I, you know, I was always told you find your husband at college. So, I didn't want to find one living in the South. I wanted to go to college in the North so I could get a husband from the North, never ever come back down here and live again.

But, you know, you can never say what you'll never do. And it was during March, my senior year in high school. I mean my father was just everything to us. I had four sisters—I'm the oldest. My mother—there are six of us, but my father wanted a son so bad. We were all girls. We all had boys' nickname[s]. I was "Bill." Now, he loved his girls but he wanted a son so bad. And when my sister was about—my youngest sister was eight, he convinced my mother to try one more time for this boy.

So, to my surprise, my senior year of high school, I thought my mother was just sick. I didn't know what was wrong with her, you know, really worried. And one day my best friend at school said, "How's your mama doing?" I said, "She just doesn't seem to be getting any better." She said, "Girl, your daddy was up at the store yesterday giving out cigars. Your mama [is] going to have a baby." He told everyone that that baby was the son. And he was, in fact, having a new home built. He was the first person to get a loan on his own to build a house. He wanted to build a brick house so bad, but they told him a black man could not borrow money to build a brick house. They had to choose blocks, you know.

So—and this new house that was being built—there were five daughters—there was this one room that was the boy's room—his son's room. He told everybody it was a boy. And, in fact, it was painted blue. And he came—he and my mother came to pick me up from school one day early to go to Albany with him to pick the furniture for this boy's room. He didn't live to see him. My brother was born two months after he died, in June of '65.

We started the movement. But before I get there, I need to tell you something . . . and I want to say this to the young people. You know, I told how I looked forward and I dreamt so much about moving north and from the farm, especially in the South, and I knew that on the night of my father's death I felt I had to do something. I had to do something in answer to what had happened.

My father wasn't the first black person to be killed. He was a leader in the community. He wasn't the first to be killed by white men in the county. But I couldn't just let his death go without doing something in answer to what happened. I made the commitment on the night of my father's death, at the age of seventeen, that I would not leave the South, that I would stay in the South and devote my life to working for change. And I've been true to that commitment all of these forty-five years.

You know, when you look at some of the things that I've done through the years and when you look at some of the things that happened—I went to school my first two years at Fort Valley—I know there are some Fort Valley graduates here, too—I did my first two years at Fort Valley but so much was happening back at home— and then I met this man, I'll tell you a little about him—that I transferred back to Albany State and did the last two years.

But two weeks after I went to school at Fort Valley, they called and told me that a bunch of white men had gathered outside of our home and burned the cross one night. Now, in the house was my mother, my four sisters, and my brother, who was born June 6—and this was September. They were all in that house that night. Well, my mother and one of my sisters went out on the porch. My mama had a gun. Another sister– you know some of this stuff, it's like movies, some of the stuff that happened through the years—I won't go into everything. I'll just tell you about this. One of my sisters got on the phone 'cause we had organized the movements starting June of '65, shortly—not long after my father's death.

That's how I met my husband. He wasn't from the North. . . . He's from up south in Virginia. But anyway my brother and my sisters got on the phone—they called other black men in the county. And it wasn't long before they had surrounded these white men. And they had to keep one young man from actually using his gun on one of them. You probably would have read about it had that happened that night. But they actually allowed those men to leave.

But I won't go into some of the other stuff that happened that night, but do know that my mother and my sister were out on the porch with a gun, and my mother said, "I see you and I know who you are." She recognized some of them. She'll tell you that she became the first black elected official in Baker County just eleven years later, and she is still serving you all. She's chair of the board of education, and she's been serving almost thirty-four years.

I didn't know how I would go about carrying out the commitment I made that night, but my husband came to Albany and started the movement there in 1961. And he stayed. You know, a lot of them went into the communities and they worked during the early part of the movement and they left. But he continued to stay in southwest Georgia, and we've done a lot of stuff through the years. . . . Some of the things that have happened to us, you'd probably be on the edge of your seat if I were to tell you about some of them. We've been in some very, very dangerous situations through the years, but we continue to work.

And, you know God is so good 'cause people like me don't get appointed to positions like state director of rural development. They just don't get these kinds of positions 'cause I've been out there at every grassroots level and I've paid some dues.

But when I . . . made the commitment years ago I didn't know how—I didn't . . . I prayed about it that night, and as our house filled with people I was back in one of the bedrooms praying and asking God to show me what I could do. I didn't have—the path wasn't laid out that night. I just made the decision that I would stay and work. And over the years things just happened. And young people: I just want you to know that when you're true to what God wants you to do the path just opens up—and things just come to you, you know. God is good—I can tell you that.

When I made that commitment, I was making that commitment to black people—and to black people only. But, you know, God will show you things and He'll put things in your path so that—that you realize that the struggle is really about poor people, you know.

The first time I was faced with having to help a white farmer save his farm, he—he took a long time talking, but he was trying to show me he was superior to me. I know what he was doing. But he had come to me for help. What he didn't know—while he was taking all that time trying to show me he was superior to me—was I was trying to decide just how much help I was going to give him.

I was struggling with the fact that so many black people have lost their farmland, and here I was faced with having to help a white person save their land. So, I didn't give him the full force of what I could do. I did enough so that when he—I—I assumed the Department of Agriculture had sent him to me, either that or the—or the Georgia Department of Agriculture. And he needed to go back and report that I did try to help him.

So I took him to a white lawyer that we had—that had . . . attended some of the training that we had provided, 'cause Chapter 12 bankruptcy had just been enacted for the family farmer. So I figured if I take him to one of them that his own kind would take care of him.

That's when it was revealed to me that, y'all, it's about poor versus those who have, and not so much about white—it is about white and black, but it's not—you know, it opened my eyes, 'cause I took him to one of his own and I put him in his hand, and felt okay, I've done my job. But, during that time we would have these injunctions against the Department of Agriculture and—so, they couldn't foreclose on him. And I want you to know that the county supervisor had done something to him that I have not seen yet that they've done to any other farmer, black or white. And what they did to him caused him to not be able to file Chapter 12 bankruptcy.

So, everything was going along fine—I'm thinking he's being taken care of by the white lawyer and then they lifted the injunction against USDA in May of '87 for two weeks and he was one of thirteen farmers in Georgia who received a foreclosure notice. He called me. I said, "Well, go on and make an appointment at the lawyer. Let me know when it is and I'll meet you there."

So we met at the lawyer's office on—on the day they had given him. And this lawyer sat there—he had been paying this lawyer, y'all. That's what got me. He had been paying the lawyer since November, and this was May. And the lawyer sat there and looked at him and said, "Well, y'all are getting old. Why don't you just let the farm go?" I could not believe he said that, so I said to the lawyer—I told him, "I can't believe you said that." I said, "It's obvious to me if he cannot file a Chapter 12 bankruptcy to—to stop this foreclosure, you have to file an 11." And the lawyer said to me, "I'll do whatever you say—whatever you think"—that's the way he put it. But he's paying him. He wasn't paying me any money, you know. So he said—the lawyer said he would work on it.

And then, about seven days before that man would have been sold at the courthouse steps, the farmer called me and said the lawyer wasn't doing anything. And that's when I spent time there in my office calling everybody I could think of to try to see—help me find the lawyer who would handle this. And finally, I remembered that I had gone to see one just 40 miles away in Americus with the black farmers.

Well, working with him made me see that it's really about those who have versus those who don't, you know. And they could be black; they could be white; they could be Hispanic. And it made me realize then that I needed to work to help poor people—those who don't have access the way others have.

I want to just share something with you and . . . I think it helps to—it—you know, when I learned this, I'm like, "Oh, my goodness." You know, back in the late seventeenth and eighteenth century, black—there were black indentured servants and white indentured servants, and they all would work for the seven years and get their freedom. And they didn't see any difference in each other—nobody worried about skin color. They married each other. You know, these were poor whites and poor blacks in the same boat, except they were slaves, but they were both slaves and both had their opportunity to work out on the slavery. Okay? But then they started looking at the injustices that they faced and started then trying—you know, the people with money—you know, they started—the . . . poor whites and poor blacks who were—they—you know, they married each other. They lived together. They were just like we would be. And they started looking at what was happening to them and decided we need to do something about it—you know, about this. Well, the people with money, the elite, decided, hey, we need to do something here to divide them.

So that's when they made black people servants for life. That's when they put laws in place forbidding them to marry each other. That's when they created the racism that we know of today. They did it to keep us divided. And they—it started working so well, they said, "Gosh, looks like we've come up on something here that can last generations." And here we are over four hundred years later, and it's still working. What we have to do is get that out of our heads. There is no difference between us. The only difference is that the folks with money want to stay in power and whether it's health care or what-ever it is, they'll do what they need to do to keep that power, you know. It's always about money, y'all. You know, I haven't seen such a mean-spirited people as I've seen lately over this issue of health care. Some of the racism we thought was buried. Didn't it surface? Now, we endured eight years of Bush and we didn't do the stuff these Republicans are doing because you have a black president.

I wanted to give you that little history—especially the young people—I want you to know they created it, you know, not just for us. But we got the brunt of it 'cause they needed to elevate what is just a little higher than us to make them think that they're so much better, and then we—they would never work with us, you know, to try to change the situation that they were all in.

But where am I going with this? You know, I couldn't say forty-five years ago—I couldn't stand here and say what I'm saying—what I will say to you tonight. Like I told you, God helped me to see that it's not just about black people, it's about poor people. And I've come a long way. I knew that I couldn't live with hate, you know. As my mother has said to so many, "If we had tried to live with hate in our hearts, we'd probably be dead now." But I've come to realize that we have to work together and—you know, it's sad that we don't have a room full of whites and blacks here tonight, 'cause we have to overcome the divisions that we have. We have to get to the point where, as Toni Morrison said, "Race exists but it doesn't matter." We have to work just as hard. I know it's—you know, that division is still here, but our communities are not going to thrive—you know, our children won't have the—the communities that they need to be able to stay in and live in and—and have a good life if we can't figure this out, you all. White people, black people, Hispanic people, we all have to do our part to make our communities a safe place, a healthy place, a good environment.

You know so that companies—why would a company want to locate in some of these places? You know, I—it's so sad that, as I go around the state, people ask me, "Where are you from?" "Yeah, I'm living in Albany." "Oh, a lot of crime they're in." You know, nothing good you could say too much about Albany anymore, and . . . a lot of it is brought on by folks who live there, you know? People who live there. You read the paper—if you read the paper and listen to the TV station there in Albany, you wouldn't want to go there and live. You know, people are still fighting each other—worse, I believe, now. Least it was open during the civil rights movement. It was a lick here and there—and my husband got in the brunt of a lot of them. But now it's . . . really in such a way that it hurts 'cause it's going to keep the jobs away.

You know, you can go to a community and you can just about tell—and I'm traveling all around where people work together, you know. You're not losing this many jobs. You're getting a few. You know, we have a beautiful country. We have a beautiful part of this state—the southern part of this state—but it's not thriving. And we need to figure out why. Well, we kind of know, but we need to work on why. And—and young folks, you know when I was growing up, you had to get home from school and go to the fields. But y'all don't have to do that no more. You should be excelling, you know. Parents, you've got to set some goals for your children, you know. You cannot allow them not to try to become the best they could be, and not study . . . you know. Y'all must love working in the chicken house. (I know they closed for one year.)

But change has to start with us and . . . somehow we've got to make the other side of town work with us. We've got to make our communities what they need to be and our young people, I'm not picking on you, but you got to, but y'all got to . . . step up to the plate. You've got to step up to the plate. You are capable of being very, very smart people. You are capable of being those doctors and lawyers. You're capable of running your own business. That's what—one of the things in the position I'm in . . . one of the things that really hurt—one of the programs we had with some of the most money in it, you know, it's with business and industry. And I sit up there and I'm signing off on six million, three million, two million—but who is it going to? Not one so far. And when I got a report on where we are with it, we're—we're approaching $80 million since October first. But not one dime to a black business—not one. You know, and I know as a young person you're thinking good times. But, hey, don't let life pass you by having a good time. You can enjoy it, but be serious, you know. And there are jobs in agriculture. There's . . .

a program, the 1890 Scholars Program and they are—they're connected with every 1890 land-grant institution, and . . . let me tell
you what that is. That's the black land-grant institutions, and there
are about seventeen and Tuskegee. They—you can actually get a
scholarship—and Fort Valley State is the main grant in Georgia,
the 1890; the 1862 is the white land-grant, that's the University of
Georgia—you can get a scholarship and every summer you work at
one of those agencies while you are in school. And when you get out,
it's an automatic job. Agencies like . . . Farm Service Agency (that's
the old Farmers Home Administration), Rural Development. . . .
Just in Rural Development nationwide, there are over six thousand
employees. But you can go up there to Washington, to the Department of Agriculture, it's on both sides of the street.

In Rural Development, there are 129 employees, and guess how
many of them are people of color? Anybody want to take a guess?
That's in Georgia. I got—there are 129 in my agency. How many?
It's more than two. Little more than twelve. There are less than
twenty of us. We have six area offices in the state and subarea offices,
and when I look at who's coming up the line in the agencies—in the
agency, there are not many of us, 'cause we think agriculture is a bad
word. We think it's working in the fields. Some of the best-paying
jobs you ever want to have, okay?

I won't keep at you with that kind of stuff. But let—just know
that you can—there's another point I want to make, though. You
know, coming out of slavery black folks used to help each other.
That's how they built the schools that we have. You know, that's how
they bought the land that we have—that we have about lost all of
it. You know that our people had over 15 million acres, and as black
people have less than 2 million acres of farm land left. And we will
sell it for nothing—for nothing.

You know, I was helping a family here recently. Five hundred fifteen acres of land, never had a drop of debt on it since the grandfather
bought it years ago and he—he died in 1974. And two cousins up in
the North, guess what they decided? They tried to force a sale of every
acre of it. And they wanted that—one of their aunts spent all of her life
on the land. She was ninety-three years old when she died. And she

died after those "For sale" signs went up out there on that farm—auction sign went up on the farm. She was in the hospital. The next month she was dead. That was January—she was dead by October.

But we kept working at it. And we found some honest lawyers—they were white—I wish I could say that about all lawyers, especially black lawyers, but they will nickel and dime you to death. I don't have—sorry—I don't have two dozen pennies for most lawyers. But anyway that land has been saved, you know. But they were trying to force a sale of all of it. They'll eventually get 62 acres of the 515. And guess what? They have a white man already lined up to buy it. But you can—what I want to say to you—you can do good. And y'all going to be smart. You're going to go on and—and get good jobs. Look, reach back and help somebody. That's what we were taught. That's what our folk did, you know. It looks like the more—the better we do, the more free we are, the more divided we become, you know. It looks like we don't care about each other anymore. You know, that's why kids can just, you know—y'all know what happened in the day. He did something wrong, everybody in the community got you, you know. Well that doesn't happen anymore. And we have to get back to that.

If we're going to rebuild our communities, if we're going to get with all of the problems we have in our communities, it will take all of us working together to solve them. We can't turn our backs. And you never know who you're helping. You could be helping the second black president of the United States.

Now, I need to tell you a little bit about Rural Development. There—there are at least forty programs at Rural Development, but I'll just talk to you briefly about a couple of them. The main one is the Housing Program. We have more money for single-family housing, direct loans—and that's loans from the agency—than we've ever had in the history of the program.

But we having trouble getting that money out the door and guess why: credit issues. They had to send me extra help from Washington to try to help—because of the stimulus money. See, we have more money, but direct loans for the low, very low income and moderate income. And guess what? Those loans—it's a 100 percent loan. You can buy the land and build a house—100 percent loans. No private mortgage insurance, those loans are directly from USDA. And folks will let a cell phone and other stuff you don't even need keeping you from being able to—to acquire an asset that you really need—which is a home. We've got to be more careful about our credit.

I was talking with a young lady, actually a relative in a major position, and she—she was letting the hospital—the hospital was getting ready to garnish her check. She works for the city. And I said, "Do you understand that goes on your credit?" . . . I said, "You could have told them 'I . . . can pay $25 a month,'" and they would have accepted that. But she didn't make that step. So now here they were getting ready to start taking it from her pay. And that goes on her credit. And I said, "You want a house one day—you'll never be able to get a house." Now, she does some foolish stuff with her money. I won't go into some of the foolish stuff.

But I—I want to say that to us and young people. You know, that's one of the things I remember from my father. He used to talk to us about business and credit. And what he said to us: "You need to always keep a good credit record. You may not have any money but you can always get some." And we need to keep that in mind. We need to stop trying to get things we don't need, you know. Take the time to get the money—you know, to save the money for what you want—and you can do that. You can do that. You *can* do that. You don't have to have everything right now, okay?

We also have in addition to the direct loans from the agency, we are . . . the guaranteed loan program for housing and . . . those loans are for people with a slightly higher income. That—that program has been so successful that we are about to run out of money. And I'm talking about all over the country. I'm talking about billions. And in Georgia, you know in 2008, they made like 1,265 guaranteed loans. Last year we did almost 4,500. And this year, if the money had not run out, if it doesn't run out—I'm hoping they're going to get some more—we might do as many as 12,000, you know. If there was ever a time for people to become homeowners, now is the time. And you can thank President Obama for that.

And I said something briefly to you about the—the business and industry money. We've got to get our act together. We got to start thinking about becoming entrepreneurs, you know. And young people, you need to think of that as you—as you mature. You know, get some education. Learn how to do it right and then think of going into business. Until our communities look at how we can grow our own businesses we'll be—we'll forever be at the mercy of these companies that will come in, use up the tax credits, and leave.

Hey, didn't y'all lose the chicken in the street, here. They will [use] up your tax credit and move on to another community and use theirs too, and leave you high and dry. We can do some—you know, you can think of creating your businesses and making those dollars flow over and over in your own community. There's also the Repair Loan Program for—for senior citizens sixty-two and over who are lower income. You can qualify for a grant of $7,500. Or, if you have repayment ability—and those payments can . . . some of them are very low, $25 a month—you get a 1 percent loan up to $20,000 to $25,000. And the—the $7,500 is only for helping safety issues, you know, like something with your bathroom or something else in the house. But if you wanted to do some renovations up to $20,000, you can get a 1 percent loan to be able to do that.

I won't go into the other programs because a lot of them [are] different types of programs for cities. And, you know, I had a visit from the mayor and your city manager and—and I've thought about y'all a lot and I'm not—my commitment is to the rural area. My commitment even more so is to south Georgia. That's where I'm from. I can't say that up in north Georgia. But they don't seem to have a problem getting the money.

Okay, I won't keep going on tonight, but just let me say there is a saying: "Life is a grindstone; but . . . whether it grinds us down or polishes us up depends on us," you know.

Thank you.

Notes

Chapter 1: "The White House Wants You Out"

2   At a time when economic good news: We at USDA Rural Development participated in the development of water and sewage treatment facilities to handle the capacity for the new Kia plant being built in West Point. A year after its opening, the Sorento CUV rolled off the line and a shift was added, raising the number of jobs created to three thousand.

2   The first sign of trouble: I never found out why I was receiving hate calls and e-mails days before Breitbart published the clip. Obviously, some people already knew about it. It turned out that Breitbart had had the tape in his possession for at least several days before he published the clip on his site.

4   Breitbart, who had published: The timeline of Monday, July 19, detailed by Media Matters (http://mediamatters.org/research/201007220004), shows a steady buildup of the incident by right-wing bloggers and Fox News throughout the day, which I was unaware of until later.

> 11:18 AM: Breitbart posts Sherrod video, calls her "racist." Fox News amplifies Breitbart's deceptively edited video.
>
> 12:13 PM: Jim Hoft (Gateway Pundit) runs with Breitbart video.
>
> 12:55 PM: HotAir's Morrissey: "Breitbart hits NAACP with promised video of racism."
>
> 1:40 PM (approximately): Fox Nation accuses Sherrod of "discrimination caught on tape."

1:49 PM: Ace of Spades picks up Sherrod story, calls it an example of "your government, working for you."

3:31 PM: Elizabeth Scalia of the blog The Anchoress raises questions about the editing of Breitbart's video.

4:01 PM: Ace of Spades reports that the CBS NYC affiliate picked up Sherrod story, declares, "Breitbart gets results."

4:28 PM (approximately): Sherrod story hits Drudge.

7:51 PM: Breitbart's Big Government links to a FoxNews.com article reporting that Sherrod had resigned and USDA repudiated her remarks.

8:21 PM: Allahpundit questions the video's editing but says he will "assume Breitbart's edit is fair to the spirit of her remarks."

8:50 PM: Bill O'Reilly airs Breitbart's Sherrod video.

9:04 PM: Fox News Alert: Hannity reports that Sherrod has resigned and discusses the incident with Gingrich.

7   when Glenn Beck said you would be the topic: Actually, Beck did not discuss me at all on his July 19 show. His program focused on an upcoming event he was planning. He didn't start talking about me until July 20, after I had resigned.

7   Finally I typed: I was so nervous that I erased the e-mail from my Black-Berry. This is my best recollection of what I wrote.

Chapter 2: Truth to Power

9   On *American Morning*: video at www.youtube.com/watch?v=KosReihC8Ts.

12 "You tell me as a reporter": You can see the interview between CNN's John King and Andrew Breitbart at www.youtube.com/watch?v=HMPBNvjcSB4.

13 With regard to the initial media coverage: This is the retraction by the NAACP:

The NAACP has a zero tolerance policy against racial discrimination, whether practiced by blacks, whites, or any other group. The NAACP also has long championed and embraced transformation by people who have moved beyond racial bias. Most notably, we have done so for late Alabama Governor George Wallace and late U.S. Senator Robert Byrd—each a man who had associated with and supported white supremacists and their cause before embracing civil rights for all.

With regard to the initial media coverage of the resignation of USDA Official Shirley Sherrod, we have come to the conclusion we were snookered by Fox News and Tea Party Activist Andrew

Breitbart into believing she had harmed white farmers because of racial bias.

Having reviewed the full tape, spoken to Ms. Sherrod, and most importantly heard the testimony of the white farmers mentioned in this story, we now believe the organization that edited the documents did so with the intention of deceiving millions of Americans. I apologized to Ms. Sherrod, clearly a committed and selfless public servant, who had been unfairly maligned.

The fact is Ms. Sherrod did help the white farmers mentioned in her speech. They personally credit her with helping to save their family farm.

Moreover, this incident and the lesson it prompted occurred more that 20 years before she went to work for USDA.

Finally, she was sharing this account as part of a story of transformation and redemption. In the full video, Ms. Sherrod says she realized that the dislocation of farmers is about "haves and have nots." "It's not just about black people, it's about poor people," says Sherrod in the speech. "We have to get to the point where race exists but it doesn't matter."

This is a teachable moment, for activists and for journalists.

Most Americans agree that racism has no place in American Society. We also believe that civil and human rights have to be measured by a single yardstick.

The NAACP has demonstrated its commitment to live by that standard.

The Tea Party Federation took a step in that direction when it expelled the Tea Party Express over the weekend. Unfortunately, we have yet to hear from other leaders in the Tea Party movement like Dick Armey and Sarah Palin, who have been virtually silent on the "internal bigotry" issue.

Next time we are confronted by a racial controversy broken by Fox News or their allies in the Tea Party like Mr. Breitbart, we will consider the source and be more deliberate in responding. The tape of Ms. Sherrod's speech at an NAACP banquet was deliberately edited to create a false impression of racial bias, and to create a controversy where none existed. This just shows the lengths to which extremist elements will go to discredit legitimate opposition.

According to the USDA, Sherrod's statements prompted her dismissal. While we understand why Secretary Vilsack believes this false controversy will impede her ability to function in the role, we urge him to reconsider.

Finally, we hope this incident will heighten Congress's urgency in dealing with the well documented findings of discrimination toward black, Latino, Asian American and Native American farmers, as well as female farmers of all races. See www.naacp.org/press/entry /naacp-statement-on-the-resignation-of-shirley-sherrod1/.

14   In one incident, Mark Williams: Mark Williams was expelled from the National Tea Party Federation after his letter was made public. However, since the Tea Party is loosely affiliated and has no centralized power structure, his expulsion had little meaning.

14   At one point I viewed: Press Secretary Robert Gibbs's press briefing. Read about it at http://politicalticker.blogs.cnn.com/2010/07/21/gibbs-sherrod-is-owed-an-apology.

14   Secretary of Agriculture Tom Vilsack: Vilsack's press conference issuing an apology can be viewed at www.youtube.com/watch?v=nAsJs_E8EKE.

18   One of the first people: Willie Nelson issued a press release on July 21, 2010: "Willie Nelson and Farm Aid Stand with Shirley Sherrod, Call for her Reinstatement by USDA," www.farmaid.org/site/apps/nlnet /content2.aspx?c=qlI5IhNVJsE&b=2792875&ct=8536593. Willie also wrote a piece for *The Huffington Post* titled "Shirley Sherrod, A Family Farmer's Friend," www.huffingtonpost.com/willie-nelson/shirley-sherrod-a-family_b_654824.html.

19   The Rural Coalition put together: The statement read as follows:

Introduction to the Compendium of Statements of Support for Shirley Sherrod, our Colleague and Friend

What follows is a compendium of the many statements of support issued by our diverse communities in support of our friend and colleague, Shirley Sherrod. We are providing the full statements in the form in which they were issued last week, as a record of the depth and breadth of support immediately generated for Ms. Sherrod, who has worked passionately without regard to race, ethnicity or gender on behalf of the producers and workers we all serve.

We recognize that since that time, apologies have been issued and Ms. Sherrod was offered a new job within the Department of Agriculture. We stand beside her in full support of whatever she decides to do next and express our willingness to work with her in any way in the continuing struggle for justice.

We also recognize that irrespective of what Ms. Sherrod decides, it is the responsibility of all of us to continue the work we have long done together with renewed energy to transform the structural injustices at the Department of Agriculture and in our society in general. We will be issuing additional calls to action and recommendations for continuing action in coming days, and will be reaching out to all who are committed to achieving equity and opportunity for everyone in the food and agriculture system and in our society. . . .

Our diverse coalition further calls on President Obama, Secretary Vilsack, and Attorney General Holder to work with us to make this a "Teachable Moment" as our colleague Edward Pennick suggests in his contribution to this compendium. We call on the press to continue probing the complexity of this story and to assure this important conversation receives continued attention involving all voices but particularly those, like Ms. Sherrod and the Spooner family, who have walked the journey the most deeply and have the most insight to share. . . .

Rural Coalition/Coalición Rural (Washington, DC)
Federation of Southern Cooperatives/Land Assistance Fund (East Point, Georgia)
Rural Advancement Fund (Orangeburg, SC)
Intertribal Agriculture Council (Billings, MT)
Farmworker Association of Florida (Apopka, FL)
National Hmong American Farmers (Fresno, CA)
National Immigrant Farmers Initiative (Washington DC)
National Latino Farmers and Ranchers Trade Association (Washington, DC)
North Carolina Association of Black Lawyers Land Loss Prevention Project (Durham, NC)
Mississippi Association of Cooperatives (Jackson, MS)
National Family Farm Coalition (Washington, DC)
Farm Aid, Inc. (Cambridge, MA)
North American Farm Alliance (Windsor, OH)
Oklahoma Black Historical Research Project (Baskerville, VA)
Organización en California de Lideres Campesinas (Oxnard, CA)
Twenty First Century Youth Leadership Movement (Eutaw, AL)
Rural Development Leadership Network (New York, NY)
Border Agricultural Workers Union (El Paso, TX)
Agriculture Missions, Inc. (New York, NY)
National Sustainable Agriculture Coalition (Washington, DC)
Flats Mentor Farm (Lancaster, MA)
League of Rural Voters (Minneapolis, MN)

Concerned Citizens of Tillery (Tillery, NC)

Black Farmers and Agriculturalists Association (Tillery, NC)

Rural School and Community Trust (Washington, DC)

American Federation of Government Employees Local 3354 (St. Louis, MO)

CASA del Llano, INC. (Hereford, TX)

New American Sustainable Agriculture Project (Portland, ME)

Taos County Economic Development Corporation (Taos, NM)

Operation Spring Plant (Oxford, NC)

Hispanic Farmers & Ranchers of America Inc (Las Cruces, NM)

CATA (The Farmworker Support Committee) (Glassboro, NJ)

Land Stewardship Project (Minneapolis, MN)

Michael Fields Agricultural Institute (East Troy, WI)

Community Food Security Coalition (Portland, OR)

American Agriculture Movement, Inc. (Springfield, CO)

Missouri Rural Crisis Center (Columbia, MO)

Rural Advancement Foundation International—USA (Pittsboro, NC)

Western Organization of Resource Councils (Billings, MT)

Family Farm Defenders (Madison, WI)

Michael Fields Agricultural Institute (Madison, WI)

Community to Community (Bellingham, WA)

Domestic Fair Trade Association (Jamaica Plain, MA)

The American Corn Growers Association (Washington, DC)

Center for New Community (Chicago, IL)

Ashtabula County Farmers Union (OH)

Arkansas Land and Farm Development Corporation (Brinkley, AR)

Religious Leaders for Coalfield Justice (Winchester, VA)

The Rural Chaplains Association

Southeast Region Agribusiness and Economic Development Corporation

Minnesota Food Association

Organic Farming Research Foundation

American Raw Milk Producers Pricing Association

Rev. Joseph D. Keesecker, Retired Former Executive Director of Agricultural Missions

Sarah Bobrow-Williams (Augusta, GA)

19 Rudy Arredondo: In addition to those mentioned here, many leaders of farm organizations wrote statements in support, including John Zippert, chairman of the Rural Coalition; Georgia Good, executive director of

the Rural Advancement Fund and vice chairman of the Rural Coalition; Chukou Thao, executive director of the National Hmong American Farmers; Savonala Horne, executive director of the Land Loss Prevention Project; Marge Townsend, a Rural Coalition board member and retired family farmer from Windsor, Ohio; Maria Moreira of Flats Mentor Farm in Lancaster, Massachusetts; Mily Trevino-Sauceda, a Rural Coalition board member; Loretta Picciano, executive director of the Rural Coalition; Pati Martinson and Terrie Bad Hand of the Taos County Economic Development Corporation in New Mexico; Mark Schultz, associate director of the Land Stewardship Project; Ferd Hoefner of the National Sustainable Agriculture Coalition; Dorothy Barker, executive director of Operation Spring Plant; Reverend Joseph D. Keesecker, retired former executive director of Agricultural Missions, Inc.; Charnell T. Green, president of the Southeast Region Agribusiness and Economic Development Corporation; and George Brosi, the editor of *Appalachian Heritage*. The Southern Rural Black Women's Initiative also wrote a letter from the executive committee: Sophia Bracy-Harris, Mikhiela Sherrod, Oleta Garrett Fitzgerald, Winifred Green, Sarah Bobrow Williams, and Carol Blackmon.

19   Of course, I had: Jerry Pennick, my longtime colleague and friend at the Federation of Southern Cooperatives, wrote a piece called "A Teachable Moment." Jerry had been one of the first people I called from my car on July 19. Federation Director Ralph Paige also wrote a piece detailing my twenty-five years working with farmers.

Chapter 3: Freedom's Whisper

27   We were still under the thumb: From the end of the Civil War through the mid-1960s, individual states passed laws meant to supplant federal civil rights regulations. They were called Jim Crow laws (Jim Crow being a character in a black minstrel show). The states varied on some of the specifics, but the scope and intent of the laws were quite similar. For more about Jim Crow laws in Georgia and nationwide, refer to the University of Dayton School of Law's series "Race, Racism and the Law," http://academic.udayton.edu/race; "Segregation," New Georgia Encyclopedia, www.georgiaencyclopedia.org/nge/Article.jsp?id=h-3610; and www.jimcrowhistory.org.

28   In 1955, Governor Talmadge published: Herman E. Talmadge, *You and Segregation* (Birmingham, Ala.: Vulcan Press, 1955); also, a review of *You and Segregation* by George W. Watson appeared in the *Harvard Crimson*, December 6, 1955.

28   The establishment church: According to Curtis Freeman, "Never Had I Been So Blind, W. A. Criswell's 'Change' on Racial Segregation," *Journal of Southern Religion* 10 (2007), in 1955 the Reverend W. A. Criswell, the most popular Southern Baptist preacher in the South, gave a fiery speech opposing integration, railing against the organized efforts by the NAACP and others and calling them "good-for-nothing fellows who are trying to upset all of the things that we love as good old Southern people and as good old Southern Baptists." See http://jsr.fsu.edu/Volume10 /Freeman.pdf. That view, however, was on its last legs. Ten years later Criswell himself was taking a more moderate view. It also bears noting that the Reverend Billy Graham never accepted segregation as being religiously defensible.

31   In 1960, Charles, along with three civil rights legends: Rock Hill, South Carolina, became a signature event in the civil rights movement and demonstrated the astonishing courage of young people. Charles Jones, one of Charles's SNCC colleagues, who went on to work with the movement in southwest Georgia, wrote about it in 2003 for "Civil Rights Movement Veterans," www.crmvet.org/info/rockhill.htm.

31   They refused bail: The "jail, no bail" policy was devised after repeated protests and sit-ins yielded little result but a financial burden of many thousands of dollars paid in bail. The idea emerged of staying in jail after an arrest, shifting the financial burden to the state and also creating the picture in the media of jails crowded with protesters, including the very young and the very old.

32   Charles was part: Recollections in Taylor Branch, *Parting the Waters: America in the King Years, 1954–63* (New York: Simon and Schuster, 1989).

32   "sons of bitches": According to the PBS *American Experience* production "Freedom Riders," May 16, 2011.

32   Use active non-violent: King spelled out his philosophy of nonviolence, drawing from the works of Gandhi and Christian faith, in an essay titled "Pilgrimage to Nonviolence," *The Christian Century*, April 13, 1960. Charles and others in the movement used points from his treatise in their organizational efforts.

35   the Albany Movement: History and timeline available at the Albany Civil Rights Institute, www.albanycivilrightsinstitute.org.

37   That event was the spark: Recounted by Charles Sherrod in *This Far by Faith: African American Spiritual Journeys* (Boston: Blackside, 2003); Clayborne Carson, "SNCC and the Albany Movement," *Journal of Southwest Georgia History* 2 (1984): 15–25; the recollections of Dr. William G. Anderson in *Eyes on the Prize: America's Civil Rights Movement 1954–1985*,

PBS, 1987; Joan Walsh, "The Civil Rights Heroism of Charles Sherrod," July 22, 2010, www.salon.com/2010/07/23/charles_sherrod_civil
_rights_hero/; Howard Zinn, *The New Abolitionists* (Boston: Beacon Press, 1965).

37 Charles saw an opportunity: Raymond Arsenault, *Freedom Riders: 1961 and the Struggle for Racial Justice* (New York: Oxford University Press, 2011).

40 Music would continue: The Freedom Singers produced an album in 1965 titled "The Freedom Singers Sing of Freedom Now." Bernice Johnson Reagon continues to offer reflections, history, music, and inspiration on her site, www.bernicejohnsonreagon.com. She recently performed at the White House and sang some of the old movement songs.

41 Finally, in December 1961: The best account of King's time in Albany was his own, as depicted in the collection of his writings: Martin Luther King, Jr., *The Autobiography of Martin Luther King, Jr.* (New York: Warner Books, 1998); chap. 16, "The Albany Movement"; numerous newspaper reports also covered King's time in Albany, including Claude Sitton, "Dr. King Is Freed Against His Will," *The New York Times*, July 13, 1962; and Hedrick Smith, "Segregation Stronghold," *The New York Times*, August 16, 1962.

42 Eighteen-year-old Ola Mae Quarterman: Quarterman was a heroine to the Albany Movement, but her heroism came at great personal cost. When she was released from jail, she was expelled by Albany State, and she later suffered a mental breakdown and was institutionalized for thirty years. She eventually married and had a child. In Albany, February 28 has been declared Ola Mae Quarterman-Clements Day in her honor, and she is recognized in the Albany Civil Rights Museum.

43 Mayor Kelley moved: Accounts of the role of Reverend Samuel Wells include Michael Chalfen, "The Way Out May Lead In: The Albany Movement Beyond Martin Luther King, Jr.," *The Georgia Historical Quarterly* 79, no. 23 (Fall 1995): 560–598; and *Deep Wells*, a play based on the life of Samuel Wells, produced at the Albany Civil Rights Institute in August 2011.

45 "the great Tift Park pool jump": The lead character in the pool jump was a young man named Randy Battle. He was wild and daring, and worked for Charles at the SNCC. He also worked for C. B. King's campaign when King ran for Congress. A few years ago, Randy told his story to Peter de Lissovoy and it was published as "The Great Pool Jump: Integrating Tift Park Pool," www.crmvet.org/nars/rbpool.htm. Peter de Lissovoy was also a SNCC worker and C. B. King advance man. He

is now a writer, editor, and teacher living in rural New Hampshire. He shared his memories of that period in "Returning to Georgia," www. reportingcivilrights.loa.org.

Chapter 4: My Father's Dream

47   Charles and several other SNCC workers: The personal account of Lucius Holloway is found in Carlene Holloway Bishop and Lucius Holloway, Sr., *The Civil Rights Movement Through the Eyes of Lucius Holloway* (Pittsburgh: Dorrance Publishing, 2008).

49   A household belonging to Carolyn Daniels: See Wesley C. Hogan, *Many Minds, One Heart: SNCC's Dream for a New America* (Chapel Hill: University of North Carolina Press, 2007).

Chapter 5: Sheriff Gator's Law

58   The trial was held: Recounted in Joseph Howell, *Civil Rights Journey* (Bloomington, Ind.: AuthorHouse, 2011).

61   Charlie Ware was a small: Ware's trial was detailed in an anonymous report published in the *Harvard Crimson* in 1963, titled "A Harvard Law Student Writes About the Recent Trial of a Local Negro." Elizabeth Holtzman, an aide to C. B. King, also recounted her experience in *Who Said It Would Be Easy?: One Woman's Life in the Political Arena* (New York: Arcade Publishing, 1996).

61   "The courthouse itself": Elizabeth Holtzman, "Shirley Sherrod and the Dark History of Baker County," July 22, 2010, http://www.huffingtonpost .com/elizabeth-holtzman/shirley-sherrod-and-the-d_b_656063.html.

66   It had been more than ten years: The long road to school desegregation in Georgia is described in Georgia Advisory Committee to the United States Commission on Civil Rights, "Desegregation of Public School Districts in Georgia," December 2007, www.usccr.gov/pubs/GADESG-FULL.pdf.

Chapter 6: Love in a Land of Hate

71   "I'm nothin but a soldier": Charles often talked about being a soldier of nonviolence. He wrote the music and lyrics to a song, "Nothin but a Soldier":

When I was a baby, black as I could be
Mama held me closely, firmly on her knee.

One day Mister Charley, needed him a maid
No more could my mother stay and rock me as her babe.

Chorus:
Nothin but a soldier, nothing but a soldier,
Nothin but a soldier can make it in.

Daddy never knew me, never wiped my tears,
Never saw me crying, never knew my fears.
Working for the white man, sun-up 'til sun-down,
Come home wet and tired, he would always wear a frown.

I became a young man, proud as I could be
Used to hear them saying, "Hang him on a tree."
Tree limb couldn't hold me, segregation tried,
Jumped the gun for freedom, getting closer every stride.

Folks say don't go marching without an alibi
But I say give me freedom before the day I die.
We don't need no H-bomb, rockets do not serve,
We have got nonviolence, packs more power for every nerve.

Hoses were a-spurting, police everywhere,
Dragged me to the wagon, stripped to underwear,
Dogs tore off my clothing, cow prods burnt my flesh,
Cops beat me with blackjacks, they were stomping on my chest.

Blood ran down my forehead, blood ran down my back,
Threw me in the jailhouse, face down on the rack,
Told Judge Jim Crow slowly, I may not be brave,
You can jail my body, but I'll never be your slave.

73 The incident that radicalized: The March Against Fear received much media attention at the time and inspired several photo and video collections, including an oral history by James Meredith for the National Visionary Leadership Project (www.visionaryproject .org/meredithjames). Meredith has always said that he wasn't a part of a movement, just an individual seeking his rights under the law. He became active in the Republican Party and once worked on the staff of Senator Jesse Helms.

74 One of the members: Joseph Howell wrote of his experience that summer in *Civil Rights Journey: The Story of a White Southerner Coming of Age During the Civil Rights Revolution* (Bloomington, Ind.: AuthorHouse, 2011). Other white former SNCC members have also written about

their experiences. One is Bob Zellner, a southerner, who said, "I didn't come South to help black people. I was already here and I got involved to free myself." Bob published his memories in *The Wrong Side of Murder Creek: A White Southerner in the Freedom Movement* (Montgomery, Ala.: NewSouth Books, 2008).

74   "The first issue": Howell, *Civil Rights Journey*, p. 97.

76   In 1967, Stokely announced: Clayborne Carson wrote about the black-white struggle within the SNCC in *In Struggle: SNCC and the Black Awakening of the 1960s* (Cambridge, Mass.: Harvard University Press, 1981).

77   Along with a group: The Southwest Georgia Project for Community Education (www.swgaproject.com) was organized as a nonprofit community services organization in 1968. It continues its work today, including, most recently, the creation of the Southwest Georgia Regional Food System (www.swgaproject.com/our-initiatives/southwest-georgia -regional-food-system/) to give access to affordable, nutritious food to the rural poor.

80   "I guess I should not": Martin Luther King, Jr., *Where Do We Go from Here: Chaos or Community?* (Boston: Beacon Press, 1968), p. 26.

82   "You start out": Lee Atwater, quoted in Alexander P. Lamis, *The Two-Party South* (New York: Oxford University Press, 1984), p. 47.

Chapter 7: At Work in the Fields

83   He introduced us: Swann, who died in 2003, was the founder of the E. F. Schumacher Society and devoted his life to developing model programs and community land trusts. He wrote *Peace, Civil Rights and the Search for Community: An Autobiography*, which can be read online at http://neweconomicsinstitute.org/publications/peace-civil-rights-and -search-community-autobiography. Chapter 20 tells the story of New Communities.

87   "The next morning": Swann, *Peace, Civil Rights and the Search for Community*.

92   We were politically active: Documents about the efforts to get blacks elected to ASCS committees are available at www.crmvets.org.

94   But in 1983, the Reagan administration: In 1999, in his ruling on *Pigford*, Judge Paul Friedman wrote that this had had a disastrous effect on civil rights claims that had been "filed [but] never processed, investigated or forwarded to the appropriate agencies for conciliation. As a result, farmers who filed complaints of discrimination never received a response, or if they did receive a response it was a cursory denial of relief. In some cases, OCREA staff simply threw discrimination complaints in the trash with-

out ever responding to or investigating them. In other cases, even if there was a finding of discrimination, the farmer never received any relief."

95   I became a part: The Rural Development Leadership Network (RDLN), a national multicultural social change organization founded in 1983, supports community-based development in poor rural areas through hands-on projects, education and skills building, leadership development, and networking. Through RDLN, emerging leaders from poor rural areas spearhead development projects and design-related study through which they may earn a certificate or academic credential (bachelor's, master's, or PhD degree). For more information go to www.ruraldevelopment.org.

95   I took a job: For more information about the Federation of Southern Cooperatives/Land Assistance Fund, go to www.federationsoutherncoop .com.

96   At the end of the Civil War: When the slaves were freed, many thousands of them left their plantations, and Union soldiers coming south were met with a dire refugee situation. General William Tecumseh Sherman saw a solution in a special land-grant program. On January 16, 1865, he gave the order that came to be known as "forty acres and a mule": "Whenever three respectable negroes, heads of families, shall desire to settle on land, and shall have selected for that purpose an island or a locality clearly defined, within the limits above designated, the Inspector of Settlements and Plantations will himself, or by such subordinate officer as he may appoint, give them a license to settle such island or district, and afford them such assistance as he can to enable them to establish a peaceable agricultural settlement. The three parties named will subdivide the land, under the supervision of the Inspector, among themselves and such others as may choose to settle near them, so that each family shall have a plot of not more than (40) forty acres of tillable ground, and when it borders on some water channel, with not more than 800 feet water front, in the possession of which land the military authorities will afford them protection, until such time as they can protect themselves, or until Congress shall regulate their title."

Chapter 8: Saving Farmers

104   Southern Alternatives Agricultural Cooperative: The cooperative has an online store where pecan products can be purchased, at www .saacgeorgia.com. A video story of the cooperative can be viewed at http://www.youtube.com/watch?v=DSIGwyrucRk.

105   That's where they met Ralph Paige: Established in 1985, Farm Aid

continues to host annual big-name concerts, and also provides an array of services to farmers, including a hotline for farmers in crisis (1-800-FARM-AID) and a citizens' advocacy group. For more information go to www.farmaid.org.

106   In 2000, I learned: The East Baker Historical Society and 21st Century Community Corporation is based in the former East Baker Elementary School, P.O. Box 738, 139 Roosevelt Ave., Newton, GA 39870. The non-profit organization was incorporated in 2002 and is governed by a board of directors. For more information go to www.eastbaker.net.

Chapter 9: At Home in the World

110   I was in line: For more information about the Kellogg Foundation and its fellowship programs, go to www.wkkf.org.

112   I chose Frances Hesselbein: Frances is a woman of amazing achievement. She is currently the president and CEO of the Leader to Leader Institute (formerly the Peter F. Drucker Foundation for Nonprofit Management) and its founding president. Hesselbein was awarded the Presidential Medal of Freedom, the United States of America's highest civilian honor, by President Clinton in 1998. The award recognized her leadership as CEO of Girl Scouts of the USA from 1976 to 1990, her role as the founding president of the Drucker Foundation, and her service as "a pioneer for women, volunteerism, diversity and opportunity." The first President Bush appointed her to two Presidential Commissions on National and Community Service. In 2011, her book *My Life in Leadership: The Journey and Lessons Learned Along the Way* was published by Wiley.

115   On my first visit to Cuba: In general, American farmers have been in favor of lifting the embargo to Cuba. Many articles have been written about this, including Roger Johnson, "Trade with Cuba Vital to U.S. Farmers," *Iowa Farmer Today*, July 14, 2010; "Cuba Remains a Strong Market for U.S. Farmers," *Corn and Soybean Digest*, March 7, 2011; Adam Davidson, "U.S. Farmers Push for Easing Embargo on Cuba," November 9, 2006, www.npr.org/templates/story/story.php?storyId=6463381; and Daniel Griswold, "Four Decades of Failure: The U.S. Embargo Against Cuba," October 12, 2005, www.cato.org/pub_display.php?pub_id=10921.

Chapter 10: A Place at the Table

119   Secretary Mike Espy commissioned: Linda L. Swanson, ed., *Racial/Ethnic Minorities in Rural Areas: Progress and Stagnation, 1980–90*, August 1996, www.ers.usda.gov/publications/aer731/aer731.pdf.

120   In 1996, Congress passed: Concerns about the 1996 Farm Bill were
      abundant among profarmer organizations and analysts. Neil E. Harl,
      Charles F. Curtiss Distinguished Professor in Agriculture and Professor
      of Economics, wrote about the damaging effects of the farm bill, cit-
      ing loss of a safety net, less economic buoyancy, and a shift in land use
      patterns. Rhonda Perry of the Missouri Rural Crisis Center concurred,
      writing, "Farm bill dupes farmers to fatten corporate profits."

121   In this case: For a history and description of *Pigford*, see Tadlock Cowan
      and Joy Feder, "The Pigford Cases: USDA Settlement of Discrimina-
      tion Suits by Black Farmers," Congressional Research Service, June 14,
      2010, www.nationalaglawcenter.org/assets/crs/RS20430.pdf.

123   In April 1999: To read the Pigford Consent Decree, go to www
      .pigfordmonitor.org/orders/19990414consent.pdf.

126   after 1999 it became increasingly clear: See Office of the Monitor, www
      .pigfordmonitor.org.

126   Finally, after years of dissent: See Federation of Southern Cooperatives,
      "Provisions in the Farm Bill Pertaining to Pigford Claims (2008)" at
      www.federationsoutherncoop.com/pigford/Pigfordfarmbilla.pdf.

Chapter 11: Joining Obama's Team

132   It had come as a result: The ruling in our case was titled *Pigford v. Vilsack/
      Brewington v. Vilsack* IN RE: The ARBITRATION OF NEW COMMU-
      NITIES, INC. ARBITRATOR'S DECISION ON REEXAMINATION.

      On Loan Restructuring.

          Having reviewed the record, the Chief Arbitrator finds that
      USDA's explanation for why it denied New Communities loan re-
      structuring was a pretext and finds no other legitimate nondiscrimi-
      natory reasons for such denial.

          On Whether plaintiff established a prima facie case that FmHA
      discriminated against New Communities in FmHA's demand for
      payment of $50,000 from the sale of timber as a precondition for an
      Emergency loan in 1982. The demand for the $50,000, realized from
      property in which Respondent had no interest, was an outrageous
      act—one totally unsupported by FmHA policy or regulation. In
      Fact, the County Supervisor, in his deposition, testified that he could
      not think of any circumstances under which FmHA would require
      such a payment. The payment smacks of nothing more than a feudal
      baron demanding additional crops from his serfs. The Chief Arbitra-
      tor finds no legitimate nondiscriminatory reasons for the demand.

Whether Plaintiff established a prima facie case that FmHa discriminated against New Communities in FmHA's demand for additional real estate without offering a loan or loan restructuring in 1983.

Regarding whether anyone outside the protected class received better treatment, New Communities presented evidence of a white farmer who received a loan in 1983; however, the arbitrator found that New Communities "made no demonstration of the types of crops or size of operation of Farmer A, nor his business dealings with USDA and thus failed to prove the fourth prong." There is sufficient evidence in the record to demonstrate that no one was required to provide additional collateral without receiving a benefit and that only New Communities had been required to do so. As previously mentioned, the County Supervisor could not recall an instance or think of any circumstances where Respondent's actions would have been appropriate.

Having found no regulatory basis for USDA's demand for collateral on New Communities without benefit and Respondent offering no contradictory evidence that *any farmers* were required to provide a Deed to Secure Debt without receiving a benefit, Arbitrator finds that New Communities has established a prima facie case for discrimination.

Considering that Respondent offered no nondiscriminatory reason for its conduct, the Chief Arbitrator finds that the USDA did discriminate against New Communities when it required Claimant to pledge additional real estate security while offering no benefit.

137   our governor, Sonny Perdue: Several southern Republican governors were quite outspoken about not wanting to take stimulus money. They were staking a position for the independence of their states. They included Texas Governor Rick Perry, Louisiana Governor Bobby Jindal, and South Carolina Governor Mark Sanford. Although Jindal refused part of the money, most of the governors eventually accepted it, in spite of their earlier remarks. So did Sonny Perdue.

137   Perdue, who'd been in office: Perdue was quite outspoken about the pride of the Confederacy, which obviously struck a sour chord with blacks and many whites as well. Once asked whether Georgia should apologize for slavery, clearly a symbolic act, he would not do even that. He left an enduring impression of insensitivity to the black experience.

137   Among the grants and loans: See the Georgia Rural Development page, www.rurdev.usda.gov/ga.

139   In March 2010: See the Appendix for the full text of my speech.

Chapter 12: Walking into the Light

146 "I did my best": CNN report: "Sherrod Turns Down Job Offer from Agriculture Department," August 24, 2010, http://articles.cnn.com/2010–08–24/politics/sherrod.agriculture.job_1_shirley-sherrod-director-of-rural-development-agriculture-secretary-tom-vilsack?_s=PM:POLITICS. A video of the press conference is available on YouTube: www.youtube.com/watch?v=zAc-EwXnHCg.

147 After the firing: For video and analysis of my appearance at the National Association of Black Journalists, go to www.nabjconvention.org/2010/2010/07/shirley-sherrod-nabj-convention-coverage/.

148 In October, several hundred pages: Peter Nicholas and Kathleen Hennessey, "Shirley Sherrod Dismissal a Rash Decision," *Los Angeles Times*, October 7, 2010, http://articles.latimes.com/2010/oct/07/nation/la-na-sherrod-usda-20101008.

151 Back in May 2010: The Jackson Lewis study is available through USDA: *Independent Assessment of the Delivery of Technical and Financial Assistance, Civil Rights Assessment, March 31, 2010*, www.usda.gov/documents/Civil_Rights_Assesssment_Executive_Summary.pdf.

152 "I hear you're back": Reporting the inaccurate story that I had returned to the USDA were Politico (Joseph Williams, "Shirley Sherrod Returns to the USDA," www.politico.com/news/stories/0511/54970.html) and CBS ("Report: Shirley Sherrod Heading Back to the USDA," www.cbsnews.com/stories/2011/05/14/earlyshow/saturday/main20062899.shtml).

Chapter 13: Seeking Justice

155 "We are in possession": Andrew Breitbart, "Video Proof: The NAACP Awards Racism—2010," July 19, 2010, http://biggovernment.com/abreitbart/2010/07/19/video-proof-the-naacp-awards-racism2010/.

156 Breitbart disputed accounts: *The Huffington Post* published a video of the spitting incident on March 28, 2010, "Congressman Spit On by Tea Party Protester," www.huffingtonpost.com/2010/03/28/congressman-spit-on-by-te_n_516300.html.

158 Leading the charge: "Steve King: Black Farmers' Settlement Is 'Slavery Reparations,'" November 30, 2010, www.tpmmuckraker.talkingpointsmemo.com/2010/11/steve_king_black_farmers_settlement_is_slaveryrep.php.

160 My decision to launch a lawsuit: Following are the lawsuit and support references, filed February 11, 2011:

COMPLAINT

1. This is an action brought by Shirley Sherrod, a former Presidential appointee and former Georgia State Director for Rural Development for the United States Department of Agriculture ("USDA") for defamation, false light and intentional infliction of emotional distress. Mrs. Sherrod was forced to resign from her job after Defendants ignited a media firestorm by publishing false and defamatory statements that Mrs. Sherrod "discriminates" against people due to their race in performing her official federal duties. Defendants drew false support for their claims from a speech given by Mrs. Sherrod that they edited, deceptively, to create the appearance that Mrs. Sherrod was admitting present-day racism. In fact, Mrs. Sherrod was describing events that occurred *twenty-three years before* she held her federal position and, in fact, was encouraging people *not* to discriminate on the basis of race.

2. This action is brought against Andrew Breitbart, author and publisher of the blog post that contained the defamatory statements; Larry O'Connor, who posted on the internet the misleading edited video segment used in the blog post; and JOHN DOE, an individual whose identity has been concealed by the other Defendants and who, according to Defendant Breitbart, was involved in the deceptive editing of the video clip and encouraged its publication with the intent to defame Mrs. Sherrod.

3. Although the defamatory blog post authored by Defendant Breitbart purported to show "video proof" that Mrs. Sherrod exhibited "racism" in the performance of her USDA job responsibilities, the short two-minute thirty-six (2:36) second video clip that Defendants embedded in the blog post as alleged "proof" of this defamatory accusation was, in truth, an edited excerpt from a much longer speech by Mrs. Sherrod that demonstrated *exactly the opposite.* In sharp contrast to the deliberately false depiction that Defendants presented in the defamatory blog post, the unabridged speech describes how, in 1986, working for a non-profit group that helped poor farmers, Mrs. Sherrod provided concern and service to a white farmer who, without her help, would almost certainly have lost his farm in rural Georgia.

4. Specifically, Defendants defamed Mrs. Sherrod by editing and publishing an intentionally false and misleading clip of Mrs. Sherrod's speech *and* added the following statements as a narrative to the clip:

- "Mrs. Sherrod admits that in her federally appointed position, overseeing over a billion dollars . . . She discriminates against people due to their race."
- Mrs. Sherrod's speech is "video evidence of racism coming from a federal appointee and NAACP award recipient."
- "[T]his federally appointed executive bureaucrat lays out in stark detail, that her federal duties are managed through the prism of race and class distinctions."
- "In the first video, Sherrod describes how she racially discriminates against a white farmer."
- Her speech is a "racist tale."

To this day, Defendant Breitbart publishes these exact same defamatory statements on his website despite his admitted knowledge of the truth. Indeed, he has subsequently stated that he "could care less about Shirley Sherrod," underscoring that Mrs. Sherrod's reputation was, at the very least, expected and acceptable collateral damage to his agenda. http://video.foxnews.com/v/4288023/racial-double-standard-in-white-house.

5. As a direct result of the highly-charged internet media environment, where misleading video segments and defamatory accusations can "go viral" and spread to a global audience in a matter of seconds, the defamatory blog post about Mrs. Sherrod—and the deceptive video segments that accompanied it—did extensive and irreparable harm to Mrs. Sherrod and her reputation. News stations across the country immediately and repeatedly aired the deceptively-edited video and echoed the false claims of Defendants. The Defendants' defamatory statements touched off a national media firestorm which led Mrs. Sherrod, under duress, to resign from her position as USDA Georgia State Director for Rural Development. In addition, as a direct result of the defamatory claims, Mrs. Sherrod has been subjected to hateful and harassing emails, telephone calls and internet commentary.

6. Mrs. Sherrod brings this action to vindicate her rights and restore her reputation. As a direct and proximate result of the Defendants' conduct, Mrs. Sherrod has suffered enduring damage to her reputation, as well as emotional distress and financial damages from the loss of her employment at the USDA. Mrs. Sherrod has been further damaged by having her integrity, impartiality, and motivations questioned, making it difficult (if not impossible) for her to continue her life's work assisting poor farmers in rural

areas. Because of these and other injuries sustained as a result of Defendants' tortious conduct, Mrs. Sherrod is entitled to compensatory damages in an amount to be determined at trial. Given the willful, malicious, intentional and reckless nature of Defendants' conduct, Mrs. Sherrod is also entitled to punitive damages.

JURISDICTION

7. This Court has jurisdiction over the subject matter of this complaint pursuant to D.C. Code §11–921.

8. This Court may exercise personal jurisdiction over each of the Defendants pursuant to D.C. Code § 13–423 because each of the Defendants caused tortious injury to Mrs. Sherrod in the District of Columbia, and because Defendants Breitbart and O'Connor regularly do business, solicit contacts, derive revenue and engage in a persistent course of conduct there. On information and belief, Defendant JOHN DOE also has sufficient contacts with the District of Columbia to support the exercise of personal jurisdiction. Moreover, the case is properly brought in this Court because significant events giving rise to Mrs. Sherrod's complaint—and significant damage to Mrs. Sherrod's reputation—occurred within the District of Columbia.

THE PARTIES

9. Plaintiff Shirley Sherrod is a resident and citizen of Georgia. A longtime advocate for civil rights and rural farmers in Georgia, Mrs. Sherrod has dedicated her entire adult life to public service. In July 2009, the Obama Administration appointed Mrs. Sherrod to serve as the USDA Georgia State Director for Rural Development, a position she held from August 17, 2009 until she was forced to resign on July 19, 2010. Mrs. Sherrod was the principal subject and target of a deceptively-edited video excerpt and defamatory blog post produced and published by Defendants on Defendant Breitbart's widely-read BigGovernment.com website.

10. Defendant Andrew Breitbart is a resident and citizen of California. Defendant Breitbart is a well-known blogger, author, publisher and media figure who owns, operates and publishes several widely-read internet websites: Breitbart.com, Breitbart.tv, BigHollywood.com, BigGovernment.com, BigJournalism.com and BigPeace.com. Defendant Breitbart has written a regular column for *The Washington Times* and regularly appears on television and radio programs as

a commentator. Defendant Breitbart also regularly appears at speaking events, conferences, conventions and rallies, including those held in the District of Columbia. Defendant Breitbart is the author of the defamatory blog post that is the subject of this lawsuit.

11. Defendant Larry O'Connor is a resident and citizen of California. Defendant O'Connor is a featured blogger at the BigHollywood .com, BigGovernment.com and BigJournalism.com websites operated by Defendant Breitbart. Defendant O'Connor also hosts "The Stage Right Show," an internet talk radio program that is available to listeners across the country, including listeners in the District of Columbia, via the internet every weeknight. Defendant O'Connor also appears at speaking events, conferences and conventions, including those held in the District of Columbia. Shortly before Defendant Breitbart published his defamatory blog post attacking Mrs. Sherrod, Defendant O'Connor posted the edited video clip of Mrs. Sherrod's speech to YouTube.com under the pseudonym "StageRightShow."

12. Defendant JOHN DOE, on information and belief, is a resident and citizen of Georgia. According to a statement made by Defendant Breitbart in a televised interview, Defendant Breitbart received the video of Mrs. Sherrod's speech from "an individual in Georgia" in "early April" of 2010 whose identity he refused to reveal. In a separate radio interview, Defendant Breitbart stated that the video of Mrs. Sherrod's speech came from "a guy down in Georgia."

FACTUAL BACKGROUND

Mrs. Sherrod Builds a Career and Good Reputation Helping Poor, Rural Farmers

13. Mrs. Sherrod was born in Baker County, Georgia in 1947. Her father was a farmer, and Mrs. Sherrod grew up, with her five siblings, working on the family farm. She attended segregated schools in Georgia until college.

14. Mrs. Sherrod's father was murdered in March of 1965, when she was only seventeen years old. The suspect, a white farmer, escaped indictment by an all-white grand jury. In the wake of her father's death, Mrs. Sherrod vowed to remain in the South to help fight for justice and change.

15. Later in 1965, Mrs. Sherrod graduated high school and attended

two years of college at Fort Valley College in Fort Valley, Georgia. Mrs. Sherrod finished college at Albany State University, where she received a degree in Sociology in 1970.

16. During her college years, Mrs. Sherrod began her involvement in the civil rights movement. Believing that building multiracial coalitions was essential to the fight for change, Mrs. Sherrod began her work with the Student Nonviolent Coordinating Committee (SNCC) in southwest Georgia. Despite her strong belief in the work of the SNCC, Mrs. Sherrod split from the group after its leader, Stokely Carmichael, publicly called for the group's expulsion of white members in 1966. Mrs. Sherrod expressed her disagreement with Mr. Carmichael's exclusionary position by leaving the group. In 1966, she co-founded her own organization, the Southwest Georgia Project for Community Education, a multiracial group that worked to support voter registration, integration, scholarships and early child care to those in need.

17. Mrs. Sherrod spent the next forty years centering her professional life on improving the lives of poor farmers in rural Georgia. From 1973 to 1985, she served at the New Communities Land Trust, where her work included managing a farmer's market, organizing farmers, helping to get representation for minority farmers on the county committees and providing opportunities for young and disadvantaged rural youth. In 1985, Mrs. Sherrod enrolled in a Masters Program at Antioch University Midwest. She received her Masters Degree in Rural Development from Antioch in 1989.

18. In 1985, Mrs. Sherrod became the Georgia Field Director of the Federation of Southern Cooperatives, an organization whose mission is to assist in land retention and development. The Federation of Southern Cooperatives operates in poor areas across the South to create cooperatives and credit unions as a collective strategy to create economic self-sufficiency. In her more than twenty-four years of service to that organization, Mrs. Sherrod assisted farmers in complying with state and federal regulations and dedicated herself to helping farmers in southwest Georgia keep their land.

19. As a result of her work helping poor farmers, Mrs. Sherrod earned and cultivated an excellent reputation in her community—and beyond—for fairness, lack of bias, decency, impartiality, even-handedness and a dedication to public service.

Mrs. Sherrod Accepts a Presidential Appointment to the USDA

20. In July 2009, as a testament to her lifelong dedication to public service and her hard-earned reputation for helping rural farmers, Mrs. Sherrod received a call from an official in President Obama's Administration offering to appoint her to the position of Georgia State Director for Rural Development, a position within the United States Department of Agriculture. The Rural Development section of the USDA administers and manages over forty housing, business and community infrastructure and facility programs as established by Congress through a network of 6,100 employees located in 500 national, state and local offices. These programs are designed to improve the economic stability of rural communities, businesses, residents, farmers and ranchers and improve the quality of life in rural America. The appointment to the position of State Director carries with it the highest government service level (GS-15) and a starting salary of $111,000.

21. The position of Georgia State Director for Rural Development was attractive to Mrs. Sherrod because it provided a greater platform from which to continue her life's work helping rural farming communities. As Georgia State Director, Mrs. Sherrod would be able to make a significant and immediate impact on rural farming communities—and help the people who live in those rural communities—by coordinating federal funding for schools, police, medical facilities, water, sewers and utilities. Mrs. Sherrod accepted the appointment.

22. On August 17, 2009, Mrs. Sherrod began her tenure as Georgia State Director for Rural Development. Among her duties as Georgia State Director, Mrs. Sherrod was in charge of numerous programs spanning various areas of community development and the overall coordination of federal assistance in rural Georgia. Among other things, she supervised grants of business loans, homeownership loans, water and sewer loans and the construction and maintenance of multi-family rental units, health care clinics, fire stations and community buildings. She oversaw a staff of more than 120 people spread among the state office, six area offices, ten sub-offices and twenty-three rural development offices. Her job required judgment, respect and impartiality.

23. Mrs. Sherrod was supervised by—and reported directly to—senior officials at USDA headquarters in Washington, D.C. The week after assuming her duties, Mrs. Sherrod attended an orientation session in Washington, D.C., along with newly appointed

State Directors for Rural Development from other states around
the country. Throughout her tenure as Georgia State Director
for Rural Development, Mrs. Sherrod reported directly to Rural
Development Deputy Undersecretaries Cheryl Cook and Vic-
tor Vasquez and, through these individuals, indirectly to United
States Secretary of Agriculture Thomas Vilsack. Through written
reports and telephone communications to USDA headquarters,
Mrs. Sherrod remained in near-continuous communication with
her supervisors in Washington.

24. With Mrs. Sherrod's federal position came more opportunities
for public speaking. In November 2009, she was asked to give the
Keynote Address at the National Community Land Trust Conference in Athens, Georgia. That same month, she was one of
several panelists at the Food Commodity Contracting Opportunity for Rural America Southeast Regional Small Business Conference at Albany State University. In these and other speeches,
Mrs. Sherrod emphasized the importance of looking beyond racial divisions to solve the economic challenges facing rural communities, farmers and small businesses.

Mrs. Sherrod Speaks to the NAACP

25. On March 27, 2010, the Georgia NAACP held its 20th Annual
Freedom Fund Banquet in Douglas, Georgia. Mrs. Sherrod was
one of several invited guests and was presented with the NAACP's
award in recognition of her lifetime of public service. Mrs. Sherrod also was invited to speak at the banquet.

26. In preparing her remarks for the NAACP Freedom Fund Banquet, Mrs. Sherrod elected to use the same speech she had given
several times before, including at a speaking engagement six
months earlier at her alma mater, Albany State University. A principal theme of the speech was to emphasize the harsh reality that,
in rural communities especially, economic hardships do not recognize racial boundaries. In delivering the speech to the NAACP
Freedom Fund Banquet, as she had done many times before, Mrs.
Sherrod underscored the importance of providing assistance to
those in need, regardless of race.

27. To emphasize this critical point of her speech, Mrs. Sherrod told
the audience a story about her experience helping two white
farmers, Roger and Eloise Spooner, save their farm from foreclosure more than twenty years earlier when she was working at
the Federation of Southern Cooperatives. In 1986, Mrs. Sherrod

was approached by Roger Spooner, a white farmer from Seminole County, Georgia who was facing the prospect of losing his farm to foreclosure. As she had done for countless other rural farmers, Mrs. Sherrod took affirmative steps over a period of many months to help Mr. Spooner and his wife Eloise keep their farm. As an initial step, Mrs. Sherrod personally accompanied the Spooners to a knowledgeable attorney who she believed could help them but, once it became clear that the attorney was providing limited (and untimely) assistance, Mrs. Sherrod personally called numerous contacts around the state, located another attorney with the relevant experience and expertise and accompanied the Spooners to multiple meetings with that second attorney. Ultimately, through the combined efforts of Mrs. Sherrod, the Spooners and the counsel that Mrs. Sherrod located for them, Mr. and Mrs. Spooner were able to save their farm from foreclosure. The Spooners have publicly credited Mrs. Sherrod with helping them save their farm and Mrs. Sherrod's assistance to them has resulted in a lifelong friendship between the families.

28. In her speech at the NAACP Freedom Fund Banquet, Mrs. Sherrod explained that, although she initially wondered whether the Spooners needed her personal attention because she was "struggling with the fact that so many black people ha[s] lost their farm land," she quickly came to realize that economic circumstance—not race—was the critical factor in determining whether people needed help and that, as described above, Mrs. Sherrod did in fact take affirmative (and successful) steps to help the Spooners save their farm.

29. Mrs. Sherrod's March 27, 2010 speech at the NAACP Freedom Fund Banquet was videotaped by the NAACP. In the weeks and months following the speech, Mrs. Sherrod's full speech was repeatedly broadcast on DCTV3, a leased access television channel dedicated to providing public, educational and government programming for the communities of Douglas and Coffee Counties.

Defendants Defame and Disparage Mrs. Sherrod by Publishing a Deceptively-Edited Video of her Speech

30. On July 19, 2010, Defendant Breitbart published an inflammatory and highly damaging blog post on his BigGovernment.com website entitled *Video Proof: The NAACP Awards Racism—2010.* Andrew Breitbart, *Video Proof: The NAACP Awards Racism—2010,* BigGovernment.com (July 19, 2010). With his post and the

"video proof" allegedly embedded within it, Defendant Breitbart apparently hoped to embarrass the NAACP and its members by demonstrating that the NAACP had condoned and rewarded "racism" and "bigotry" in its ranks by inviting Mrs. Sherrod to speak at its event and applauding her "racist tale" of interaction with the Spooners.

31. The "video proof" described in the inflammatory headline—and the centerpiece of the post itself—was a short, heavily-edited two-minute thirty-six second (2:36) segment of Mrs. Sherrod's March 27, 2010 speech at the NAACP Freedom Fund Banquet. Defendants misleadingly and deceptively edited the content of the video segment—and annotated it with additional text to underscore their defamatory allegation—to falsely state, directly contrary to the central premise and overall message of Mrs. Sherrod's speech to the NAACP, that Mrs. Sherrod had "racially discriminated" in carrying out her *federal job.*

32. The misleading video segment of Mrs. Sherrod's speech that Defendants embedded in the blog post included five introductory slides containing false statements of fact regarding Mrs. Sherrod—and hammered home the false and defamatory conclusion that Defendants wished their viewers to draw about Mrs. Sherrod. The first introductory slide states:

> On July 25, 2009
> Agriculture Secretary
> Tom Vilsack appointed
> Shirley Sherrod
> as Georgia Director
> of Rural Development

33. The second introductory slide states:

> USDA Rural Development
> spends over $1.2 Billion
> in the State of Georgia
> each year.

34. The third introductory slide states:

> On March 27, 2010,
> while speaking at the
> NAACP Freedom
> Fund Banquet...

35. The fourth introductory slide states:

> Ms. Sherrod admits
> that in her federally

appointed position,
overseeing over a
billion dollars...

36. The fifth introductory slide states:
    She discriminates
    against people due
    to their race.

37. These introductory slides—and the text that Defendants added to the video segment—defame and disparage Mrs. Sherrod by falsely stating that, in carrying out her duties as a federal government official, Mrs. Sherrod "discriminates against people due to their race." The introductory slides and text further defamed Mrs. Sherrod by presenting a preconceived conclusion that Defendants wished viewers to reach when viewing the segment.

38. None of these five introductory slides—or the defamatory text that appears on them—were present on the video of Mrs. Sherrod's speech prepared by the NAACP, or the video of the full speech that had been broadcast repeatedly on DCTV3 in Douglas and Coffee Counties. On information and belief, Defendants O'Connor and/or DOE, at the specific direction and with the full knowledge and consent of Defendant Breitbart, added the introductory slides and defamatory text to the video clip embedded in the blog post. Defendant Breitbart then repeated, republished and adopted as his own the false and defamatory statements in the introductory slides when he embedded the video clip containing those introductory slides and text into his independently defamatory blog post—and published the slides and text to a worldwide internet audience on BigGovernment.com.

39. In addition to the false and defamatory statements directed specifically to Mrs. Sherrod, the introductory slides that the Defendants added to the video segment contained false statements of fact about the position that Mrs. Sherrod held at the time that she allegedly "discriminate[d] against people due to their race." Despite the fact that Mrs. Sherrod's story regarding her dealings with the Spooners described events that had occurred in 1986—twenty-three years before she was appointed to her federal position—the introductory text falsely states that Mrs. Sherrod "discriminates against people due to their race" in "her federally appointed position," in the course of administering "over a billion dollars" of federal funds. Only later, after Defendants' deceptive editing of the video was publicly revealed, did Defendants add a

"disclaimer" box to the introductory slides that stated: "While Ms. Sherrod made these remarks while she held a federally appointed position, the story she tells refers to actions she took before she held that federal position." The disclaimer did not appear on the video at the time it was initially embedded and published and at the time that the media firestorm ensued.

40. Defendants knowingly and intentionally edited the video of Mrs. Sherrod's speech in a false, deceptive and misleading manner, with the specific intent of creating a video clip to support the conclusion that Mrs. Sherrod "discriminates against people due to their race" in the performance of her government job duties. In truth, Mrs. Sherrod's story demonstrated exactly the opposite point. Specifically, Defendants knowingly and intentionally edited the video of Mrs. Sherrod's speech to conceal Mrs. Sherrod's true message and instead misleadingly presented only a short excerpt of the speech in which Mrs. Sherrod recounted her initial, internal struggle about helping a "white farmer." Defendants' selectively-edited video segment intentionally left out critical statements in the speech both before and after the portion that was presented.

41. Defendants knowingly and intentionally removed critical introductory statements by Mrs. Sherrod—spoken *just seconds before* her story about the Spooners—expressly identifying the point of the story and stating, without regard to race, that "the struggle is really about poor people." NAACP Videos, *Shirley Sherrod: the FULL Video*, at 16:53–16:58 (July 20, 2010), http://www.youtube .com/watch?v=E9NcCa_KjXk&feature=related. Instead of providing this essential introduction, Defendants deliberately edited the video to begin, misleadingly, with out-of-context statements that, when she was first confronted with the task of helping a "white farmer" save his farm, Mrs. Sherrod "didn't give him the full force of what [she] could do" and instead took the white farmer "to one of his own." Defendants deliberately edited the video to present these statements in a false and misleading manner, without the introductory statements immediately preceding them, thereby defaming Mrs. Sherrod and casting her in a false and damaging light.

42. Defendants also knowingly and intentionally removed many other critical statements from the video of Mrs. Sherrod's speech—some coming *just after* her story about the Spooners— that had made clear the central premise and main theme of her

speech. Indeed, the edited video clip cuts Mrs. Sherrod's story off mid-sentence. Moreover, in a portion of Mrs. Sherrod's speech that came *after* the segment deceptively excerpted by Defendants, Mrs. Sherrod clearly stated the point of her story regarding the Spooners—and emphasized to the audience that the story was intended to reinforce her firm stance *against* the exercise of power in a racially discriminatory manner. Specifically, she told the NAACP audience: "Well, working with [Roger Spooner] made me see that it's really about those who have versus those who don't, you know. And they could be black and they could be white. They could be Hispanic. And it made me realize then that I needed to work to help poor people, those who don't have access the way others have." *Id.* at 21:00–21:25. Defendants knowingly, intentionally and recklessly omitted this critical statement from the video clip featured in the defamatory blog post.

43. Indeed, throughout the entirety of her forty-three minute speech to the NAACP, Mrs. Sherrod stressed the need for racial unity and repeatedly emphasized that poverty, not race, must be the critical factor for helping those in need. The following additional excerpts from Mrs. Sherrod's speech—all intentionally and recklessly omitted by Defendants in the misleading video segment embedded in the defamatory blog post— make the true message of Mrs. Sherrod's speech abundantly clear:

- "God will show you things and he'll put things in your path so that you realize that the struggle is really about poor people."
- "What we have to do is get [racism] out of our heads. There is no difference between us." *Id.* at 23:24–23:31.
- "It's sad that we don't have a room full of whites and blacks here tonight, because we have to overcome the divisions that we have. We have to get to the point where, as Toni Morrison said, race exists but it doesn't matter." *Id.* at 25:55–26:13.
- "Our communities are not going to thrive. Our children won't have the communities that they need to be able to stay and live in and have a good life if we can't figure this out, you all. White people, black people, Hispanic people, we all have to do our part to make our communities a safe place, a healthy place, a good environment." *Id.* at 26:24–26:53.

44. Defendants intentionally and recklessly omitted these (and many

other) critical statements from the short segment of the speech featured in the defamatory blog post, each of which makes clear that Mrs. Sherrod does not condone or practice racism, or any form of racial discrimination, in the exercise of her job responsibilities.

45. Through these and other deceptive editing techniques, Defendants deliberately edited the full video of Mrs. Sherrod's forty-three minute speech down to a short, highly misleading two-and-a-half minute clip that Defendants knew, or should have known, would portray Mrs. Sherrod in a false and defamatory manner. Given the extensive and misleading nature of Defendants' edits to the video, the addition of defamatory introductory slides and the inflammatory placement of the deceptive video segment amid defamatory text and headlines in the blog post, it is abundantly clear that Defendants' defamation and disparagement of Mrs. Sherrod was done intentionally and with actual malice.

46. Defendants Breitbart and O'Connor actively induced, encouraged and aided and abetted Defendant JOHN DOE in obtaining the full video of Mrs. Sherrod's speech, editing the video in a deceptive and intentionally misleading manner, adding inflammatory and factually inaccurate text to the introduction of the edited video segment, preparing the edited video segment for inclusion in the blog post and embedding the edited video in the defamatory post. Upon information and belief, Defendant JOHN DOE sent the video of Mrs. Sherrod's speech to Defendants Breitbart and O'Connor with the knowledge and intention that it be used to mislead the public about the content of Mrs. Sherrod's speech and to defame her reputation. On July 18, 2010, Defendant O'Connor published the deceptively-edited video on YouTube under his pseudonym, "StageRightShow." One day later, Defendant Breitbart published the same deceptively-edited video on the BigGovernment.com website.

Defendant Breitbart Further Defames and Disparages Mrs. Sherrod in the Text of the *Video Proof* Blog Post

47. The defamation and disparagement of Mrs. Sherrod was not limited to the posting of the deceptively-edited video clip. Defendant Breitbart embedded the video clip in a 1,396 word blog post, published under his name and picture, entitled *Video Proof: The NAACP Awards Racism—2010*. The headline and text of Defendant Breitbart's blog post further defamed and disparaged

Mrs. Sherrod by making additional false and defamatory allegations—and reinforcing the false statements and themes of the deceptively-edited video.

48. Ironically, Defendant Breitbart begins his defamatory blog post with the statement that "[c]ontext is everything." *Video Proof: The NAACP Awards Racism—2010.* Defendant Breitbart then states the defamatory conclusion he wishes his readers to reach from the remainder of the post: "In this piece you will see video evidence of racism coming from a federal appointee and NAACP award recipient . . . ." *Id.* He then celebrates his defamation by including a cartoon depiction of a "race card," featuring symbols of a "black power" hand gesture. The inflammatory preamble appears on the BigGovernment.com website as follows:

> Context is everything.
> In this piece you will see video evidence
> of racism coming from a federal appointee and
> NAACP award recipient and in another clip from
> the same event a perfect rationalization for why
> the Tea Party needs to exist.

49. Next, Defendant Breitbart claims to be "in possession of a video" in which Mrs. Sherrod, whom he identifies with her then-current title of "USDA Georgia Director of Rural Development," gives a "meandering speech" to an "all-black audience." *Id.* Defendant Breitbart then falsely states that the video shows that Mrs. Sherrod "lays out in stark detail" how "her *federal duties are managed through the prism of race and class distinctions*." *Id.*[1]

50. Defendant Breitbart further states that the video clip showed Mrs. Sherrod "describ[ing] how she *racially discriminates* against a white farmer" and telling a *"racist tale." Id.*

51. Although the text of the blog post does, in one stray reference, concede that Mrs. Sherrod gave some help to the farmer, even this statement is portrayed in a deliberately misleading and incomplete manner. The blog post mentions only the first part of Mrs. Sherrod's assistance—that Mrs. Sherrod initially referred the farmer to a white lawyer, noting sarcastically that Mrs. Sherrod had "decide[d] that he should get help from 'one of his own kind,'" taking yet another quote out of context from Mrs. Sher-

---

1 Emphasis added unless otherwise noted.

rod's speech. *Id.* Defendant Breitbart knowingly and intentionally excluded the remaining part of Mrs. Sherrod's story where she explains the extraordinary additional steps she took to help the Spooners after learning that the first lawyer was not providing adequate or timely assistance.

52. To drive his point home, Mr. Breitbart then embedded into the blog post the selectively-edited video clip described above, prefaced by additional false and defamatory introductory statements: "Mrs. Sherrod admits that in her federally appointed position, overseeing over a billion dollars . . . [s]he discriminates against people due to their race." *NAACP Bigotry in their ranks.*

53. Defendant Breitbart ends his post by drawing a comparison between the "real video evidence" and the "mainstream media's straight faced reportage of the NAACP's baseless accusations [of racism]." *Video Proof: The NAACP Awards Racism—2010.*

54. Nowhere in his post did Defendant Breitbart explain the true content of Mrs. Sherrod's speech or how Mrs. Sherrod took extraordinary steps to help the Spooners and prevent them from losing their farm. Instead, Mr. Breitbart sensationalized and exaggerated the misleading content of the edited video clip with false and defamatory statements to convince his readers that Mrs. Sherrod had exercised—and continued to exercise—her federal job duties in a racist manner.

55. Indeed, Defendant Breitbart falsely stated that Mrs. Sherrod's racially discriminatory conduct in the exercise of her job duties is ongoing. The blog post falsely states in the present tense that Mrs. Sherrod's "federal duties *are managed* through the prism of race and class distinctions." *Id.* This, despite the readily discernable facts that:

   • Mrs. Sherrod did not hold a federal position at the time the events in her story unfolded;
   • Mrs. Sherrod was talking about events that occurred 23 years earlier; and, most importantly,
   • Mrs. Sherrod was actually saying that one should *not* offer or withhold help on the basis of racial distinctions.

   Defendant Breitbart describes Mrs. Sherrod's story as a "racist tale" when, in fact, it is exactly the opposite: a parable *against* racism.

56. Defendants worked together to obtain the full video of Mrs. Sherrod's speech, edit the video in a deceptive and intentionally misleading manner, add inflammatory and factually inaccurate text to the introduction of the edited video segment, prepare the

edited video segment for inclusion in the defamatory blog post and embed the video segment in the blog post.

57. Defendant JOHN DOE contacted Defendant Breitbart with the express purpose of enlisting Defendant Breitbart's help in accusing Mrs. Sherrod of exercising her federal position in a racist manner and publicizing these defamatory allegations. On information and belief, as a resident of Georgia, Defendant JOHN DOE had access to and had seen the local television broadcast that aired the full version of Mrs. Sherrod's speech. Indeed, Defendant Breitbart has stated that Defendant JOHN DOE attempted to send the full content of the speech to him as early as April 2010. http://www .foxnews.com/story/0,2933,597324,00.html.

58. Defendant Breitbart also has admitted in a radio interview that he directed Defendant JOHN DOE to "cut the pertinent information" from the full speech. http://www.youtube.com /watch?v=hYqr8yPMIA0. Both individuals acted with full awareness that the edited clip published on Defendant Breitbart's blog was false and defamatory. On information and belief, Defendant JOHN DOE published his own version of the edited video clip on YouTube as early as July 15, 2010.

59. As a frequent contributor to three of Defendant Breitbart's websites and Editor-in-Chief of Breitbart.TV, Defendant O'Connor was a close associate to Defendant Breitbart. The day immediately prior to the publication of Defendant Breitbart's blog post, Defendant O'Connor separately posted the edited video clip to YouTube.com under the name "StageRightShow." Defendant O'Connor's posting of the defamatory video on YouTube is a stand-alone defamation of Mrs. Sherrod and provided Defendant Breitbart with the necessary digital ammunition for his defamatory blog post. The YouTube clip posted by Defendant O'Connor and the video clip on Defendant Breitbart's post are exactly the same. Indeed, Defendant Breitbart's blog post embeds and directly links to the video clip that Defendant O'Connor posted on YouTube.

Defendant Breitbart Publicizes his Defamatory Blog Post (and Further Defames and Disparages Mrs. Sherrod) on Twitter

60. On July 19, 2010, the same day that he published the deceptively-edited video segment and defamatory blog post, Defendant Breitbart publicized and compounded his defamation of Mrs. Sherrod by publishing a Twitter message, or "tweet," making clear that

Mrs. Sherrod was indeed the intended target of the Defendants'
malicious acts. At 9:31 am on July 19, 2010, Defendant Breitbart
"tweeted" the following message: "Will Eric Holder's DOJ hold
accountable fed appointee Shirley Sherrod for admitting *practicing racial discrimination*?" Andrew Breitbart, *Will Eric Holder's
DOJ hold accountable fed appointee Shirley Sherrod for admitting
practicing racial discrimination?*, Twitter (July 19, 2010), http://
twitter.com/AndrewBreitbart/status/18928307285.

61. Defendant Breitbart's Twitter message contains undeniable falsehoods: Mrs. Sherrod never admitted "practicing racial discrimination" and certainly never admitted doing so in her position as
a "fed[eral] appointee." Moreover, by inciting Attorney General
Holder to "hold accountable" Mrs. Sherrod, Defendant Breitbart clearly insinuated that she had done something worthy of
prosecution or retribution by the federal government. Defendant
Breitbart's Twitter message directly illustrates his intent to accuse
Mrs. Sherrod of unlawful activity and to provoke and instigate
financial and reputational damage to Mrs. Sherrod.

Defendants Acted with Actual Malice

62. Angered by the NAACP's claims of racism against the Tea Party,
Defendant Breitbart used Mrs. Sherrod to further his own agenda
of counter-attacking the NAACP with claims of racism. In doing
so, he and his associates acted with actual malice, reckless intent
and gross indifference to the false and misleading nature of the
edited clip posted on his blog and the effects that the posting
would have on Mrs. Sherrod.

63. On its face, it is blatantly obvious that the clip posted to Defendant Breitbart's website is an excerpt from a longer speech. In
fact, by stating that he asked Defendant JOHN DOE to "cut the
pertinent information," Defendant Breitbart has admitted that he
knew the clip was edited from a longer speech at the moment he
published it. http://www.youtube.com/watch?v=hYqr8yPMIA0.
Indeed, amidst his post-publication excuses, Defendant Breitbart acknowledged in a July 2010 interview with Newsweek
that he "should have waited for the full video . . . ." http://www
.newsweek.com/blogs/thegaggle/2010/07/30/breitbart-i-d-like
-to-speak-with-sherrod-in-private.html.

64. Despite Defendant Breitbart's knowledge of the full content of
the video, or—at the very least—knowledge that he only had a
fraction of the story and that the clip was heavily edited, he know-

ingly and intentionally published it with full awareness that he was publicly branding Mrs. Sherrod as someone who "discriminates" against people due to their race. Defendant Breitbart's concession that he "should have waited for the full video to get to me" underscores his acknowledgement that his conduct was wrongful and harmful towards Mrs. Sherrod. *Id.*

65. Defendant Breitbart's own comments reveal that he and his associates acted with full awareness of the falsity of their statements. In his own public statements, Defendant Breitbart admitted that he had seen more of the tape than he posted on his website. In a July 20, 2010 interview with CNN's John King, Defendant Breitbart stated that "the more video that we've seen, that we ***haven't even offered,*** there's even more racism on these tapes. This is deeply problematic." http://www.youtube.com /watch?v=DxcBIEV8bmI. Defendant Breitbart later said falsely in the same interview that "there's ***more racist sentiment in the video.***" *Id.*

66. Indeed, in a later post to his BigGovernment.com website, Defendant Breitbart has admitted that he had been in possession of the tape of Mrs. Sherrod's speech as early as July 15, 2010—meaning that for at least four days, he either knew the full content of Mrs. Sherrod's speech and published the misleadingly-edited and defamatory video clips anyway, or had ample time to investigate the veracity of the clips and made a conscious decision not to do so. Defendant Breitbart made this clear by describing the threat he made to NAACP President Ben Jealous on July 15, 2010: "On Thursday, July 15th, I warned NAACP president Ben Jealous to stop the race-baiting. I directed my ire at Jealous on the Scott Hennen radio show: 'I have tapes, a tape, of racism, and it's an NAACP dinner. You want to play with fire? I have evidence of racism, and it's coming from the NAACP.'" http://biggovernment .com/abreitbart/2010/12/06/me-mrs-sherrod-and-the-pigford -ii-black-farmers-settlement/. Defendant Breitbart's reckless decision to threaten the NAACP with the video—instead of using his communication with the NAACP to determine the accuracy and completeness of the video—provides additional evidence of his malice.

67. In addition to his own statements and admissions, external facts leave little doubt as to the knowledge and defamatory intent of Defendant Breitbart and his associates. It is plainly obvious from even the edited version of the tape that Mrs. Sherrod was describ-

ing events in the distant past. To give just one example, in the video clip, Mrs. Sherrod mentions that when Mr. Spooner came to her for help, "Chapter 12 bankruptcy had just been enacted for the family farm." *NAACP Bigotry in their ranks*. A quick web search easily reveals that Chapter 12 was added to the Bankruptcy Code in 1986. Thus, Mrs. Sherrod could not have been describing actions taken in the course of her federal duties, which did not begin until 2009.

68. Defendants also recklessly disregarded numerous readily-available sources that would have quickly demonstrated the false and defamatory nature of the selectively-edited videos—and the defamatory blog post in which they planned to use them. Defendants made no effort to contact Mrs. Sherrod to verify the accuracy of the video clips or whether they accurately reflected her views and conduct, made no effort to contact the NAACP to obtain a copy of the full, unedited tape, made no effort to contact the local television stations in Georgia to obtain a copy of the full, unedited tape, and made no effort to obtain the full speech from other sources.

69. To this date neither Defendant Breitbart nor the other Defendants have ever issued an apology to Mrs. Sherrod. Tellingly, Defendant Breitbart has left the defamatory blog post on the internet, amounting to daily republication, despite now knowing the full context of Mrs. Sherrod's story. Defendant Breitbart's only concession was to post a small "correction" on the blog post to address the fact that Mrs. Sherrod's story "refers to actions she took before she held that federal position." *Video Proof: The NAACP Awards Racism—2010*. Defendants have not removed or withdrawn the blog post or video clip, and their daily republication has caused ongoing and serious harm to Mrs. Sherrod.

Defendants' Defamatory Statements are Repeated and Republished in Other Media Outlets, Compounding the Harm to Mrs. Sherrod

70. Defendants' publication of the deceptively-edited video segment and the blog post set off a media firestorm. Prompted and encouraged by Defendant Breitbart, national and local media outlets across the country republished and amplified the false and defamatory statements. For example:

   • On July 19, FoxNews.com reported: "Days after the NAACP clashed with Tea Party members over allegations of racism, a video has surfaced showing an

Agriculture Department official regaling an NAACP audience with a story about how she withheld help to a white farmer facing bankruptcy." http://www .foxnews.com/politics/2010/07/19/clip-shows-usda -official-admitting-withheld-help-white-farmer/.

- On July 19, 2010, in a Gateway Pundit post titled, *More Racism at NAACP: Radical Obama Official Admits That She Openly Discriminates Against Whites,* Jim Hoft posted Breitbart's video clip and wrote: Sherrod "admits in a speech at the NAACP that she discriminated against farmers because they were white." http://gatewaypundit.rightnetwork.com/2010/07 /more-racism-at-naacp-radical-obama-official -admits-to-leftist-group-that-she-openly-discriminates -against-whites-video/.

- On July 19, 2010, the Drudge Report linked to a CBS New York City affiliate's story on Mrs. Sherrod with the headline, *SHOCK: Video Suggests Racism At NAACP Event.* http://www.drudgereportarchives.com /data/2010/07/19/20100719_212852.htm.

- On July 19, 2010, CNN reporter Joe Johns reported on Mrs. Sherrod's resignation, stating that Mrs. Sherrod "has resigned after a YouTube video surfaced showing her describing to an NAACP audience how she withheld help to a white farmer," and airing a portion of her comments taken from the Breitbart clip. http:// transcripts.cnn.com/TRANSCRIPTS/1007/19/acd.01 .html.

- On July 20, 2010, MSNBC's Morning Joe aired the edited Sherrod clip and reported that Secretary Vilsack accepted Mrs. Sherrod's resignation. Co-host Joe Scarborough then said that "a narrative is going to emerge . . . certainly on the right with this tape that's just come out—and you'll be hearing this the next couple of days. I think its relevance relates back to the New Black Panthers tapes that have been out there." http://mediamatters.org /mmtv/201007200046.

71. Defendant Breitbart himself conducted at least three interviews on July 20, 2010:

- In an interview with CNN's John King, Defendant Breitbart said Mrs. Sherrod " . . . expresses a discrimina-

tory attitude towards white people" and the audience is
" . . . applauding her overt racism she is representing."
http://www.youtube.com/watch?v=DxcBIEV8bmI.

- In an interview on 971 FM Talk, Defendant Breitbart
said Mrs. Sherrod was "speaking in a racist language
and the audience is accepting it, and laughing at it, and
applauding it, and that is deeply offensive and it's ten
times more evidence, matter of fact, it's a billion times
more evidence than the main stream media has been
able to compile over a year and a half of trying to falsely
frame the tea party as racist." He continued, "Can you
imagine CNN right now going wall-to-wall with the
Shirley Sherrod story? If Shirley Sherrod were white?
And Shirley Sherrod had said those racial things, trying to find exculpatory evidence saying well maybe
later in the tape, later in the tape, what? She's talking
in racist terms, she refers to whites as the other and
everybody in the audience nods in laughter, she was
speaking in present tense, she was not talking about
I used to, she was skeptical of white people, throughout the entire thing, the full video will show that she
sees things through a racial prism and that is what
the NAACP has been about it." http://www.youtube
.com/watch?v=AM7WqVrcBew&p=3EC2C5A88A2F
76B0&playnext=1&index=11.
- In a third interview on Fox News with Hannity, Mr.
Breitbart said: ". . . I'm agnostic on the issue [of her
being fired] . . . I could care less about Shirley Sherrod."
http://video.foxnews.com/v/4288023/racial-double
-standard-in-white-house.blogpost.

Mrs. Sherrod Is Forced to Resign

72. Mrs. Sherrod's phone started ringing off the hook with calls from
the media asking for her reaction to the post. Mrs. Sherrod immediately notified the media department at the USDA and was
told that "someone from D.C. would be calling" her back with
specific instructions.

73. Meanwhile, at USDA headquarters, the agency's response to
the Breitbart post was frantic and harsh. Shortly after learning
of the blog post and video clip, USDA Communications Director Chris Mather advised colleagues "THIS IS HORRIBLE."

http://articles.latimes.com/2010/oct/07/nation/la-na-sherrod-usda-20101008. Other USDA officials described Secretary Vilsack as "absolutely sick and mad" about the situation. *Id.* Internal USDA emails indicate that upon learning of the selectively-edited clip, Secretary Vilsack stated that it was the worst thing that had happened during his tenure at the agency.

74. The same day, at approximately 3:38 pm, while attending a meeting in west Georgia, Mrs. Sherrod received a phone call from Cheryl Cook in Washington. Ms. Cook, Deputy Under Secretary for Rural Development, told Mrs. Sherrod that she has been placed on administrative leave and advised her to go home. Mrs. Sherrod began the long, seven-hour drive to Athens, Georgia to return her government property to the office before continuing home to Albany, Georgia.

75. At approximately 4:42 pm, while driving, Mrs. Sherrod received a second call from Ms. Cook asking where Mrs. Sherrod was.

76. At approximately 5:56 pm, while still driving, Mrs. Sherrod received a third telephone call from Ms. Cook. Ms. Cook told Mrs. Sherrod that the White House wanted her resignation.

77. At approximately 6:35 pm, while still driving, Mrs. Sherrod received a fourth telephone call from Ms. Cook. Ms. Cook told Mrs. Sherrod that they could not wait any longer for her resignation and instructed her to pull over to the side of the road to email her resignation from her BlackBerry. Mrs. Sherrod, under duress, did as she was requested and sent her resignation at 6:55 pm.

78. On the morning of Tuesday, July 20, 2010, Mrs. Sherrod awoke to several media trucks parked outside of her home and repeated requests from reporters to enter her house. Her phones were ringing so often that it had to be taken off the hook.

79. Later that day, Secretary Vilsack defended the decision to demand the resignation of Mrs. Sherrod because her ability to do her job was compromised: "[S]tate rural development directors make many decisions and are often called to use their discretion. The controversy surrounding her comments would create situations where her decisions, rightly or wrongly, would be called into question making it difficult for her to bring jobs to Georgia." http://content.usatoday.com/communities/theoval/post/2010/07/obama-white-house-dragged-into-agdepartmentnaacp-flap/1; *see also* http://www.youtube.com/watch?v=FZfGDEqhVqM.

The Full Video Surfaces

80. On Tuesday, July 20, 2010, at approximately 7:45 pm, the NAACP released the full video of Mrs. Sherrod's speech at the Freedom Fund Banquet. The NAACP quickly recognized and stated that Defendant Breitbart's deceptively-edited video "didn't tell the full story" and was "selectively edited to cast her in a negative light." http://www.naacp.org/news/entry/video_sherrod.

81. The local TV station in Albany, Georgia also began airing the similar speech Mrs. Sherrod had given at Albany State.

82. Realizing that Defendant Breitbart's edited video and defamatory statements had deceived them, senior White House and other administration officials began to apologize to Mrs. Sherrod for their earlier rush to judgment. On July 21, 2010 Press Secretary Robert Gibbs apologized to Mrs. Sherrod during a White House press briefing. Later that day, Secretary Vilsack held a press conference that included an apology to Mrs. Sherrod. On July 22, 2010, President Obama apologized to Mrs. Sherrod.

83. Many national media figures and other leaders also followed with apologies. For example, a leading talk show host, Bill O'Reilly, apologized, stating "So I owe Mrs. Sherrod an apology for not doing my homework, for not putting her remarks into the proper context."   http://www.foxnews.com/on-air/oreilly/transcript/who-shirley-sherrod-and-why-was-she-unjustly-fired-obama-administration.

Defendant Breitbart Defiantly Refuses to Apologize to Mrs. Sherrod, Retract the Defamatory Blog Post, or Remove it from his Website

84. Despite widespread recognition that Breitbart's blog post, at the very least, created a false impression of Mrs. Sherrod, to date, none of the Defendants have apologized to Mrs. Sherrod or published a retraction of the defamatory video or blog post. Even more striking is the fact that Defendant Breitbart has not removed the defamatory content from his blog. His original blog post remains available on BigGovernment.com exactly as it was on July 19, complete with the deceptively-edited version of Mrs. Sherrod's speech and the introductory slides stating that she "discriminates against people due to their race" in her federal position. This despite the fact that the complete version of Mrs. Sherrod's speech has been available for many months.

85. Similarly, throughout the media firestorm that ultimately forced Mrs. Sherrod's resignation, Defendant JOHN DOE, who un-

questionably knew the full content and true message of Mrs. Sherrod's speech, stood silent and took no action to identify himself or correct the false reports. Instead, Defendant JOHN DOE sat idly by and watched while Mrs. Sherrod's career and hard-earned reputation were destroyed.

Mrs. Sherrod has Suffered Severe Reputational and Financial Harm and has Been Subjected to Severe Emotional Distress

86. As a direct and proximate result of Defendants' conduct, Mrs. Sherrod has suffered serious reputational, financial and professional damage. Mrs. Sherrod was forced to resign from her position at the USDA, which had paid her approximately $111,000 a year.

87. Beyond the financial damage, however, Mrs. Sherrod has suffered irreparable reputational and career damage. Despite the fact that the Obama Administration and various news outlets have offered Mrs. Sherrod their apologies, she remains known by countless persons nationwide for her allegedly "racist" remarks. To make matters worse, even after the full video surfaced, numerous blogs and internet sites continued to rely on—and link to—Defendants' blog post to viciously accuse Mrs. Sherrod of being a racist.

88. Most difficult for Mrs. Sherrod is her inability to continue in the career that she loved. With her objectivity, independence and intentions called into question, and with her name so closely tied to issues of racial discrimination, Mrs. Sherrod is no longer able to effectively discharge her former duties as the Georgia State Director for Rural Development.

89. Mrs. Sherrod has also been forced to deal with unwanted and unwelcome attention. Unwillingly thrust into the spotlight by Defendant Breitbart's allegations, Mrs. Sherrod is now constantly approached by strangers who recognize her exclusively from the controversy sparked by Defendant Breitbart's blog post. Dealing with this public attention has caused Mrs. Sherrod to suffer exhaustion and has forced her to alter daily plans. Because Mrs. Sherrod has been subjected to this unwanted attention, harassment and heckling as a result of Defendant Breitbart's post, she has been forced to take extra security precautions.

90. Moreover, Mrs. Sherrod has suffered continued severe emotional distress as a result of the defamation. She has received harassing phone calls in the middle of the night, interrupting her sleep, as

well as harassing emails. Mrs. Sherrod who, at age 63, already suffered from diabetes, also has had problems sleeping and increasingly severe back pain.

DEFENDANTS' CONDUCT WARRANTS PUNITIVE DAMAGES

91. Defendants' conduct warrants the imposition of punitive damages. The factors justifying punitive damages include, at a mini-
mum, the following:

   a. Defendants knowingly and intentionally edited the
      video of Mrs. Sherrod's speech to give the misleading
      impression that Mrs. Sherrod exercised her job duties
      in a racist manner;

   b. Defendants added false commentary into the video stat-
      ing that Mrs. Sherrod "discriminates against people due
      to race" "in her federally appointed position";

   c. Defendants acted with actual malice in altering the
      video—that is, acted with actual knowledge of the falsity
      of the speech or reckless disregard of it;

   d. Defendants intentionally and/or recklessly ascribed to
      Mrs. Sherrod conduct and characteristics that would
      adversely affect her fitness for her profession;

   e. Defendants edited the video of Mrs. Sherrod's speech
      with the purpose of publishing it and disseminating it;

   f. Defendants targeted Mrs. Sherrod in order to make her
      an example of alleged NAACP racism;

   g. Defendant JOHN DOE sent the video of Mrs. Sher-
      rod's full speech to Defendants Breitbart and O'Connor
      with the intention that it be used to mislead the public
      about the true content of the speech and to defame her
      reputation;

   h. Defendant O'Connor knowingly and intentionally and/
      or recklessly or negligently posted the edited version of
      Mrs. Sherrod's speech to YouTube in order to give the
      impression that Mrs. Sherrod exercised her job duties in
      a racist manner;

   i. Defendant Breitbart knowingly and intentionally and/
      or recklessly or negligently posted the edited version of
      Mrs. Sherrod's speech to his blog in order to give the
      impression that Mrs. Sherrod exercised her job duties
      in a racist manner;

j. Defendant Breitbart added additional commentary describing Mrs. Sherrod's speech in which he falsely stated that Mrs. Sherrod's "federal duties are managed through the prism of race and class distinctions," and in which he falsely accuses her of "describ[ing] how she racially discriminates against a white farmer" and telling a "racist tale";

k. Defendant Breitbart acted with actual malice authoring his blog post—that is, he acted with actual knowledge of the falsity of the speech or reckless disregard of it;

l. Defendants intentionally and/or recklessly ascribed to Mrs. Sherrod conduct and characteristics that would adversely affect her fitness for her profession;

m. Defendant Breitbart acted with actual malice in posting a Twitter message encouraging Attorney General Holder to "hold accountable" "fed appointee" Mrs. Sherrod for "admitting practicing racial discrimination"; herein.

n. Defendant Breitbart continues to republish the defamatory blog post even with undisputed actual knowledge of its falsity;

o. Defendants refuse to apologize to Mrs. Sherrod and refuse to issue a retraction.

COUNT I: DEFAMATION

92. Plaintiff incorporates all preceding paragraphs of the Complaint as fully set forth herein.

93. Through the editing of the video of Mrs. Sherrod's speech and the publication of falsehoods on BigGovernment.com, YouTube.com and Twitter.com, Defendants have defamed Mrs. Sherrod in at least the following ways:

a. By falsely stating, both directly and by implication, that Mrs. Sherrod exercised her federal job duties in a racially discriminatory manner;

b. By falsely stating, both directly and by implication, that Mrs. Sherrod presently discriminates against white farmers in the course of her federal employment;

c. By falsely stating, both directly and by implication, that Mrs. Sherrod condones and encourages racism.

94. Specifically, Defendants have defamed Mrs. Sherrod by editing

and publishing an intentionally misleading clip of Mrs. Sherrod's speech and by making at least the following statements:

- "Mrs. Sherrod admits that in her federally appointed position, overseeing over a billion dollars . . . . She discriminates against people due to their race."
- The clip shows "video evidence of racism coming from a federal appointee and NAACP award recipient."
- "[T]his federally appointed executive bureaucrat lays out in stark detail, that her federal duties are managed through the prism of race and class distinctions."
- "In the first video, Sherrod describes how she racially discriminates against a white farmer." Through the editing of the video of Mrs. Sherrod's speech and the publication of herein.
- Her speech is a "racist tale."
- "Will Eric Holder's DOJ hold accountable fed appointee Shirley Sherrod for admitting practicing racial discrimination?"

95. These defamatory falsehoods were of and concerning Mrs. Sherrod and specifically impugned Mrs. Sherrod's professional reputation. They ascribe to her conduct that would adversely affect her fitness for the proper conduct of her profession.

96. These defamatory falsehoods were made with actual malice by Defendants inasmuch as they knew of their falsity or recklessly disregarded their truth or falsity.

97. These defamatory statements made with actual malice were published on BigGovernment.com, YouTube.com and Twitter.com, accessible to millions of people. Those statements were amplified in many other media outlets and internet locations.

98. These defamatory falsehoods have and will actually injure Mrs. Sherrod in at least the following ways:
    a. By impugning Mrs. Sherrod's professional reputation;
    b. By ascribing to her conduct that would adversely affect her fitness for the proper conduct of her profession;
    c. By causing Mrs. Sherrod's forced resignation from the USDA;
    d. By inhibiting Mrs. Sherrod's successful performance of her previous job duties;
    e. By limiting Mrs. Sherrod's future career prospects;
    f. By subjecting Mrs. Sherrod to unwanted attention, harassment and persecution.

COUNT II: FALSE LIGHT

99. Plaintiff incorporates all preceding paragraphs of the Complaint as fully set forth herein.

100. Defendants published false statements, representations, and/or imputations of and concerning Mrs. Sherrod. Those include at least:

   a. False statements, both direct and by implication, that Mrs. Sherrod exercised her federal job duties in a racially discriminatory manner;

   b. False statements, both direct and by implication, that Mrs. Sherrod presently discriminates against white farmers in the course of her federal employment;

   c. False statements, both directly and by implication, that Mrs. Sherrod condones and encourages racism.

101. Specifically, Defendants have represented Mrs. Sherrod in false light by publishing an intentionally misleading, edited clip of Mrs. Sherrod's speech and by making at least the following statements:

   • "Mrs. Sherrod admits that in her federally appointed position, overseeing over a billion dollars . . . . She discriminates against people due to their race."

   • The clip shows "video evidence of racism coming from a federal appointee and NAACP award recipient."

   • "[T]his federally appointed executive bureaucrat lays out in stark detail, that her federal duties are managed through the prism of race and class distinctions."

   • "In the first video, Sherrod describes how she racially discriminates against a white farmer."

   • Her speech is a "racist tale."

   • "Will Eric Holder's DOJ hold accountable fed appointee Shirley Sherrod for admitting practicing racial discrimination?"

102. These statements placed Mrs. Sherrod in a false light that would be highly offensive to a reasonable person.

103. The Defendants had knowledge of or acted in reckless disregard as to the falsity of the publicized matter and the false light in which Mrs. Sherrod would be placed.

104. These defamatory falsehoods have and will actually injure Mrs. Sherrod in at least the following ways:

   a. By impugning Mrs. Sherrod's professional reputation; herein.

b. By ascribing to her conduct that would adversely affect her fitness for the proper conduct of her profession;

c. By causing Mrs. Sherrod's forced resignation from the USDA;

d. By inhibiting Mrs. Sherrod's successful performance of her previous job duties;

e. By limiting Mrs. Sherrod's future career prospects;

f. By subjecting Mrs. Sherrod to unwanted attention, harassment, and heckling.

COUNT III: INTENTIONAL INFLICTION OF EMOTIONAL DISTRESS

105. Plaintiff incorporates all preceding paragraphs of the Complaint as fully set forth herein.

106. Defendants' defamatory and false statements, intentionally misleading editing, and wide publication constituted extreme and outrageous conduct.

107. Defendants' actions were done intentionally and/or recklessly in conscious disregard of the high probability that Mrs. Sherrod's mental distress would follow.

108. As a result of Defendants' actions, Mrs. Sherrod suffered severe emotional distress resulting in sleeping problems and mental anguish.

PUNITIVE DAMAGES

109. The actions or omissions of Defendants set forth in this Complaint demonstrate malice, egregious defamation, and insult. Such actions or omissions by Defendants were undertaken with either (1) maliciousness, spite, ill will, vengeance or deliberate intent to harm the Plaintiff; or (2) reckless disregard of the falsity of the speech and its effects on Plaintiff. Accordingly, Plaintiff requests an award of punitive damages and attorneys' fees beyond and in excess of those damages necessary to compensate Plaintiff for injuries resulting from Defendants' conduct.

PRAYER FOR RELIEF

Plaintiff prays that this Court provide the following relief:

(1) An order requiring Defendant Breitbart to remove the defamatory language and video from his blog;

(2) An order requiring Defendant O'Connor to remove the defamatory video clips from YouTube.com;

(3) An order enjoining Defendants from engaging in future tortious conduct against Mrs. Sherrod;

(4) Compensatory and consequential damages for detraction from good name and reputation, for mental anguish, distress and humiliation, and for injuries to Plaintiff's occupation in an amount of no less than $5,001;

(5) Punitive damages to punish Defendants' reprehensible conduct and to deter its future occurrence;

(6) Costs and fees incurred in the prosecution of this action; and

(7) Further relief as this Court shall deem just and proper.

JURY DEMAND

110. Plaintiff requests a trial by jury on any and all issues raised by this Complaint which are triable by right of a jury.

162   "We are a confused bunch": http://keyconversationsradio.com/?p=621.

163   Not long ago: Andrew Ferguson, "The Boy from Yazoo City: Haley Barbour, Mississippi's Favorite Son," *The Weekly Standard*, December 27, 2010, www.weeklystandard.com/articles/boy-yazoo-city_523551.html.

163   "fired signers of the integration petition": Halberstam, "The White Citizens Councils: Respectable Means for Unrespectable Ends," *Commentary*, October 1956, www.commentarymagazine.com/article/the-white-citizens-councils-respectable-means-for-unrespectable-ends/.

164   "Slavery had a disastrous impact": After a huge storm of protest, the Family Leader group removed the slavery language from its pledge, but that doesn't acquit the presidential candidates who signed it with the original language. See www.thefamilyleader.com/wp-content/uploads/2011/07/themarriagevow.final_.7.7.111.pdf.

164   The 2010 Multi-State Survey: The study was performed under the auspices of the University of Washington Wiser Institute for the Study of Ethnicity, Race & Sexuality. It is available at www.depts.washington.edu/uwiser/racepolitics.html.

164   "It's really a matter": See http://depts.washington.edu/uwiser/mssrp_table.pdf.

Chapter 14: Planting Hope

170   As we investigated the history: *Historical Collections of the Georgia Chapters Daughters of the American Revolution*, vol. 4, *Old Bible Records & Land Lotteries, 1932*, included information from a family Bible of the Hartwell Hill Tarver family; Hartwell Hill Tarver was a son of Andrew Tarver and

Elizabeth Hartwell, born in 1791 in Brunswick County, Virginia. He married Ann R. Wimberly on May 15, 1823, and had Paul E. in 1824; the Hartwells lost an infant daughter, Rebecca, according to Stephanie Lincecum, "The Death of a Child (Tombstone Tuesday!)," http:// blog.southerngraves.net/2011/04/death-of-child-tombstone-tuesday .html; Jack F. Cox, compiler, *The 1850 Census of Georgia Slave Owners* (Baltimore: Clearfield, 1999) lists the Tarvers as owning many slaves in southwest Georgia.

171   "At last we stopped": John Brown, *Slave Life in Georgia: A Narrative of the Life, Sufferings, and Escape of John Brown, a Fugitive Slave, Now in England,* ed. Louis Alexis Chamerovzow (London:1854), pp. 19–30.

171   Paul Tarver died: "Signs of the Times with the Death of Paul Tarver," http://rosehillcemeterymacongeorgia.blogspot.com/2011/04/signs-of -times-with-death-of-paul.html.

171   there is a record of an estate sale: "Slave Auction 1859," www.eyewitness-tohistory.com/slaveauction.htm; Annette Holmes, "The Weeping Time; Butler Slave Auction," www.glynngen.com/slaverec/butler.htm.

172   "150 NEGROES FOR SALE": "Signs of the Times with the Death of Paul Tarver," http://rosehillcemeterymacongeorgia.blogspot .com/2011/04/signs-of-times-with-death-of-paul.html.

174   "It is part life experience": Spencer Perkins, "Playing the Grace Card," *Christianity Today,* July 13, 1998, www.ctlibrary.com/ct/1998 /july13/8t8040.html.

Bibliography

Alexander, Amy. *Uncovering Race: A Black Journalist's Story of Reporting and Reinvention*. Boston: Beacon Press, 2011.

Branch, Taylor. *Parting the Waters: America in the King Years, 1954–1963*. New York: Simon and Schuster, 1989.

Brown-Nagin, Tomiko. *Courage to Dissent: Atlanta and the Long History of the Civil Rights Movement*. New York: Oxford University Press USA, 2011.

Carawan, Cande and Guy. *Sing for Freedom: The Story of the Civil Rights Movement Through Its Songs*. Montgomery, Ala.: New South Books, 2008.

Chafe, William Henry, Raymond Gavins, and Robert Korstad, eds. *Remembering Jim Crow: African Americans Tell About Life in the Segregated South*. New York: New Press, 2008.

Dyson, Michael Eric. *Can You Hear Me Now?: The Inspiration, Wisdom, and Insight of Michael Eric Dyson*. New York: Basic Civitas Books, 2009.

——. *Race Rules: Navigating the Color Line*. New York: Basic Civitas Books, 2012.

Ficara, John Francis. *Black Farmers in America*. Lexington: University Press of Kentucky, 2006.

Gates, Henry Louis, Jr. *Life Upon These Shores: Looking at African American History, 1513–2008*. New York: Knopf, 2011.

Gillespie, Andra. *Whose Black Politics?: Cases in Post-racial Black Leadership*. New York: Routledge, 2009.

Grant, Donald L. and Jonathan. *The Way It Was in the South: The Black Experience in Georgia*. Athens: University of Georgia Press, 2001.

Holsaert, Faith S., Martha Prescod Noonan, Judy Richardson, and Betty Garman

Robinson, eds. *Hands on the Freedom Plow: Personal Accounts by Women in SNCC.* Champaign: University of Illinois Press, 2010.

Holt, Thomas C. *Children of Fire: A History of African Americans.* New York: Hill and Wang, 2011.

Kaplan, Roy H. *The Myth of Post-racial America: Searching for Equality in the Age of Materialism.* Lanham, Md.: Rowman & Littlefield Education, 2011.

Klarman, Michael J. *From Jim Crow to Civil Rights: The Supreme Court and the Struggle for Racial Equality.* New York: Oxford University Press USA, 2006.

Lemon, Don. *Transparent.* Las Vegas: Farrah Gray Foundation, 2011.

McWhorter, Diane. *Carry Me Home: Birmingham, Alabama, the Climactic Battle of the Civil Rights Revolution.* New York: Simon and Schuster, 2001.

Norris, Michele. *The Grace of Silence: A Memoir.* New York: Pantheon, 2010.

Obama, Barack. *Dreams from My Father: A Story of Race and Inheritance.* New York: Broadway Books, 2004 (paperback).

Rank, Mark Robert. *One Nation, Underprivileged: Why American Poverty Affects Us All.* New York: Oxford University Press USA, 2005.

Risen, Clay. *A Nation on Fire: America in the Wake of the King Assassination.* New York: John Wiley, 2009.

Robinson, Eugene. *Disintegration: The Splintering of Black America.* New York: Doubleday, 2010.

Smiley, Tavis. *What I Know for Sure: My Story of Growing Up in America.* New York: Doubleday, 2006.

Squires, Catherine. *African Americans and the Media.* Polity, 2009.

Tatum, Beverly. *Can We Talk About Race?: And Other Conversations in an Era of School Resegregation.* Boston: Beacon Press, 2008.

Tesler, Michael, and David O. Sears. *Obama's Race: The 2008 Election and the Dream of a Post-racial America.* Chicago: University of Chicago Press, 2010.

Tuck, Stephen G. N. *Beyond Atlanta: The Struggle for Racial Equality in Georgia.* Athens: University of Georgia Press, 2001.

Walker, Melissa. *Southern Families and Their Stories.* Lexington: University of Kentucky Press, 2006.

Watson, Bruce. *Freedom Summer: The Savage Season That Made Mississippi Burn and Made America a Democracy.* New York: Viking, 2010.

Wilkerson, Isabel. *The Warmth of Other Suns: The Epic Story of America's Great Migration.* New York: Random House, 2010.

Wise, Tim. *Between Barack and a Hard Place: Racism and White Denial in the Age of Obama.* San Francisco: City Lights Publishers, 2009.

———. *Colorblind: The Rise of Post-racial Politics and the Retreat from Racial Equity.* San Francisco: City Lights Publishers, 2010.

Zinn, Howard. *The Southern Mystique.* South End Press, 2002.